Women in Science

Women in Science

∾ CAREER PROCESSES
AND OUTCOMES

YU XIE

KIMBERLEE A. SHAUMAN

HARVARD UNIVERSITY PRESS

Cambridge, Massachusetts, and London, England

First Harvard University Press paperback edition, 2005

Library of Congress Cataloging-in-Publication Data

Xie, Yu, 1959–
    Women in science : career processes and outcomes / Yu Xie, Kimberlee A. Shauman.
      p. cm.
    Includes bibliographical references and index.
    ISBN 0-674-01034-5 (cloth)
    ISBN 0-674-01859-1 (pbk.)
    1. Women in science. 2. Women scientists. I. Shauman, Kimberlee A., 1969–
II. Title.

Q130.Z54 2003
305.43'5—dc21   2003045274

To our children, Raissa,
Kevin, and Lucy

Contents

Figures and Tables

Tables

Acknowledgments

As sociologists, we are keenly aware of the importance of social influence, both intellectually and emotionally. This book is a product of a ten-year journey in our professional lives, and during that period we benefited from countless interactions with mentors, colleagues, and other professional friends. In particular, we wish to express our sincere appreciation to the following scholars for their encouragement and support: Julia Adams, Christopher Bettinger, John Bound, Mary Brinton, Mary Corcoran, Thomas DiPrete, Reynolds Farley, William Frey, David Grusky, David Harris, Robert Hauser, Sandra Hofferth, Alice Hogan, James House, Mary Jackman, Valerie Lee, Richard Lempert, J. Scott Long, Charles Manski, Robert Mare, Peggy Marini, Bill McCarthy, Mark Mizruchi, Laurie Morgan, Susan Murphy, Charles Peek, Adrian Raftery, Pamela Smock, Arland Thornton, and Christopher Winship.

Our special thanks go to Kimberly Goyette for her contributions to this book. She coauthored Chapters 7 and 10 and served as an invaluable resource for various matters throughout the project. We also wish to acknowledge previous versions of portions of the text.

- Material from Chapters 2–4 was drawn heavily from Kimberlee Shauman's dissertation, "The Education of Scientists: Gender Differences during the Early Life Course," at the University of Michigan (1997).

• Chapter 8 was revised from Kimberlee Shauman and Yu Xie's article, "Geographic Mobility of Scientists: Sex Differences and Family Constraints," published in *Demography* 33:455–468 (1996).

• Chapter 9 was revised from Yu Xie and Kimberlee Shauman's "Sex Differences in Research Productivity: New Evidence about an Old Puzzle," published in *American Sociological Review* 63:847–870 (1998).

• Chapter 10 was revised from an article by Kimberly Goyette and Yu Xie, "The Intersection of Immigration and Gender: Labor Force Outcomes of Immigrant Women Scientists," *Social Science Quarterly* 80:395–408 (1999), copyright © 1999 by the University of Texas Press; all rights reserved.

Able research assistance for the project was provided by Pamela Bennett, Judy Rosenstein, and Zhen Zeng. Pamela Bennett, Pat Preston, and Zhen Zeng proofread earlier drafts of the book. Their careful reading and valuable suggestions prompted significant improvements and saved us from publishing some embarrassing mistakes. We are grateful to Judy Mullin and Rhonda Moats for their excellent clerical support. We also acknowledge the occasional programming assistance provided by Albert Anderson and Lisa Neidert.

The research reported in this book was supported by a combination of grants and fellowships: a research grant and a Young Investigator Award from the National Science Foundation, a Spencer Fellowship from the National Academy of Education to Yu Xie, and a Spencer Fellowship from the National Academy of Education to Kimberlee Shauman. Substantial work for this book was done by Kimberlee Shauman as part of her dissertation research, which was supported by an NICHD traineeship and Rackham Dissertation Finishing Grant while she was a graduate student at the Population Studies Center of the University of Michigan. The general support from the University of Michigan and from the University of California–Davis facilitated the project. We also thank the National Center for Education Statistics (NCES) for its cooperation in allowing us to access several restricted datasets (see Appendix A).

Two anonymous reviewers provided thorough and very useful comments that helped us improve the manuscript. Michael Aronson at

Harvard University Press played a critical role in making this book a reality. While always supportive of the project, he was also patient through its various delays. Kate Schmit did an excellent job of copyediting the manuscript. Benno Weisberg at the Press was helpful in facilitating the final production of the book.

Finally and most importantly, we are deeply indebted to the members of our families for their unreserved support during the long journey from the start to the conclusion of our project. Without their support, the progress of our work would be much delayed and the completion of this book would be impossible. We dedicate this book to our children, for whom we wish limitless opportunities to develop their talents and pursue their goals.

CHAPTER ONE

Introduction

This book is about the career processes and outcomes of women in science. The brevity of this statement belies the complexity of the topic and the scope of the study that we present in the pages that follow. The underrepresentation of women is a hallmark characteristic of science and has persisted in spite of the rapid improvement of women's social and economic status over the past few decades. During this period the gender gap in overall educational attainment in the United States has closed (Bae et al. 2000), and women have made significant inroads into many other high-status professions, such as medicine, the law, and the arts (Reskin and Roos 1990). In trend analyses of occupational segregation by sex, science and engineering stand out as the stubborn exceptions to the general trend of significant progress toward gender equity.

Why is it that science and engineering occupations seem less responsive to the social forces that have successfully effected progress toward gender equality in other professional occupations? Is science the "final frontier" for occupational gender equality? Is it simply that more time is needed, or is science so unique that it defies the trend toward gender equality witnessed in other professional occupations? Our task in this book is to shed new light on the question of why women continue to be underrepresented in science by systematically examining and documenting the career processes and outcomes of women scientists and comparing their experiences with those of men.

We accomplish this task by departing from the common "science pipeline" approach and adopting the life course approach to the study of science careers. By calling attention to the multidimensionality of human lives as well as to the multiple levels of influences that combine to affect career trajectories and outcomes, the life course perspective provides a new conceptual and methodological framework that guides our study of women in science.

At the risk of oversimplification, let us borrow the economist's language and classify factors that affect women's underrepresentation in science as "demand" factors and "supply" factors. Demand factors are characteristics associated with jobs and employers that discourage women from entering an occupation. Such characteristics could include overt or covert gender discrimination. Supply factors are individual-level characteristics that deter women from pursuing science careers and/or encourage their pursuit of another type of career. Supply factors include educational background, career preferences, and family status. This dichotomy is illustrative and far too simplistic, for there can be important interactions between demand and supply influences. For example, women may consciously avoid attaining the prerequisite scientific education if they anticipate future difficulties, such as gender discrimination, in pursuing science careers.

We contend that the relatively slow movement of women into science and engineering occupations is caused by the forces of both supply and demand. This is significant because much of the blame for women's underrepresentation in science has been attributed to the practice of science per se or to the actions of male scientists. As we will demonstrate throughout the book, the inadequate supply of interested and qualified women has been as much, if not more, of a hindrance to the feminization of science as has the influence of demand factors. In other words, in our view, it would be naïve to presume that science and engineering occupations are closed to women simply through discriminatory practices and structural barriers. Despite a trend toward convergence, it remains true that women trail men in their desire and persistence in pursuing scientific careers. Among those who do pursue science, however, a significant portion of women achieve a level of success on par with their male colleagues.

The persistent enigma of women's underrepresentation in science has fueled a vast body of research. Scholars have examined a variety of questions about women's participation in, exclusion from, and contributions to the fields of science and engineering. Despite the significant breadth and depth of this research, much of it suffers from conceptual and methodological limitations that restrict the significance and usefulness of its findings. As a consequence, we have only limited knowledge of the processes that produce the gender differentials in science participation and attainment. In this book, we address the gap by presenting the first systematic examination of gender differences in the science career trajectory throughout the life course: from middle school through the career years. Our research explores both the early life course processes of selection into and out of the science educational track and the stratifying influences that operate after entry into the science labor market. The results of this study contribute to the literature on women in science, as well as to the broader literature on gender inequality in the labor force.

Our study encompasses the entirety of a career trajectory and provides a comprehensive, updated, and systematic empirical account of where and how women fall behind men in pursuing scientific careers and in practicing science. However simple this task may seem, it is in fact extremely difficult to execute. The project has required us to analyze seventeen large, nationally representative datasets (including the 1960–1990 U.S. censuses) at the individual level. Any empirical social scientist would surely appreciate the sheer scale of the project. Throughout the project, our philosophy has been to learn as much as we can about the empirical world and to impart this valuable knowledge to our readers, each of whom may come to our book with different orientations and may act in different ways on the information conveyed in these pages. In this respect, our approach is decidedly demographic, for it values empirical knowledge for its own sake while allowing for alternative interpretations. In our view, the large literature on women in science has been plagued by broad discussions that pay insufficient attention to factual information. We hope to balance this tendency of the literature on women in science by providing the necessary empirical foundation for the discussions to move forward.

The design of our study addresses many of the conceptual and methodological limitations of previous research on women in science. We depart from the common "pipeline approach" to the study of science careers and instead draw on the life course perspective to frame our research and to guide the organization of this book. The result is a study of career processes and outcomes that emphasizes the human ecology of career development. We examine, for example, the causal influence of prior experiences on later career outcomes and the interactions of the multiple domains of an individual's life, such as career and the family. We accomplish this by relying extensively on the statistical analysis of longitudinal data and, in places where true longitudinal data are lacking, "synthetic" cohorts constructed by piecing together information from different sources pertaining to different periods of the life course.

Although limited to science and engineering professions, our study is a concrete example of how to understand gender differences in career processes and outcomes in the general labor force. The innovative and expansive design of our study can be easily adapted for the study of gender inequities in other professions. The empirical findings reported in this book have important implications for, if not direct generalizability to, gender differences in other high-status occupations. It has long been recognized by researchers and felt by individual women that gender differences in career trajectories are intimately linked to gender differences in the timing of events, prioritizing of roles, and social relations across the life course (Hochschild 1994; Maccoby 1995). Our research analyzes a career trajectory in its entirety in an attempt to illuminate the life course processes that at some times facilitate and at other times inhibit the career development of women relative to men.

Why Study Women in Science?

There are two primary social problems motivating the study of women in science. The first is the persistence of gender inequality in the labor force and the role of the gender segregation of occupations (including scientific and engineering occupations) in its maintenance. Stratification researchers have long documented that science is one of the most prestigious segments of the labor force (Hodge, Siegel, and Rossi 1964) and that women's low rates of participation in science contribute to, in aggregate, the lower social status of women relative to men (Jacobs 1989; Reskin 1984; Reskin and Hartmann 1986). An increase in the representation of women in science would lessen occupational segregation and reduce the level of gender inequality in the labor force. Theoretically speaking, one may expect women's entry into science to be relatively easy, given that science is lauded as relying on universalistic criteria for the evaluation and commendation of its members and their work (Cole 1979; Cole and Cole 1973; Merton 1973). If universalism is truly a norm in science, the problem of sex discrimination should be absent or at least less prevalent there than in other occupations (Xie 1989). We should, therefore, expect women to prefer science as a channel for upward social mobility. In reality, women's relatively slow movement into science suggests that career processes in science are influenced by multifaceted social forces far more complicated than those dictated by the simplistic universalism principle.

Concern in the United States about the supply of science labor provides the second motivation for studying women in science. To a large extent, the booming U.S. economy of the past half-century has been driven by advances in science and technology. Keeping pace with these advances and ensuring their continuation requires the maintenance of a scientific labor force of adequate size and quality. Concern is frequently raised about a possible shortage of scientists in the United States (Atkinson 1990).[1] Recruiting more women (along with underrepresented minorities) into science is often proposed as an effective way to expand the talent pool and therefore to increase the supply of scientists (National Science Foundation 1999). An implicit assumption underlying this policy approach is that the distribution of talent for scientific work is unrelated to gender, although recruitment into science traditionally has been. All available evidence suggests that innate differences in scientific ability between men and women are nonexistent or very small (Maccoby and Jacklin 1974). Most scholars attribute women's lower representation and lesser success in science to social structural, social psychological, and family-related barriers (Sonnert 1999; Valian 1999; Zuckerman 1991). Thus the argument is: If we could remove or lower these barriers, we would expand the talent pool and increase the supply of well-trained scientists and engineers.

As social scientists and private citizens, we see gender-based inequality in the labor force as a social problem requiring remedy. We would like to see women's talent tapped more fully for science, both for the personal satisfaction of individual talented women as well as for the benefit of society as a whole. Although our research is motivated by these personal preconceptions, their influence stops there. We try to be objective and "value-free" (in so far as it is possible) in our empirical research. We conducted the statistical analyses for this study with great care, and we make every effort to report the empirical results in a balanced manner. In many places, we resist the temptation to impute our subjective interpretation into data, preferring instead to draw empirically grounded conclusions that are informed by the life course perspective. Since we wish to reach a wide audience, complicated statistical results are compressed and reported only in summary form in the main text. Detailed information about statistical results and data analysis is available in the appendices.

Previous Research on Women in Science: The Legacy of the Pipeline

The past two decades have witnessed a proliferation of literature on women in science. Indeed, a casual search in a major research library would easily yield more than a dozen book titles specifically addressing women in science, most of which were published after Cole's 1979 landmark book, *Fair Science: Women in the Scientific Community.* (See Davis et al. 1996; Gornick 1990; Hanson 1996; Kahle 1985; Long 2001; McIlwee and Robinson 1992; Pattatucci 1998; Schiebinger 1999; Selby 1999; Sonnert 1995a, 1995b; Wasserman 2000; and Zuckerman, Cole, and Bruer 1991.) A search of scholarly journals in sociology, psychology, history, and women's studies would add a plethora of articles that address topics ranging from the existence and extent of gender differences in math-related brain functioning (e.g., Haier and Benbow 1995) to the influence of family characteristics on participation in math courses during high school (e.g., Eccles, Jacobs, and Harold 1990), and from gender differences in publication productivity (e.g., Xie and Shauman 1998) to the impact of feminization on salaries in specific academic disciplines (e.g., Bellas 1994). In addition to this body of academic research, government agencies have periodically published reports full of statistical information that measure the participation and progress of women in science education and occupations (e.g., Committee on Women in Science and Engineering 1991; National Science Foundation 1986, 1992, 1994, 1996, 1999, 2000).

The sheer size of this literature indicates that there is a great deal of interest in the subject of women in science in both the scholarly community and the public at large. This large and growing body of research has illuminated many aspects of women's careers in science and the ways in which the careers of men and women scientists differ. Some scholarship also argues that women's participation in science itself enriches scientific thinking by bringing more subjectivity, more empathy, more reliance on intuition, more holism, and perhaps more passion to science than has been practiced by men.[2] We will not address the philosophical issues of women's increased involvement in science in this book. Instead, our research engages the literature that focuses on gender differences in science career trajectories and their causes. Owing to conceptual drawbacks and associated methodological limitations, the extant research on the careers of women in science has failed to answer many old questions, and indeed it has raised new ones. In the sections that follow, we briefly discuss some of the inadequacies of the literature before describing our approach to the study of women in science.

Limitations of the "Science Pipeline"

The major conceptual limitation of the literature on women in science is the predominance of the "pipeline" model. According to this model, the process of becoming a scientist can be conceptualized as a pipeline, called the "science pipeline." The image of the science pipeline is used to illustrate a structured set of educational and employment stages that comprise a science career. The pipeline typically refers to the sequence of college-track math and science courses in middle and high school, followed by science concentration in undergraduate college, science graduate study, and/or employment in a science occupation. The pipeline conceptualization posits a straight and narrow connection between education and occupation and prompts the conscious consideration of the career as a developmental process encompassing both educational and occupational outcomes. A common conclusion drawn from this conceptual perspective is that the underrepresentation of women in science is attributable to women's relatively higher rates of attrition from the science pipeline. Hence, the implication of the model is that, to increase women's representation in science, policies must be devised to "block" the leakage at those points where the pipeline loses more women than men.

Berryman's (1983) introduction of the pipeline model to empirical analysis was a major innovation that facilitated the examination of gender differences across the entire process of becoming a scientist, instead of focusing on single career stages in abstraction. For example, Berryman analyzed gender and racial differences in the science career trajectory by compiling detailed statistics by gender and race that pertain to attainment of sequential levels of science education. From this analysis, Berryman (1983, p. 5) concluded that "For women, the losses are concentrated at the end of the pipeline: at the Ph.D. level." We note that Berryman's study was based on cross-sectional data, as are most other studies that are based on the pipeline conceptualization.

Since Berryman's study, the pipeline model has become so widespread that it is commonly accepted as the dominant, if not the standard, conceptual framework within which to organize studies of the science educational and career trajectory. For instance, an overview article published in *Science* was provocatively entitled "The Pipeline Is Leaking Women All the Way Along" (Alper 1993), and two recent reviews (Schiebinger 1999; Sonnert 1999) also include "pipeline" as part of a major heading. With the exception of Hanson (1996, p. 4), the pervasive use of the pipeline model has gone unquestioned. This is unfortunate, since the pipeline model, while a useful conceptual framework, has limited empirical research by restricting the kinds of questions that are asked by researchers.

To argue that the pipeline framework should not dictate the research agenda, we point to three major limitations. First, the pipeline model does not capture the complexity of the educational and career processes of becoming a scientist. It refers to a unidirectional, orderly, and rigid series of stages, and it equates noncompliance with the normative career trajectory to "leaking" or "dropping out" of the pipeline. This characterization is reified by research that narrowly focuses on gender differences in exits from science/engineering (denoted as S/E) at the expense of not studying the actual, often complicated, pathways followed by men and women in the pursuit of science careers.[3]

Second, in the pipeline framework, persistence across different stages of the educational and career trajectory is assumed to represent progress along the science pipeline. In other words, the pipeline model is a developmental framework in which the successful completion of all stages within an ideal time schedule means a positive outcome. Nonparticipation at any stage is equated with dropping out of the pipeline, and movement back into the pipeline after dropout is assumed to be structurally improbable or impossible. Thus, the narrowness of this model has precluded the consideration of alternative educational and career trajectories, neglecting, for example, a thorough examination of the possibility and implications of "late" entry into S/E and whether the existence or nonexistence of such a career path influences gender differences in participation.

Third, other life course events, such as family formation, that coincide and interact with the science career trajectory are absent from the pipeline conceptualization. By not situating the science career in the context of other life course events, pipeline researchers have implicitly assumed that the pipeline is independent of the timing and character of other life course events. As a result, past research is mostly individual-centered and overlooks the role of the family, whereas gender differences in family expectations and the demands of familial roles may have a significant impact on the timing and sequencing of women's science careers.

Methodological Limitations

Associated with the conceptual drawbacks of the extant literature are some common methodological limitations. First, the current literature on women in science pays inadequate attention to the complexity of measuring career processes and outcomes. Since the processes and outcomes that comprise a career are multifaceted, it is a gross over-simplification to focus on just one or two aspects of the career in investigating women's experiences in science. To be sure, a few studies have been very thorough (e.g., Ahern and Scott 1981; Cole 1979; Long 2001; Sonnert 1995a). These studies, however, are each based on a single data source and are consequently narrow in scope. The career outcomes typically considered are productivity, rank, and salary. In our study, we attempt to address gender differences in career processes and outcomes using a variety of measures within a single broad conceptual framework. In doing so, we update old results and produce new findings.

A second methodological limitation is the widespread use of select, nonrepresentative samples.[4] For example, Sonnert's (1995a, 1995b) two influential books were based on a database about former post-doctoral fellows who received prestigious fellowships from the National Science Foundation or the National Research Council. Other examples include the study by Etzkowitz and colleagues (1994), who collected data in four departments at a single research university, and

Wasserman's (2000) project, which is based on interviews with women who have been elected to the National Academy of Sciences. These focused studies do provide good insight into why women trail men in science careers. In some ways, they may be better than large, nationally representative databases at enabling a deeper examination of the institutional, cultural, and structural barriers that women scientists may face. At the same time, however, studies based on nonrepresentative samples have the irremediable shortcoming of producing results that are not generalizable to the reference population of women scientists.

The widespread use of nonrepresentative, nonrandom samples in studies of women in science underscores the difficulty of conducting a formal statistical analysis of women scientists: there are relatively few of them in the population. Random sampling of the national population is therefore an extremely inefficient way to collect the necessary data. Researchers therefore often collect data from a well-defined subpopulation, such as recipients of doctoral degrees in science (e.g., Cole 1979; Long, Allison, and McGinnis 1993). While sampling from a subpopulation is effective—indeed it is an approach that is also adopted to a large extent in this book—it is important to realize that this approach also carries some methodological risks in light of the dynamic nature of career processes and outcomes.

One methodological problem with sampling from a subpopulation is the arbitrariness inherent in defining a static subpopulation in a dynamic process. Whether or not someone happens to be included in a subpopulation at a given time is undoubtedly affected by chance, and this approach allows chance to play too large a role in defining the sampling frame. When we draw a sample from all doctoral recipients in a specific year, we exclude not only individuals who obtained their degrees in the adjacent years but also those who have not obtained (and will not obtain) a doctoral degree but who are making important scientific contributions. Similarly, when we study academic scientists, we exclude scientists who work in the government and industrial sectors, scientists who have recently moved out of academia, and scientists who are temporarily out of the labor force. If the element of chance is entirely random in its effects on who is included in a particular subpopulation at a particular time, the problem is only a nuisance but does not introduce a serious bias to statistical results. Unfortunately, individuals with certain characteristics may be differentially affected by this uncertainty. We discuss this problem in greater detail below but wish to emphasize here that sampling from a subpopulation is not a simple matter, since determining at what point of the career process a sample should be drawn is a consequential decision.

A related methodological risk is the potential problem of selectivity due to what is commonly called "left censoring": only individuals who have successfully progressed to a certain career stage are included in a sampling frame, and these individuals may differ systematically from those who previously dropped out for whatever reason. For example, when very few women worked in science, it was reasonable to assume that these women may have possessed characteristics that distinguished them from the vast majority of women who did not work in science. Since women have increased their representation in science, the degree of distinction between women working in science and those working in nonscience may have decreased. In this sense, we may want to say that the population of women scientists has become less selective with the increased representation of women in science. Theoretically speaking at least, selectivity could seriously bias statistical results based on observational data and thus render the results unreliable. Unfortunately, selectivity bias is always a potential threat to any study of scientists, because scientists constitute only a very small (albeit increasing) proportion of the labor force.

We do not claim to solve these methodological problems in this book. In the broad scheme, these problems are not solvable with observational data. Our solution is to be comprehensive and pragmatic: we analyze samples that are drawn at different stages of the life course, starting from a very early age. In so doing, we benefit from having rich information about a certain segment of the educational and career trajectory from a single sample. We then juxtapose statistical results from different samples to gain a fuller understanding of the issues. Since our study covers the career trajectory from middle school onward, we gain knowledge about gender differences in earlier career stages before proceeding to analyze gender differences in career outcomes at later stages. Thus, although each separate analysis in our book may suffer from the common problems of left-censoring and selectivity bias, the project itself addresses the problem by using multiple data sources to cover the entire career process.

Another common methodological problem in the literature on women in science is the overreliance on cross-sectional data, despite the fact that most hypotheses in the literature are about dynamic processes that require the analysis of longitudinal data. A prime example is Berryman's (1983) study, which provides excellent snapshots of women's representation in the science pipeline at different educational stages. As we argued earlier, the science career should be conceptualized as a dynamic process. Given the dynamic nature of the subject matter, longitudinal data should in principle always be preferred over cross-sectional data, although we recognize the limited availability of longitudinal data suitable for the study of women in science.

Finally, much of the earlier research on women in science has relied on simple, descriptive statistics (for example, Ahern and Scott 1981, Berryman 1983, Davis et al. 1996, and the special reports by the Committee on Women in Science and Engineering 1991 and the National Science Foundation 1999). While studies reporting descriptive statistics are informative, they can be misleading owing to the possibility that observed gender differences in career outcomes may be confounded by other factors that are related to both gender and career outcomes. In a later section of this chapter, we illustrate the importance of multivariate analysis for controlling factors that mediate the observed association between gender and a career outcome. Throughout the book, we attempt to examine the net effect of gender in a multivariate framework and to compare multivariate results with descriptive results.

Life Course Perspective

The life course perspective frames our examination of the career processes and outcomes of women in science and organizes the presentation of this book. The life course perspective shares with the pipeline perspective an attention to the sequencing and interdependence of educational and occupational events, but the similarity is a superficial one. Whereas the pipeline perspective assumes the science career to be an exceptionally rigid structure, the life course perspective allows for a more multidimensional and nuanced understanding of career processes and outcomes. In a nutshell, the life course perspective posits that the significant events and transitions in an individual's life are age-dependent, interrelated, and contingent on (but not determined by) earlier experiences and societal forces.

Researchers have long recognized that inequality in the labor force is the manifestation of a process of stratification that occurs throughout the life course (e.g., Merton's [1973] theory of cumulative advantage). In particular, the persistent effect of educational attainment on subsequent occupational attainments has been a core subject of traditional social stratification research. However, empirical analyses of specific career lines have tended to separate the educational career from the labor force career and thus have failed to connect them in a life course conceptualization. To understand gender differences in science careers, career lines must be recognized as "lifetime trajectories which result from stratification processes occurring in both educational and labor force settings" (Kerckhoff 1996, p. 38). In this study, we conceptualize the S/E career trajectory as a life course process that begins with S/E education and extends to S/E labor force participation. Our investigation is aimed at understanding and gauging gender disparities during different periods of the life course and examining how early gender differences establish and reinforce gender inequalities later in life.

Conceptualizing the S/E career trajectory as a life course process highlights the need to model explicitly the dynamic processes that lead to the attainment of educational credentials in science, placement in scientific occupations, and the experience of successive career outcomes. The emphasis on the dynamic processes of the life course has guided our research in four ways.

First, the life course perspective recognizes the interactive effects of institutional-level and individual-level influences on the course of career trajectories. That is, "which individuals follow which trajectories is determined by the intersection of individual and institutional actions" (Kerckhoff 1996, p. 38). We argue that gender inequalities in S/E careers are produced by the interaction of structural allocation and self-selection processes. We use the word *self-selection* because we assume that humans lead purposive lives: individuals set both short-term and long-term goals about the roles they intend to fill, and they act to achieve those goals (Clausen 1986). However, it is also important to recognize that the range of considered options is largely constrained by the social and cultural norms that are reflected in the social structure and reinforced by the significant actors in one's life (Clausen 1986; MacLeod 1987; Sewell, Haller, and Portes 1969; Xie and Shauman 1997). Individuals perceive their options through their unique "matrix of social characteristics" (Xie 1989, p. 4). The objective of this research is to discover how certain configurations of factors lead some individuals, but not others, to believe that the scientist role is desirable and attainable, to maintain and act on that belief through an extended period of the life course, and why this sorting of individuals into S/E and non-S/E pools so neatly divides along gender lines.

Second, the life course perspective attempts to model the complexity of human lives by recognizing that the life course is composed of multiple trajectories in the domains of education, family, and work. Progress in a career trajectory is always accompanied, and may be influenced, by developments in other life course trajectories (Elder 1977; O'Rand 1996; O'Rand and Krecker 1990). Thus, educational and occupational achievements and choices are affected by developments in the family domain as well as by individual and structural influences that are associated directly with education and occupation. Events in one domain of the life course can affect the course of trajectories in other domains through their effects on one's available time, interest, energy, and material resources.

Third, the life course perspective recognizes the existence of "career lines," or relatively structured and frequently traveled pathways through multiple transitions to particular life course outcomes, but it also emphasizes individual-level variation in career tracks. It is assumed that there are normative pathways linking social-structural origins to career destinations, but the life course perspective also directs us to recognize that there are many other viable career tracks. In fact, as we show in this book, for women the less-traveled pathways may be important routes to science. The research agenda set by the life course perspective aims to identify the "most frequently traveled pathways" to S/E careers (Kerckhoff 1996, p. 38) and to understand the systematic variation at the individual level in these paths.

Fourth, the life course perspective points to the cumulative nature of life events, the way small differences at particular points in time can deflect trajectories and subsequently generate large differences in career outcomes. The idea that the stratification of career outcomes is the culmination of small differences at earlier points in the life course was introduced by Robert Merton's (1973) cumulative advantage hypothesis (also see Cole and Singer 1991). Kerckhoff's (1993) work documents that modest influences can accumulate into substantial "deflections" over the life course. Deflections are produced and reinforced at the institutional level through structural allocation, and at the individual level through socialization, actualization, and self-legitimization. Accurately identifying the causes of gender differences in career trajectories requires a holistic research design that examines a significant span of the life course and multiple levels of social influences.

In short, a key strength of the life course perspective is its recognition of the multidimensionality of individuals' lives. It encourages social researchers to take into account the multiple roles that characterize individual lives, the layers of forces that influence an individual's life course, and the succession of events and outcomes that comprise a "career." For our study, we outline a schematic model that specifies the dynamics of a particular set of social determinants that operate over the course of someone's life and affect his or her educational and occupational outcomes. For convenience, we group these social determinants by the level of aggregation into individual influences, familial influences, and broader social influences. We propose that the impact of these determinants gradually shifts in measurable and predictable ways as individuals move through the life course (Maccoby 1995). We also propose a set of career processes and outcomes that are appropriate to particular periods of the life course. While the set of career processes and outcomes we include in this study falls far short of complete coverage, the events we examine are theoretically important "points of deflection" in the S/E career. This schematic model serves as a heuristic guide for our empirical study rather than as the theory to be supported or rejected. In the following subsections, we discuss the three groups of social determinants in greater detail and present the sequence of career processes and outcomes that organize our life course analysis of women's careers in science.

Individual Influences

Early in the life course, certain individual characteristics, such as intelligence or career ambition, should matter a great deal for educational outcomes. For example, influential throughout primary and secondary school is an individual's demonstrated aptitude, that is, her/his ability to learn and to perform well on classroom work and achievement tests. Later in the life course, academic performance remains influential, but the character of its influence changes. As an individual progresses from high school to college and the labor force, his/her educational and occupational trajectory is influenced less by aptitude and more by mastery of the skill to perform specific tasks. As new scientists enter the labor force, their career prospects are judged more by the credentials they have attained in formal education than by any measure of cognitive ability. Needless to say, attainment of educational credentials depends on cognitive ability. However, the causal effects of cognitive ability on educational credentials are by no means deterministic. What we argue here is that most of the effects of cognitive ability on science careers are indirect, mediated by formal education. Furthermore, some new individual characteristics emerge as influential as individuals begin to participate in a labor market. For example, characteristics such as the time between bachelor's degree and doctorate and access to research funding are factors that become influential for career paths only at or after entry into the labor force.

The expected shifts in individual influences throughout the life course inform our analysis and are reflected in the selection of explanatory and outcome variables for each chapter of the book. In the early chapters we explicitly examine gender differences in measured achievement in math and science and then go on to analyze the influence of math and science achievement on other outcomes, such as the formation of S/E career aspirations and the choice of an S/E college major. These chapters also include measures of affective characteristics, such as comfort with math and science and attitudes about the perceived future usefulness of math achievement. The later chapters of the book address gender differences in labor force experiences and outcomes. The analyses of these later chapters include explanatory variables that are expected to be most relevant for individuals participating in the S/E labor market. For example, the analysis of gender differences in publication productivity in Chapter 9 examines the influence of individual characteristics such as time to degree, access to research funding and assistance, and time spent on classroom teaching.

Familial Influences

Changes also occur in the nature of the familial influences. A general trend is that the locus of familial influences shifts from the family of origin (i.e., the natal family) to the family of formation (i.e., the primary family) as the individual progresses from childhood to adulthood (Maccoby 1995). Early in the life course, one's parents are the primary socializing agents. Youth learn the social rules and norms and are oriented to their world and taught their place in it by their parents and other members of the natal family. Parents make most decisions for their children, and the few decisions that children make on their own are strongly influenced by the beliefs of their parents. As the individual matures, his/her parents modify their treatment (Maccoby and Jacklin 1974), slowly yielding their authority and gradually reducing their influence. Eventually, individuals find themselves making their own decisions. As this transition occurs, the direct influence of parents wanes, and life decisions are increasingly influenced by an individual's conceptions of his/her own current and future social roles. Prominent among these conceptions is one's orientation to the gender roles society prescribes, especially the roles associated with marriage and family. As individuals later marry and begin to have children, their life decisions become increasingly influenced by the familial roles they assume and the needs of the other members of the primary family.

Before individuals marry and start a family of their own, the influence of familial concerns is manifest in the influence of sex-role socialization on a young person's perceptions of the current and future social costs of pursuing a career in science. The anticipated conflict between a demanding career and childrearing may be a salient issue for girls early in the life course, long before they actually experience childbearing and childrearing. For young girls who plan to combine work and family roles, the heavy human capital investments and anticipated time demands of S/E occupations may squelch their interest in an S/E career (Sandberg et al. 1987; Wolfe and Betz 1981). Later in the S/E career trajectory, familial influence is manifest in the tension between actual familial life and the commitment to a career that requires heavy investment in education, training, and role performance. Reflecting this shift in familial influences, variables measuring the expected timing of family formation and the relative importance of familial roles are central to the analyses of the early life course presented in Chapters 2, 3, and 4. Beginning with the analysis of bachelor's degree attainment in Chapter 4, we introduce marital and parental statuses as explanatory factors and include them in later chapters whenever data permit.

Social Influences

Although parents and the family lay the foundation for career development, individuals are also exposed to influences through social institutions that operate outside the family. When individuals are young, they are mostly affected by the school system. As schooling ends and work begins, the locus of social influences shifts from schools to the labor force.

Schools exert their influence in a variety of ways: the availability of courses, sporting facilities, and extracurricular activities; the quality of teaching, teachers' expectations, and guidance; the availability and orientation of guidance counselors; and the characteristics of the student's peers. Although in principle it is possible for schools to initiate social change by treating girls and boys equally, in practice schools often serve to reinforce traditional gender stereotypes. This is true because schools often reflect the social structure of the larger society. For example, very few science and math teachers are women, and both male and female teachers report having higher expectations for girls than boys in language-related tasks and higher expectations for boys than girls in math and science activities (Reid and Paludi 1993). Whereas the influence of the educational structure is limited to the period of direct contact, the influence of the labor force structure may begin even before individuals officially enter it. Students are aware of the structure of the labor force and use that information to plan their further education and careers and to assess the appropriateness of their aspirations (Xie and Shauman 1997). Students' career aspirations reflect their perceptions of the careers that are appropriate for and attainable by them. Therefore, gender differences in aspirations reveal the degree to which young men and women perceive different opportunity structures for themselves (Laws 1976; Marini and Brinton 1984). The fact that young women are much less likely than young men to aspire to an S/E career indicates that a significant proportion of young women do not perceive S/E occupations to be within their realm of possibility, and this perception is reinforced by the structure of the labor force.

Once individuals make the transition into the labor force, their actions, access to resources, and achievement-related goals are influenced by their work setting and their coworkers. Different work environments lead to different and unequal career outcomes. For example, women academic scientists are more likely than men to be found in teaching colleges rather than in research universities (Fox 1995, p. 212; Long 2001; Long and Fox 1995), and this helps explain gender differences in publication productivity (see Chapter 9).

Processes and Outcomes in S/E Careers

Just as the life course perspective draws our attention to the multiple levels of influences that operate throughout the course of a career, it also calls for an examination of career processes and outcomes that is appropriate to particular stages of the career trajectory. A distinct feature of this study is our attention to the multifaceted nature of career processes and outcomes. This feature reflects our belief that gender differences in S/E career processes and outcomes accumulate over the life course and manifest themselves at different points in time. We cannot, however, include everything that is relevant to this subject. Some topics are excluded from the book because they are relatively less important than those that we choose to study. Other topics are omitted because we do not have satisfactory data with which to address them. The aspects of career processes and outcomes that we study are:

1. Academic achievement in science and mathematics before college.
2. The expectation of enrolling in an S/E major in college.
3. The likelihood of obtaining an S/E degree at the bachelor's level.
4. Career outcomes following the completion of a bachelor's degree in S/E.
5. Career outcomes following the completion of a master's degree in S/E.
6. The demographic and labor force characteristics of scientists/engineers.
7. Geographic mobility of doctoral scientists/engineers.
8. Research productivity among academic scientists.
9. Immigrant women scientists.

Clearly, the above list falls far short of exhausting all the possible topics that can be considered as career processes and outcomes. Another caveat is that, although we earlier discussed the influence of social determinants in connection with the life course approach, our analysis of educational outcomes in S/E is mainly concerned with in-dividual-level and family-level influences. We do not examine school-level and other broad social influences in our study. Our decision to limit the scope of this research prevents us from directly testing the hypothesis that gender differences in S/E education are affected by such school-level social influences as teacher behavior, instructional style, and classroom atmosphere. Rather, we can only indirectly infer the influence of the school from the effects of individual attributes and family characteristics. Our decision is based on the limitations of our data as well as our desire to accomplish a thorough investigation of individual and familial influences. We leave the role of the school-level influences to be explored by other researchers.

Methodological Issues

Implementing this study of the career processes and outcomes of women in science required many decisions about the research design, concept definitions, and methodological issues. Essentially, the book consists of nine separate analyses targeted at different topics. While a specific analysis often required unique methodological decisions, some common methodological issues permeate the entire project. In this section we address the methodological concerns and elements of the research design that are common to all of the component analyses of the study.

Synthetic Cohorts

From the previous discussion, it should be clear that the life course framework calls for longitudinal data covering individuals' educa-tional and career histories. In reality, however, we have access only to cross-sectional or longitudinal data of limited duration. To overcome this difficulty, we devised a demographic approach to studying the de-velopmental process of becoming a scientist/engineer that follows a synthetic cohort through the formative years of career development. The approach is dynamic rather than static in the sense that it traces changes over the different career stages of a cohort.

In a classic article, Ryder (1965, p. 845) defined a cohort "as the ag-gregate of individuals (within some population definition) who expe-rienced the same event within the same time interval." For example, all individuals born at the same time (say, within a given calendar year) make up a birth cohort. Similarly, events such as marriage and school entry define marriage and school cohorts. Ideally, we would like to observe all career changes of a real cohort for its entire history, from childhood to retirement. This would allow us to construct an accurate model of life course career processes of the cohort. Such longitudinal designs, however, are unrealistic in practice not only because they are too expensive and would yield extremely small samples of practicing scientists, but also because they take a lifetime to complete and thus cannot yield even tentative answers to important questions that society currently faces.

One common solution to this dilemma, often adopted by demographers in studies of fertility and mortality, is to construct age-specific vital rates from a cross-section and then assume them to be experienced by a hypothetical cohort. For instance, the total fertility rate (TFR) is the expected total number of children a woman would have if she followed the entire age-specific fertility schedule of a given period, and life expectancy is the expected total number of years a newborn child would live if she/he were subject to the age-specific mortality schedule of a given time and place. Berryman's study (1983) is an application of this approach. As we discussed above, however, this approach does not allow researchers to uncover dynamic processes underlying the cross-sectional data. For example, Berryman was unable to examine the changes in enrollment status and field of study and their variations across gender and race, even though she clearly realized the importance of such transitions.

Limited longitudinal studies, a middle ground between purely cross-sectional designs and ideal longitudinal designs, have gained more popularity and acceptance in recent years. By "limited longitudinal studies" we mean that a group of subjects is followed only for a limited duration. Examples are the National Longitudinal Study of the Class of 1972 (NLS-72), Longitudinal Study of American Youth (LSAY), High School and Beyond (HSB), National Education Longitudinal Survey (NELS), and the 1982–1989 Survey of Natural and Social Scientists and Engineers (SSE). We use these limited longitudinal studies for our research and describe them in Appendix A.

Limited longitudinal studies could be cohort-based, such as NLS-72, LSAY, HSB, and NELS, or population-based, such as SSE. While the sampling frames of NLS-72, LSAY, HSB, and NELS were school cohorts, the sampling frame of SSE was the population of scientists

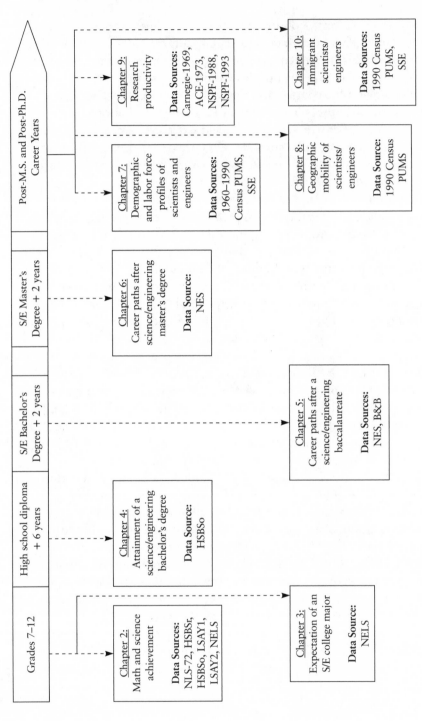

Figure 1.1. The life course of a synthetic cohort of individuals on the science/engineering trajectory, including the career processes and outcomes examined in this book and the data sources used for the analyses

identified by the 1980 U.S. census. Because there are currently many large, nationally representative, cohort-based limited longitudinal studies available, we piece together the experiences of different cohorts to form a synthetic cohort. Here we define a synthetic cohort as a hypothetical cohort whose life history is constructed from different real cohorts in a supplementary manner. Although the synthetic cohort is not real, segments of the cohort's experiences are real. A major advantage of this approach is that it allows us to study the "social dynamics" of individuals' transitions into and out of different educational and career states (Tuma and Hannan 1984).

Unfortunately, even limited longitudinal studies with reasonable sample sizes are difficult to come by. For some important phases of career development and some important career outcomes, we do not have access to even limited longitudinal studies. When this is the case, we resort to using cross-sectional data for snapshots of dynamic processes, and we sometimes rely on respondents' recall of retrospective information. Despite the limitations of cross-sectional data, we believe that empirical findings from such data can be very informative. We therefore supplement longitudinal data with cross-sectional data in some chapters in this book. Together, the information from many different datasets contributes to a composite portrait of the career processes and outcomes of women in science. This composite portrait does not belong to any real person, nor any real cohort, but to a synthetic cohort. See Figure 1.1 for an illustration of the segments in the life course that we examine and the various datasets we use.

Synthesizing results pertaining to different cohorts as if they belong to a single cohort requires the assumption that the career process is mainly age-dependent rather than cohort- or period-dependent. This assumption is called "stationarity," referring to the robustness of age patterns across different cohorts and historical periods. Over fifty years ago Ginzberg and his associates (Ginzberg et al. 1951) observed that the career process is generally an age-dependent developmental process. As we show in this book, however, women's careers in science have changed rapidly in recent decades, and the assumption of stationarity required for interpreting the results as if they pertain to a synthetic cohort is likely to be violated in reality. Thus, the reader should treat the synthetic cohort approach discussed in this section as a heuristic device that aids in the interpretation of the empirical results from many datasets. Indeed, the empirical results reported in the book are meaningful in and by themselves, and the interpretation of them does not hinge on one's acceptance of the synthetic cohort approach.

Definition of Scientists/Engineers

Before we can proceed further, we need to define what we mean by the terms *scientists* and *engineers*. At first glance, the task seems straightforward, for the terms are commonly used. In practice, however, defining scientists/engineers is a difficult task facing all researchers who study the population (Citro and Kalton 1989).

There are at least three approaches to defining scientists/engineers. Let us call the three resulting definitions the substantive definition, the credential definition, and the behavioral definition. The substantive definition recognizes the existence of "invisible colleges" (Crane 1972)—the scientific community—in which scientists communicate with each other through formal and informal publication channels. The ultimate criterion for the substantive definition is one's contribution to a common body of scientific knowledge and thus one's involvement in scientific communication. The main problem with this approach is the difficulty of measuring contribution. In contrast, the credential definition is based on one's formal credentials, such as an S/E degree. This definition is also called the "education-based" or "supply-based" definition, as it defines the "supply" of scientists. The main problem with the credential definition is that not everyone with the requisite credentials is actually involved in scientific activities. Lastly, the behavioral definition takes the "demand" perspective and relies on information about activities that individuals actually perform in their jobs. We call this definition "occupation-based" or "demand-based" since it defines a person as a scientist if he or she reports holding a scientific job. The populations of "scientists" identified by these three definitions do not coincide. A person may be labeled a scientist according to one definition but a nonscientist according to another. For example, it is possible to find a small number of people actually doing scientific work even though they neither hold formal degrees nor publish scientific papers. More often than not, however, an individual is identified as a scientist by all three definitions.

The National Science Foundation (e.g., NSF 1986, p. 39) had a long-standing, eclectic practice that combined information pertaining to the three definitions.[5] Roughly speaking, it defined someone as a scientist/engineer if at least two of the following three criteria were met: (1) the person's highest degree is in science/engineering; (2) the person is employed in a scientific/engineering occupation; and (3) the person professionally identifies himself/herself as a scientist/engineer on the basis of total education and work experience. There are a number of problems with this hybrid definition. The most serious of all is that it does not have a clear theoretical interpretation. Another is the difficulty of maintaining consistency across datasets. Finally, the third criterion, self-identification as a scientist, gives too much room to individual subjectivity.

We adopt two alternative definitions of scientists/engineers: the credential (education-based or supply-based) definition and the behavioral (occupation-based or demand-based) definition, following the recommendation of Citro and Kalton (1989). In practice, the occupation-based definition specifies that the incumbents of S/E occupations are scientists/engineers. The education-based definition considers individuals with or working toward S/E educational degrees as scientists/engineers or potential scientists/engineers. In the first part of the book, we are primarily concerned with education in science and engineering and thus rely on the education-based definition. In the second part of the book, where the focus is on career outcomes of scientists/engineers, we shift to the occupation-based definition. Although this strategy provides only a vague specification of whom we ultimately wish to define as scientists/engineers, it allows us to define the most appropriate population for the analysis of each specific aspect of career processes and outcomes that we study.

Measuring Gender Differences

Although we are mainly interested in the experiences and outcomes of women in science, we believe it is essential to include men in our analysis. While a few studies (e.g., Wasserman 2000) of women in science have been based on data from women alone, such studies are inherently limited in their ability to identify barriers unique to women's careers in science and engineering. As in most studies on women in science, we treat men as the natural reference group with whom to compare women. We maintain this focus on gender comparison throughout the statistical analyses reported in this book. Indeed, whenever feasible, we present only those statistics that contrast women and men. In this section, we discuss the pros and cons of several single-number measures summarizing gender differences.[6]

Correlation. Earlier work on women scientists (e.g., Blackburn,

Behymer, and Hall 1978; Cole 1979) used the correlation coefficient as the primary measure of gender differences. To use this measure, the researcher typically codes sex as a dummy variable and then computes the Pearson correlation coefficient (r) between sex and a continuous outcome variable. The Pearson correlation involving a dummy variable for sex (X) and a continuous variable (Y) can be calculated easily from the sex-specific sample means of Y, the sex composition in the sample, and the standard deviation of Y (S_y). More specifically (Stuart and Ord 1991, p. 995),

$$(1.1) \qquad r = \sqrt{pq}(\overline{Y}_F - \overline{Y}_M)/S_y,$$

where p and q denote the proportions of female scientists and male scientists in the sample and $\overline{Y}_F$ and $\overline{Y}_M$, respectively, represent the means for female and male scientists. Equation 1.1 reveals that the correlation between X and Y is *not* invariant with respect to the sex composition in the sample. Specifically, the correlation reaches the maximum possible value when the sex composition is balanced at 50 percent female and 50 percent male and declines when the sex composition is unbalanced. This is so even though the essential information (i.e., sex-specific means) in the data remains unchanged. For this reason, correlation generally is not a desirable statistic for measuring gender differences, especially in the field of S/E, where gender composition has been unequal but changing rapidly in recent decades.

Means Ratio. Since conditional means by sex convey the most essential information on sex differences, we can measure sex differences simply by taking the ratio between sex-specific means:

$$(1.2) \qquad R = \overline{Y}_F / \overline{Y}_M.$$

The sex ratio of means (R) is invariant to changes in the sex composition. For most research questions, this invariance is desirable, and thus R is preferable to r. Indeed, this is the measure used in the studies of gender differences in publication productivity by Cole and Zuckerman (1984) and Long (1992). Easy to compute and interpret, the ratio expressed by equation 1.2 has been the standard measure used in the labor force literature studying sex differences in earnings (e.g., Bianchi and Spain 1986). As will be shown later, this measure can also be computed easily from multivariate regression models with the logarithm of Y as the dependent variable.

Probability Ratio. The outcome variable (*Y*) itself may also be a dummy variable, taking the value of 1 or 0. An example is whether or not a person completes a bachelor's degree in S/E. When this is the case, equation 1.2 changes to a probability ratio:

(1.3) $PR = P(Y = 1|F)/P(Y = 1|M),$

where $P(Y = 1|F)$ is the probability among females and $P(Y = 1|M)$ is the probability among males. The probability ratio is also called the relative risk (Powers and Xie 2000, pp. 94–95). Although the measure can be straightforwardly defined as an extension of the means ratio, it has the drawback of asymmetry. We know that the 0–1 coding for a dummy variable is arbitrary. Thus, an ideal measure of sex differences should not vary however we code the outcome variable *Y*. Unfortunately, the probability ratio is not invariant to which category of the dichotomous outcome variable is coded to 1 (versus 0) (Powers and Xie 2000, p. 95). This drawback makes the measure a poor candidate for summarizing gender differences.

Odds Ratio. For dichotomous outcome variables, we resort to the odds ratio (*OR*) to measure gender differences. Simply put, an odds ratio is the ratio of odds instead of probabilities, with odds (*O*) defined as

(1.4) $O = P(Y = 1)/P(Y = 0).$

The odds ratio measuring gender differences in the likelihood of $Y = 1$ versus the likelihood $Y = 0$ is:

(1.5) $OR = [P(Y = 1|F)/P(Y = 0|F)]/ [P(Y = 1|M)/P(Y = 0|M)].$

Unlike a probability ratio, an odds ratio is symmetric around the 0.5 probability point and invariant to changes in the coding of the outcome variable: a switch in the coding of $Y = 1$ and $Y = 0$ simply means the inversion of the odds ratio. If $P(Y = 1)$ is very small, and $P(Y = 0)$ is therefore close to 1, the probability ratio and the odds ratio are about the same.

What is particularly attractive about odds ratios is that they can be retrieved easily from multivariate logit regression models. This is true because the dependent variable in a logit regression model is the logarithm of odds. Hence, we can compare observed odds ratios with adjusted odds ratios after controlling for covariates. In Chapter 7, we will also explore the relationship between an odds ratio as defined above and a representation ratio.

Explaining Gender Differences: The Multivariate Approach

Given our primary interest in comparing women and men, can we simply present statistics (such as R or OR) that pertain to gender differences on average? That is, can we conduct bivariate analyses showing relationships between gender and relevant outcome variables? The answer is no, although for the sake of parsimony we would like to do so.

The danger in drawing conclusions based on simple female-male comparisons is that such comparisons may be confounded by other relevant factors. To illustrate this point, consider the example of gender differences in earnings. Women earn less than men in part because women are more likely to work part-time, and part-time workers earn less than full-time workers on average. A simple comparison of the average earnings of women and men thus would be misleading. In general, to tease out confounding factors that mediate between gender on one hand and educational and career outcomes on the other hand, it is necessary to conduct multivariate analyses involving more than these two variables. In our study, we take a multivariate approach to statistical analyses of individual-level data.

Our multivariate approach can be easily demonstrated with the language of direct, indirect, and total effects used in path analysis and structural equation modeling (Alwin and Hauser 1975). In Figure 1.2, we give an unrealistically simple presentation for illustrative purposes. Let X denote the variable of sex (coded as female = 1, male = 0) and Y denote the outcome variable. The bivariate effect of sex, shown as A^* in Figure 1.2a, is called the total effect. In Figure 1.2b, this total effect of sex on Y is decomposed into two components: a direct effect (A) and an indirect effect through covariate Z (paths C and B).[7]

It should be noted that sex (X) is causally prior to potential covariates (Z) and that Z represents all possible mediating variables between X and Y. In this simple setup, we are interested in the relative importance of the indirect effect of X on Y through Z. When the indirect effect constitutes a large part of the total effect of X on Y, we attain a good understanding of how the total effect of X on Y operates. It is in this context that we say that Z "explains" the effect of X.

Not all potential covariates serve to mediate the total effect of sex (X). To illustrate this point, let A* be negative, signifying that the outcome variable has a lower mean for women than for men. When covariate Z serves to mediate women's disadvantage in Y, one of the following two scenarios is indicated:

> *Both* of the following two conditions are satisfied: (1) Z positively affects Y and (2) Z is negatively associated with sex, with women having a lower mean of Z than men. *Or,*
> *Both* of the following two conditions are satisfied: (1) Z negatively affects Y and (2) Z is positively associated with sex, with women having a higher mean of Z than men.

We call (1) the relevance condition and (2) the correlation condition (in either scenario). A covariate may confound the bivariate relationship between sex and an outcome variable *only if* the covariate is relevant to the outcome variable *and* correlated with sex.

One should not mechanically apply the relevance and correlation conditions, however. Doing so would lead to the inclusion of too many covariates in a multivariate analysis and erroneous conclusions if the covariates are "pseudocontrols" (Lieberson 1985). It is critical

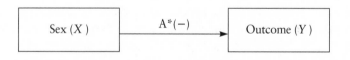

Figure 1.2a. Bivariate approach to explaining gender differences

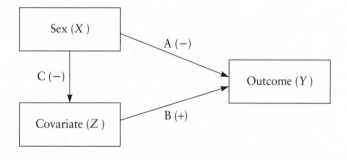

Figure 1.2b. Multivariate approach to explaining gender differences

to select covariates that are appropriate for each particular research context. Each chapter that follows addresses a specific question about gender differences in S/E career processes and outcomes and in that context considers a set of covariates that may serve as explanatory factors.

As we discussed earlier, we can easily compute the sex ratio of means (R) and sex ratios of odds (OR) from regression models with logged mean and logged odds, respectively, as the dependent variable. In such cases, R or OR is simply the exponentiated coefficient of the sex variable, $\exp(b_{sex})$. Since sex is a dummy variable coded 0 for male and 1 for female, $\exp(b_{sex})$ is called the female-to-male ratio (or odds ratio) in tables reporting results from multivariate analyses. When women are disadvantaged relative to men for a positive career outcome, b_{sex} is negative and $\exp(b_{sex})$ is lower than one. As covariates are added, the magnitude of $\exp(b_{sex})$ changes. If the covariates included indeed help explain the total effect of sex on the outcome, $\exp(b_{sex})$ increases in value toward one. The increase in $\exp(b_{sex})$ over its value in the baseline bivariate model (i.e., with no other controls) yields a sensible measure of the extent to which the explanatory variables included in a statistical model "explain" the raw bivariate sex difference in the outcome. However, the size of the change in $\exp(b_{sex})$ depends on what other variables are present in the model. In Appendix B, we describe a method that allows us to estimate the independent contribution of an explanatory variable in accounting for changes in $\exp(b_{sex})$. We use this decomposition methodology in several chapters.

Outline of the Book

This book is divided into two parts. In the first part, we focus on gender differences along the S/E educational trajectory. We begin with academic achievement in science and math in the precollege years in Chapter 2 and then move to the expectation of enrolling in an S/E major in college in Chapter 3. In Chapter 4, we document gender differences in the likelihood of obtaining an S/E degree at the bachelor's level; here we pay attention to aggregate transition rates leading to the attainment of S/E degrees as well as individual-level determinants. In Chapters 5 and 6, we are concerned with career transitions following the completion of an S/E degree respectively at the bachelor's level and at the master's level. Beginning with Chapter 7, we shift our attention from career processes to career outcomes, with an empirical portrait of the demographic and labor force outcomes of men and women scientists. In Chapter 8, we focus on the likelihood of geographic mobility among all scientists. Research productivity among academic scientists is the subject of Chapter 9. In Chapter 10, we explore the consequences of immigration on the gender composition of scientists and on the gender differences in labor force outcomes among scientists.

CHAPTER TWO

Math and Science Achievement

According to the pipeline perspective, a young student's interest in a scientific career and his or her ability to achieve such a goal depend largely on the student's experiences in math and science education during middle and high school. Failing to build a solid foundation of mathematics coursework and achievement in these years may therefore close the door to college coursework in an S/E field. At the very least, redressing inadequate math and science preparation through remedial coursework is likely to delay the completion of S/E postsecondary education. Thus, gender disparities in science and engineering postsecondary education and careers are widely believed, among academic researchers and the public alike, to originate with gender differences in math and science achievement among middle and high school students.

If we are to be satisfied that gender differences in the S/E educational trajectory and labor force participation are explained by gender differences in math and science achievement, two corollaries of this explanation need to be empirically affirmed. First, the magnitude of the gender differences in math and science achievement and their stability over time must be established. Second, the causal connection between gender differences in achievement and gender differences in participation in the S/E educational and occupational trajectories must be empirically measured. In this chapter we address the first of these two corollaries. We examine the magnitude of gender differences in student performance on standardized math and science achievement tests at successive points in the educational trajectory from the seventh to the twelfth grade, focusing on the trends in these gender differences from the early 1970s to the early 1990s. We then use multivariate analyses to assess the power of individual and familial influences to explain gender differences in math and science achievement.

Measuring Gender Differences in Math and Science Achievement

There is a large body of research devoted to the measurement and explanation of gender differences in mathematics achievement (e.g., Armstrong 1985; Benbow 1983, 1988, 1992; Benbow and Stanley 1980, 1983a; Entwisle, Alexander, and Olson 1994; Fennema 1980, 1984; Friedman 1989; Hyde, Fennema, and Lamon 1990; International Association for the Evaluation of Educational Achievement 1985; Leahey and Guo 2001; Meyer 1989; Nowell and Hedges 1998; Oakes 1990). The majority of this research has focused on gender differences in average performance on math and science achievement tests and has relied on measures of central tendency to assess those differences. Although the research results vary somewhat depending on the characteristics of the sample used (Hyde, Fennema, and Lamon 1990), the general consensus from studies using broadly representative samples and meta-analyses is that gender differences are nonexistent or slightly favor females prior to adolescence, whereupon a male advantage emerges and grows in magnitude through the high school years (Feingold 1988; Friedman 1989; Hyde, Fennema, and Lamon 1990; Leahey and Guo 2001; Linn and Hyde 1989; Nowell and Hedges 1998).[1] The emergent gender gap favoring males is limited to certain types of math skills, such as quantitative reasoning and some types of spatial visualization (Friedman 1989; Hyde, Fennema, and Lamon 1990; Jacklin 1989; Maccoby and Jacklin 1974), and, though statistically significant, the gender differential in average performance is small compared with the variation within each gender group. In addition, analyses of the recent historical trends in the mathematics achievement gender gap have unanimously reported significant decreases in the magnitude of the differential over the past twenty years (Feingold 1988; Friedman 1989; Hyde 1981; Linn and Hyde 1989; NSF 1994).

Researchers examining science achievement have found a somewhat different pattern of gender differences: the differential in science achievement favors boys even at young ages and appears to be consistent across grade levels and over recent history. The magnitude of the gender disparity in science achievement also varies with the content or subject matter of the tests: achievement differences in biology and general science are found to be significantly smaller than those in physics (Becker 1989; Lee and Burkam 1996; Lee, Burkam, and Smerdon 1997; Steinkamp and Maehr 1983, 1984). A study by Linn and Hyde (1989), however, contradicts the assertion that gender differences in science achievement have been invariant over time. They report that the gender gap in science achievement, like that in mathematics achievement, has dwindled to insignificance over the past two decades.

The extant literature on gender differences in math and science achievement is very large and spans many disciplines. However, our knowledge of gender differences is still incomplete because most studies focus on differences in mean performance and typically overlook gender differences in the variability of test scores. Researchers have long pointed to the importance of examining differences in variance and extreme scores. For example, extensive reviews and meta-analyses of gender differences show that the magnitude of measured gender differences increases with the selectivity of study samples (Becker and Hedges 1984; Hyde, Fennema, and Lamon 1990; Maccoby and Jacklin 1974). If males and females attain the same scores on average, but they differ in the variability of test scores, members of the sex with the greater variability will be more likely to achieve both very high and very low scores (Feingold 1992).

Studies have consistently found greater variance in achievement among males than among females (Feingold 1988, 1992, 1994; Hedges and Nowell 1995; Leahey and Guo 2001; Nowell and Hedges 1998). Moreover, the combination of a relatively small male advantage in mean performance with a larger male variance results in a significant overrepresentation of males among high-scoring students (Feingold 1992).[2] So, although gender differences in central tendency are small and may have decreased to insignificance in recent years, the greater variability of achievement among males means that females continue to be underrepresented among the highest achievers. If extremely high achievement is a strong predictor of participation and success in the S/E educational trajectory, the underrepresentation of women at the highest levels of performance may help explain gender differences in participation in science and engineering.

While researchers generally accept the existence of gender differences in science and math achievement, especially among late-adolescent and high-scoring students, there is disagreement about the magnitude of the differences, the timing of their emergence, and their stability over time. Researchers also disagree about the practical significance of the math and science achievement differentials. The ostensible gender differences are thought to be significant because of their presumed implications for occupational sex segregation and wage inequality. Indeed, such implications are arguably the most frequently cited justification for continuing to study math and science gender gaps. However, many researchers contend that the magnitude of gender differences in math and science achievement is too small to be practically meaningful (Fennema and Sherman 1978; Friedman 1989; Hyde 1981; Linn and Hyde 1989). They argue that these gender differences are not large enough to explain gender differences in participation in math and science education and in the scientific labor market later in the life course. We address the question of the predictive power of the gender differences in general math and science achievement in the chapters that follow.

Describing Gender Differences in Math and Science Achievement

To describe gender differences in science and math achievement, we examine disparities in both the mean and the variability of achievement test scores. Mean gender differences are measured using the d-statistic (Cohen 1977). The d-statistic is defined as the mean achievement score for females minus the mean achievement score for males, divided by the pooled within-gender standard deviation. Hence, a positive value of d indicates a female advantage, and a negative value of d indicates a male advantage in average achievement. Generally speaking, d values of ± 0.20, ± 0.50, and ± 0.80 indicate small, medium, and large effects, respectively (Cohen 1977). We assess gender differences in representation among the highest math and science achievers using a high achievement ratio, *AR*, defined as the female-to-male ratio of the odds of scoring in the top 5 percent of the pooled distribution of achievement test scores. For this descriptive analysis, we use data from four nationally representative longitudinal studies: the National Longitudinal Study of the Class of 1972 (NLS-72), the High School and Beyond Sophomore and Senior Cohorts (HSBSo, HSBSr), the National Education Longitudinal Study of 1988 (NELS), and both cohorts of the Longitudinal Study of American Youth (LSAY1, LSAY2). The dependent variables for the analyses presented in this chapter are math and science achievement, measured by students' scores on the standardized tests administered as part of each of the studies.[3] All of the data sources are used to describe gender differences in math achievement. The analysis of science achievement is based only on data from the HSBSo, LSAY1, LSAY2, and NELS, since the other studies did not include tests of science achievement. See Appendix A for a full description of each of the data sources as well as a detailed description and comparison of the achievement tests. Cases with missing data on the dependent variables are excluded from all analyses. The sample sizes of the data used for the descriptive analysis are presented in Appendix Table D2.a. This collection of data sources allows us to examine the age trajectory of gender differences in achievement as well as the historical trends in grade-specific gender differences. We track the age profile of gender differences by following each cohort of students over time. The trends from the 1970s to the early 1990s are described by comparing the grade-specific measures of achievement for the six different cohorts observed.

The standardized mean gender differences in mathematics and science achievement scores are presented by cohort and grade in Table 2.1. The school cohort identifier presented in the first column of this table refers to the modal year in which its members would have started elementary school. The values of *d* in each row of the table represent standardized mean gender differences in math and science achievement at sequential grades in the educational trajectory of each cohort. The columns present the cross-cohort changes in the magnitude of grade-specific gender differences in math and science achievement.

Our results confirm that male students tend to outperform female students on both math and science achievement tests. Males have

Table 2.1 Standardized mean gender difference of math and science achievement scores by grade and cohort

School cohort	Mean difference (*d*) in grade						Data source
	7	8	9	10	11	12	
Panel A: Math achievement							
1960						−0.25***	NLS-72
1968						−0.22***	HSBSr
1970				−0.09***		−0.15***	HSBSo
1978				−0.04	−0.07	−0.13**	LSAY1
1980		−0.03***		−0.03*		−0.09***	NELS
1981	0.14***	0.16***	0.12**	0.09*	0.06		LSAY2
Panel B: Science achievement							
1960							NLS-72
1968							HSBSr
1970				−0.26***		−0.30***	HSBSo
1978				−0.28***	−0.11˙	−0.25***	LSAY1
1980		−0.14***		−0.27***		−0.31***	NELS
1981	−0.15***	0.05	−0.07	−0.01	−0.07		LSAY2

Note: Index *d* is defined as the standardized difference in achievement between males and females, measured in standard deviations. Negative values of *d* indicate that the average achievement score for females is less than the average achievement score for males.

*$p < .05$, **$p < .01$, ***$p < .001$ (two-tailed test), for the hypothesis that there is no mean difference between males and females.

higher math and science achievement scores at each grade level for all except the youngest cohort. Panel A of Table 2.1 shows that the male advantage in math achievement is very small early in the educational trajectory but increases during the last years of high school.[4] For the youngest cohort (LSAY2), significant gender differences favoring girls are found from grade 7 to grade 10. This female advantage declined with age, but the male advantage seen among other cohorts had not emerged even when this cohort was in grade 11. Since the gender differences in both math and science achievement for the LSAY2 cohort are somewhat anomalous, we bracket the findings for this cohort from our discussion of the trends.

As shown in the last column, the gender gap among high school seniors declined substantially between 1972 and 1992. For the NLS-72 cohort, the mean mathematics achievement score for males is a quarter of a standard deviation greater than the mean among their female classmates ($d = -0.25$). The magnitude of the gender gap declines 64 percent by 1992 (NELS cohort), when $d = -0.09$.[5] These results therefore confirm the findings of declining gender differences in math achievement reported by other researchers.[6] The values of d measured at each grade level for these cohorts are comparable to those reported by other researchers who have conducted meta-analyses (Feingold 1988; Friedman 1989; Hyde 1981). It is important to note that even the greatest value of d (-0.25) found in Panel A should be interpreted as a small difference according to Cohen's (1977) criteria.

The patterns of gender differences in science achievement, presented in Panel B of Table 2.1, are somewhat different from those observed for math achievement. The male advantage in science achievement is greater in magnitude than that observed for math achievement, and it exhibits neither a clear age pattern nor a clear trend across cohorts. The magnitude of d for science achievement increases with grade for the NELS cohort (from -0.14 in grade 8 to -0.31 in grade 12). The increase, however, is slight between grades 10 and 12, the period of significant increases in the gender gap in math achievement. The value of d increases slightly for the HSBSo cohort, from -0.26 to -0.30, during the last two years of high school. For the LSAY1 cohort, the value of d fluctuates and slightly decreases between grades 10 and 12.

Although gender differences in average math and science scores are small, we find relatively large gender differences in the variance of the distribution of achievement scores. For all cohorts at every grade level and for both math and science achievement scores, we observe that the variance of females' achievement scores is on average about 20 percent less than the variance of the achievement scores of pre-college male students. Appendix Table D2.b presents the grade-specific female-to-male variance ratios (Feingold 1992). This gender difference in variability, coupled with the small gender gap in mean performance, may produce a disproportionately high representation of males among the top math and science achievers. To measure the extent and significance of gender differences in representation among the top performers, we use an achievement ratio, *AR*, defined as the female-to-male ratio of the odds of achieving in the top 5 percent of the distribution. The values of *AR* are presented by grade and school cohort in Table 2.2. An *AR* of one indicates that female and male students are equally represented at and above the 95th percentile.[7] Ratios of less than one indicate the degree to which females are underrepresented among students who score in the top 5 percent of the achievement distribution.

The values of *AR* presented in Table 2.2 confirm that females are significantly underrepresented at the upper tail of both the math (Panel A) and science (Panel B) achievement score distributions. For math achievement, female underrepresentation in the top 5 percent of the distribution becomes more pronounced with age, mirroring the age-dependent growth of the male advantage in mean math achievement. Among the 1981 school cohort, for example, the disparity measured in grades 7 and 8 is not significant (at 0.72 and 0.77), but it becomes significant during high school (0.48 to 0.42). However, no clear pattern of cohort differences emerges. For science achievement, the gender gap is large and significant at every grade level for all cohorts, and no clear cohort or age pattern is evident.

The results of this descriptive analysis reinforce the general consen-

Table 2.2 Female-to-male high achievement ratio for math and science by grade and cohort

School cohort	High achievement ratio (*AR*) in grade						Data source
	7	8	9	10	11	12	
Panel A: Math Achievement							
1960						0.45**	NLS-72
1968						0.47**	HSBSr
1970				0.52**		0.48**	HSBSo
1978				0.46**	0.27**	0.25**	LSAY1
1980		0.78**		0.74**		0.60**	NELS
1981	0.72	0.77	0.48**	0.48**	0.42**		LSAY2
Panel B: Science achievement							
1960							NLS-72
1968							HSBSr
1970				0.50***		0.39***	HSBSo
1978				0.45***	0.38***	0.22***	LSAY1
1980		0.54***		0.41***		0.38***	NELS
1981	0.33***	0.69*	0.38***	0.38***	0.40***		LSAY2

Note: Index *AR* is defined as the female-to-male ratio of the odds of achieving in the top 5 percent of the distribution of achievement test scores.

$*p < .05$, $**p < .01$, $***p < .001$ (two-tailed test), for the hypothesis that there is no proportional difference between males and females.

sus of earlier research: gender differences in mathematical achievement tend to favor males, but the magnitude of the differences is small and has declined significantly over the past 20 years. Further, we have shown that the magnitude of gender differences is greater in science than in math. Contrary to the assertion made by Linn and Hyde (1989), however, we do not find any evidence of a declining trend in the magnitude of gender differences in science achievement. Our results for both math and science achievement support Feingold's (1992, 1994) assertion that the variance of the distribution of math and science achievement scores is greater for males than for females and that females are consequently underrepresented among the highest achievers.

Explaining Gender Differences in Math and Science Achievement

The literature devoted to understanding the causes of gender differences in math and science achievement is extensive and multidisciplinary. In general, this literature shows that the gender gap in achievement is affected by a diverse and multilevel complex of individual, familial, and social factors whose influences shift in character and prominence across the life course. In the following subsections, we discuss the factors proposed in the literature as explanations of gender differences in achievement. Using data from the base year, first follow-up, and second follow-up waves of the NELS, we test the influence of many, but not all, of the hypothesized explanatory factors. The objective of our analysis is to account for gender differences in mean achievement scores, as well as in the probability of being in the top 5 percent of the distribution of achievement scores, by considering the gender differences in the distribution of individual and familial characteristics. Appendix Table D2.c presents the descriptive statistics, by sex, of the variables that we use in the explanatory analysis.

Individual Influences

The potential individual-level influences that may generate gender differences in science and math achievement include individual attributes, such as cognitive and affective characteristics, and individual behaviors, such as participation and performance in math and science courses.

Biological Influences. Whether or not gender differences in math and science achievement are due to biological causes is the subject of a longstanding debate. In their much publicized work on gifted children, Benbow and Stanley (1980, 1983a) claim that males have "superior" innate math ability relative to females. In the search for a concrete mechanism for the biological cause, much research has focused on gender differences in spatial ability. Spatial ability refers to the capacity to process spatial information and is thought to be a cognitive skill that is fundamental to the understanding of mathematical and scientific concepts. It is thus hypothesized that biologically based gender differences in spatial ability are an important cause of observed gender differences in mathematics achievement. However, the existence, causes, and consequences of gender differences in spatial abilities are subject to debate (Caplan, MacPherson, and Tobin 1985).[8] Where found, the sex differences on average performance of spatial tasks are often modest in magnitude and depend on the measurement instrument used. Reviewers of the literature emphasize the small magnitude of detected sex-related differences (Caplan, MacPherson, and Tobin 1985; Hyde 1981) as well as the significant overlap in the sex-specific distributions of spatial abilities. Furthermore, even if the sexes differ in spatial ability, it is unclear whether the differences can be attributed to biological, rather than social, causes (Halpern 1986; Kavrell and Petersen 1984; Linn and Peterson 1985; Rogers 2001; Sharps, Price, and Williams 1994).

Recently, researchers have argued that the biological explanation is supported by brain-scanning studies showing that men and women utilize somewhat different regions of their brains at rest (Gur et al. 1995) and when performing mathematical and language tasks (Haier and Benbow 1995; Shaywitz et al. 1995). However, this line of research has serious limitations that prevent its results from being interpreted as unambiguous evidence of a biological basis for gender differences in math and science achievement. For the biological interpretation to hold, it is necessary that *both* of the following two assumptions be true:

1. The relationship between the measured aspects of brain functioning and math/science achievement is causal.
2. Gender differences in these aspects of brain functioning are biologically based.

Neither of these two assumptions is supported by the scientific evidence. Concerning the first, the causal link between the locus of brain activity and cognition has not been established. Detectable brain activity may not be a valid measure of cognition since, even under experimental conditions, it is not possible to relate brain activity to a specific cognitive function. For example, it is possible that differences in brain activity associated with math performance may actually reflect differences in emotional responses (i.e., an effect) rather than biological differences in the ability to process information (i.e., a cause). Concerning the second, it is unclear that the observed gender differences in brain functioning are due to biological (i.e., genetic or hormonal) causes rather than social causes (Rogers 1983, 2001; Rogers and Walsh 1982). Social causes are plausible because we know that brain functioning responds to social environments and past experiences (i.e., socialization).

Critics of biological explanations propose more complicated models that capture "the mutual interaction between the genetic program and experience (or learning), occurring at all stages of development and [that is] always subject to further change . . . [in which] genes have a role, but it is neither central nor primary" (Rogers 2001, p. 32). There is scientific evidence suggesting a reciprocal, rather than unidirectionally causal, relationship between biological influences on the one hand and brain functioning and behavior on the other hand (Rogers 2001). According to this view, the development of sex differences is not orchestrated innately according to a predetermined genetic and hormonal map, but instead it is realized only through interaction with one's social environment and with particular social actors such as mothers and fathers (Rogers 2001). Indeed, the variation in both the direction and the magnitude of gender differences in math and science achievement across different studies reinforces the interpretation that the social and cultural contexts play an important role in their development (Baker and Jones 1993; Finn 1980; Harnisch 1984). The data we use for our study do not allow us to assess the relative importance of social versus biological influences. However, since the literature suggests that biological factors are not the sole, perhaps not even the major, causes of observed gender differences in math and science achievement, our effort to identify the social factors that may explain these differences is justified.

Attitudes about Math and Science. Sociocultural explanations of gender differences in mathematics and science achievement focus on the influence of individual affective factors such as attitudes toward math and science, confidence in these abilities, and perceptions about the relevance of math and science knowledge to one's own future. As an example, Eccles' (1989, 1994) "expectancy-value" model emphasizes that achievement in specific substantive areas, such as math and science, and the development of specialized knowledge are themselves short-term goals that individuals consciously work toward. Achievement-related goals—such as course selections in school, early career aspirations, persistence on difficult tasks, and the allocation of time and effort to various activities—are directly affected by "the individual's expectations for success and the importance or value the individual attaches to the various options perceived by the individual as available" (Eccles 1994, p. 587). Furthermore, both the individual's expectations and perceptions of the value of various tasks are influenced by cultural norms and the attitudes of their significant others, such as parents, as well as by their own aptitudes and past experiences.

Affective factors influence gender differences in math and science achievement both directly and indirectly through their effects on gender differences in participation in S/E courses and extracurricular activities. Interest in a particular educational subject and confidence in one's performance in that area are positive determinants of participation and achievement (Reyes 1984; Schunk 1981, 1982). Past research has consistently shown that girls lag behind boys in level of interest, expectations for success, and confidence in their ability in math and science. These gender differences appear during middle school and grow over the course of high school (Eccles 1989; Wigfield and Eccles 1992). For example, although girls are as likely as boys to report liking mathematics (Chipman and Wilson 1985; Gilbert 1996; Hyde et al. 1990), girls are less likely than boys to perceive math and science coursework as relevant to their future goals (Brush 1985; Eccles, Adler, and Meece 1984; Eccles et al. 1985; Sherman and Fennema 1977) and more likely to express a desire to avoid taking math and science classes (Hyde et al. 1990; Mullis and Jenkins 1988). Both boys and girls tend to believe that math is more useful and important for males than for females (Brush 1985; Eccles et al. 1985; Fennema and Sherman 1977, 1978; Hyde et al. 1990). Girls consistently report a lower level of confidence in their ability to perform mathematics tasks than do boys (Catsambis 1994; Chipman and Wilson 1985; Fennema and Sherman 1977, 1978; Hyde et al. 1990; Linn and Hyde 1989; Meyer and Koehler 1990; Terwilliger and Titus 1995). Girls also report expending more effort to do well in math than do boys (Eccles et al. 1985) and are more likely to attribute their success in math to effort (Gilbert 1996; Kloosterman 1990; Meyer and Koehler 1990).

We include indicators of students' attitudes about math and science in our explanatory analysis of the gender differences in achievement for the NELS students at grades 8 and 10. The eighth-grade analysis includes binary indicators of the students' agreement or disagreement with three statements regarding their attitudes toward both math and science: "Math/science will be useful in my future," "I usually look forward to math/science class," and "I am often afraid to ask questions in math/science class." The tenth-grade analysis includes indicators of students' agreement, ambivalence, or disagreement with a series of statements about math. The statements included: "Math is one of my best subjects," "I have always done well in math," and "I get good marks in math."[9]

Course Participation and Performance. Course-taking is predictive of students' achievement and their readiness for college-level work (Welch, Anderson, and Harris 1982). For this reason, participation in mathematics and science courses in high school has been characterized as a "critical filter" that regulates entry into S/E concentrations in higher education (Casserly and Rock 1985; Lee and Burkam 1996). If girls are less likely than boys to take math and science courses, differential patterns of course-taking by sex may well explain sex differences in math and science achievement (Fennema and Sherman 1977). This proposition is known as the "differential course-taking hypothesis." Although much research has been devoted to testing this hypothesis, results have been ambiguous (Benbow and Stanley 1983b; Lee, Burkam, and Smerdon 1997; Pallas and Alexander 1983). The inconclusiveness of the literature is not surprising given the varying nature of the gender gap in course participation. In the 1970s, there was a significant gender gap in mathematics course-taking in favor of boys, but it has narrowed substantially since then. Data from the 1990s show only a slight gender gap in high school math and science course participation (Bae et al. 2000; NSF 1999). Girls are still slightly less likely than boys to take calculus, physics, and computer science, especially at the advanced placement level, but their participation in all other science and math courses is equal to or exceeds that of boys (Bae et al. 2000). The near equity in course participation renders the "differential course-taking hypothesis" limited as a potential explanation of gender differences in achievement.

How much a student actually learns from a math/science class depends not only on participation but also on performance in the class, but the role of performance in math and science courses in explaining gender achievement gaps in math and science is ambiguous. On the one hand, grades in math and science courses are positively associated with achievement on standardized math and science tests. On the other hand, although course grades are not standardized across teachers and schools, research has shown that girls' math and science course grades are as high as, or even exceed, those of boys (Benbow and Stanley 1980; Lee, Burkam, and Smerdon 1997; Pallas and Alexander 1983). The higher course grades of girls, however, may reflect teachers' reaction to the more compliant behavior typical of girls rather than a female advantage in academic performance. If this is true, accounting for gender differences in course grades should not explain the gender gap in achievement scores.

We use three measures of participation and performance in high school mathematics and science courses to estimate the influence of high school education on achievement at grades 10 and 12. First, we use information from the NELS transcript data to measure whether or not a student has taken high school math courses in: (1) algebra 1, (2) geometry, (3) algebra 2, (4) trigonometry, (5) precalculus, and (6) calculus. Second, we measure student participation in six types of science courses: (1) earth science, (2) biology, (3) chemistry, (4) physics, (5) advanced biology courses, and (6) advanced chemistry courses.[10] Codebook A (posted at www.yuxie.com) lists the program codes and titles for the specific high school courses in each type of math and science course. Third, we assess participation using a categorical indicator of the high school year during which a student took his/her final math or science course. For course performance, we use the average of the students' grades in the math or science courses they had taken up to the point at which achievement is measured as our indicator of performance in high school math and science courses. The average grade is calculated only for those who enrolled in any math or science course and is measured on a continuous scale that ranges from a low grade of 33 to a high of 99.[11]

Familial Influences

Sociocultural explanations have also called attention to familial influences that may generate gender differences in math and science achievement. Familial influences originate from two different generational locales: (1) an individual's family of origin, i.e., the characteristics of the family into which he or she is born; and (2) the family formed by an individual. Early in the life course this second locale of familial influence is manifest in expectations about the characteristics of the family the student intends to form, about future family roles, attitudes about family and work, and his/her current dating behavior.

Family of Origin Influences. Despite a strong association between family socioeconomic status and children's math and science achievement, such family characteristics are unlikely to explain gender differences in science and math achievement because they are independent of the sex of the children in the family. Other family characteristics are related to children's gender and may therefore help explain gender differences. For example, parental behavior that differs toward male and female children can engender differences in math and science achievement. We know that parents', and particularly mothers', beliefs about their children's abilities have a great influence on their children's educational attitudes (Eccles and Jacobs 1986; Jacobs and Eccles 1992; Yee and Eccles 1988). When it comes to math and science learning, parents encourage and expect higher levels of achievement and persistence from boys than girls (Eccles and Jacobs 1986; Eccles, Jacobs, and Harold 1990; Maccoby and Jacklin 1974), and they tend to believe that doing well and taking advanced courses in math and science are more important for boys than for girls (Casserly 1980; Eccles and Jacobs 1986). Girls seem to be aware of their parents' lower expectations and to adjust their attitudes, aspirations, and performance accordingly (Armstrong and Price 1982; Eccles and Jacobs 1986; Fennema and Sherman 1978; Jacobs and Eccles 1992). Furthermore, parents' gender-specific attitudes and expectations may also operate through their influence on the placement of their children in educational tracks or ability groups (Useem 1992).

Resources within the home, such as a home computer, can significantly influence the development of mathematical and science skills and positive attitudes toward science and math. If access to and utilization of computers is positively associated with achievement in technical subjects, gender differences in access may help explain gender differences in achievement. There is some evidence that girls who have no siblings or who have sisters only are less likely to have access to computers at home (Littleton 1996; Straker 1986). Other studies show no gender differences in students' reported access to computers when home and school access are not distinguished, but that there are gender differences in usage (Bae et al. 2000; NSF 1999). Female students are most likely to use computers for word processing, whereas male students have higher levels of computer literacy and are more likely than females to use computers to solve math problems and to take computer science courses (NSF 1999, p. 12).

In this study, we do not have detailed measures of parental attitudes. We attempt to capture the explanatory power of parental influences using a broad indicator of parental expectations: the students' perceptions of their parents' expectations for their educational attainment. Specifically, we compare the expectation for less than a college degree with the expectation for a four-year college or more advanced degree. We also include variables indicating whether or not each student's mother and father attained at least a bachelor's degree. Family investment in educational resources is measured by a variable indicating whether the student has access to a computer at home. Each of these variables is measured at multiple points in the longitudinal study, and their values therefore can vary with time. We control for family income by including a categorical variable that measures family income at the base year of the study.

Student's Attitudes about Dating, Family, and Work. As discussed in Chapter 1, one prominent departure of the life course approach from the "pipeline" approach is the contention that the progress of an S/E career is not isolated from the development of other dimensions in the life course. In particular, we argue that an individual's progress along the S/E career line is complicated and often constrained by concerns, needs, and responsibilities in his/her family life. For most high school students, the influence of one's primary family on career plans and progress is manifest only through attitudes and expectations about future family life (since most have not yet formed a family). Given the perception that an S/E career may conflict with family life, the expectation for early family formation and the desire for prioritizing family over work may exert a negative influence on math and science achievement. An *anticipated* conflict between family and work roles at this early stage is plausible given that an S/E career is known to take a long time to develop and to demand long hours to sustain.

If an S/E career is perceived to be in conflict with investment in family life, women are especially affected. This is true because responsibility for household and childcare labor falls primarily on women in traditional as well as "egalitarian" families (Becker, G. S. 1981; Hertz 1986; Williams 2000). Research has shown that girls perceive their future family roles as incompatible with S/E careers (McLure and Piel 1978; Rossi 1965; Seymour and Hewitt 1997). Given the demanding nature of the S/E career track, it may be rational for girls not to invest heavily in difficult subjects such as math and science. In this sense, even girls who plan to combine work and family may underinvest in math and science education because they view the S/E career track as inhospitable to a full family life while other career options offer more leeway. In addition, S/E subjects are considered masculine domains (Armstrong 1981; Fennema and Sherman 1977, 1978; Hyde et al. 1990; Meece et al. 1982), so high performance in those subjects may be threatening to a girl's feminine gender identity. There is some evidence that girls who enroll in high-level science courses report seeing themselves as less feminine, attractive, popular, and sociable (Matyas 1985).[12] Thus, girls who are oriented toward traditional norms of femininity may avoid possible negative social consequences by forgoing extensive participation and high achievement in math and science.

In our analysis, we attempt to capture these "own family" influences by including variables measuring students' attitudes about dating and about their future family roles. To measure students' attitudes about dating, we use student responses to the question, "How important is it to have a steady boy/girlfriend?" Student responses to this question are coded as "Not important," "Somewhat important," or "Very important" and are included in the analyses of achievement in grades 10 and 12. Students' orientations toward familial roles are measured in two ways: (1) the age at which they expect to marry for the first time and the age at which they expect to begin childbearing, and (2) a family vs. work attitude scale that contrasts their expectations about the future importance of work and family in their lives.

Expected age at first marriage and expected age at first birth are continuous variables.[13] The family vs. work attitude scale is constructed using variables measuring students' attitudes about the importance of family and work to their lives.[14] Respondents who indicate that family is relatively more important than career and financial success have positive values on the scale, and students ranking work-related aspects of life as more important have a negative value. The family-work scale score is included as an unlagged variable in all the tenth- and twelfth-grade models of math and science achievement (i.e., it was measured at the same time as math and science achievement).

Social Influences

The gender gap in math and science achievement may also be influenced by many social factors that are distinct from individual and familial influences. School-level social influences have been shown to affect gender differences in students' orientation toward science and math and their performance on math and science achievement tests. These include differences that male and female students are subject to in the academic expectations of teachers (Becker, J. R. 1981; Eccles 1984); in the teaching style (Lee and Burkam 1996; Lee, Burkam, and Smerdon 1997; Peterson and Fennema 1985); in the use of laboratory materials (AAUW 1992); in school climate (Lee, Chen, and Smerdon 1995); in the advice and encouragement, or discouragement, offered by teachers and counselors; and in the mere presence of role models, such as teachers in high school math and science courses (Kahle and Matyas 1987; Stake and Granger 1978). For example, teachers tend to give more attention to male students than to female students in math and science courses (Eccles et al. 1985; Lee, Marks, and Byrd 1994; Sadker and Sadker 1995; Tobin and Garnett 1987). In addition, there is some evidence that the gender gap in achievement may be affected by neighborhood resources and influences that are independent of the family and school-level influences (Entwisle, Alexander, and Olson 1994).

Although a model of gender differences in achievement is incomplete without these neighborhood-, school-, and teacher-level influences, we are not able to include them in this analysis. The NELS dataset we use for these analyses does not include useful information at these levels of measurement. The NELS includes some general measures of school- and teacher-level influences, but the measures are unsuitable for our purpose because they are not linked to individual students' attributes. Since we cannot ascertain school-level or teacher-level practices that differ between male and female students, including school- or teacher-level factors in this analysis would not further our understanding of the determinants of gender gaps in math and science achievement. Indeed, research by Hanson (1996) shows that such variables do not hold much power to explain gender differences in either participation or achievement in science and math. We therefore focus this research on the explanatory power of individual and familial influences.

Methods

Following the explanatory framework outlined in Chapter 1, we attempt to explain the observed gender differences in math and science achievement by controlling for the hypothesized intervening influences in statistical models. We use linear regression models to examine mean gender differences and binary logit models to examine gender differences in the probability of being a top achiever. In linear regression models with the standardized achievement score as the dependent variable, the estimated coefficient of gender is tantamount to the d-statistic, the standardized difference between the male and female test scores.[15] Similarly, the achievement ratio (AR), the female-to-male ratio of the odds of attaining high achievement, can be easily computed as the exponentiated coefficient of sex in the logit models predicting representation among top scorers. Models are estimated separately for math and science achievement at grades 8, 10, and 12 using weighted data. For each grade-specific achievement measure, we focus on a pair of models: a baseline model with sex as the sole predictor and a full model including all relevant explanatory variables.[16] The difference in the estimated gender gap between two contrasted models indicates the degree to which the observed gender gap is attributable to the independent variables. Although we aimed for strictly parallel grade-specific models, variations in the survey items across waves of the NELS data collection result in grade-specific sets of variables measuring individual and familial influences that are only approximately parallel.

In addition to the individual and familial variables we described above, each model includes a set of control variables measuring the student's racial/ethnic identification, an indicator of the high school program or curriculum in which a student was enrolled or expected to be enrolled, and the student's educational aspirations. Race/ethnicity is coded as a four-category variable: white, black, Hispanic, and other. The "other" category includes students who identified themselves as "Asian or Pacific Islander" or "Native American Indian."[17] The indicator of high school program contrasts college preparatory (i.e., academic) and general/vocational-technical programs. For the analysis of achievement at grade 8, "High school program" refers to the student's expectations about intended high school program. Educational aspirations are coded as a dichotomous variable that contrasts the expectation of four years or more of postsecondary education with the expectation of less than four years of college. High school program and the student's educational aspirations are included as unlagged, time-varying variables in the models of achievement.

Results

Table 2.3 presents the unadjusted and adjusted values of d and AR for both math and science achievement at each grade level. The unadjusted measures of gender differences, d and AR, are computed from the baseline regression models with sex as the sole covariate, and they deviate only slightly from the descriptive results presented in Tables 2.1 and 2.2 for the NELS cohort.[18] The adjusted estimates of the gender differences are obtained from the regression models that include all of the individual and familial influence covariates indicated with a check mark in the lower part of the table. The estimated coefficients for the full models are presented in Appendix Tables D2.d–D2.f.

The results show that gender differences favoring boys remain significant even after accounting for the effects of the individual and familial covariates that are expected to intervene between gender and achievement. In fact, controlling for the complete set of covariates tends to inflate both d and AR. Only among eighth-grade students did controlling for familial and individual influences explain some portion of the observed gender gap in either d or AR for math and science achievement. For sophomores and seniors, accounting for the influence of familial and individual characteristics exacerbates the estimated gender differences in average and high achievement for both math and science. For example, among twelfth-grade students the magnitude of the mean gender difference in math achievement increases from -0.09 to -0.15, and the value of the female-to-male

Table 2.3 Adjusted mean gender difference (*d*) and female-to-male high achievement ratio (*AR*) from regression models of math and science achievement in 8th, 10th, and 12th grades

	8th grade	10th grade	12th grade
Math			
Mean gender difference (*d*)			
Unadjusted	−0.03*	−0.04	−0.09***
Adjusted	−0.02*	−0.09***	−0.15***
Female-to-male high achievement ratio (*AR*)			
Unadjusted	0.76***	0.70***	0.65***
Adjusted	0.81***	0.62***	0.52***
Science			
Mean gender difference (*d*)			
Unadjusted	−0.15***	−0.28***	−0.30***
Adjusted	−0.14***	−0.35***	−0.34***
Female-to-male high achievement ratio (*AR*)			
Unadjusted	0.53***	0.41***	0.39***
Adjusted	0.55***	0.34***	0.35***
Control variables included in the model			
Background characteristics			
Race/ethnicity	√	√	√
High school program	√	√	√
Educational aspirations	√	√	√
Family of origin influences			
Father's educational attainment	√	√	√
Mother's educational attainment	√	√	√
Parental expectations for student's educational attainment	√	√	√
Family income	√	√	√
Family owns a computer	√	√	√
Student's dating attitudes, family expectations, and family vs. work attitudes			
How important is it to have a steady girl/boyfriend		√	√
Expected age at first marriage			√
Expected age at first birth			√
Family vs. work attitude scale		√	√
High school math/science course participation and grades			
Math/science courses taken high school		√	√
Average math course grades		√	√
Grade during which student took last math/science course			√

Table 2.3 (continued)

	8th grade	10th grade	12th grade
Student attitudes about math/science			
Math/science will be useful in my future	√		
I am often afraid to ask questions in math/ science class	√		
I usually look forward to math/science class	√		
Math is one of my best subjects		√	
I have always done well in math class		√	
I have always gotten good grades in math		√	

Source: NELS, Base Year in 1988 to Second Follow-up in 1992.

$*p < .05$, $**p < .01$, $***p < .001$ (two-tailed test), for the hypothesis that there is no difference between males and females.

high achievement ratio decreases from 0.65 to 0.52 (i.e., an increase in the gender gap in representation among the top 5 percent of the achievement distribution). Note that the magnitude of adjusted d values for grades 10 and 12, albeit greater than the magnitude of the unadjusted ones, represents statistically significant but substantively small gender differences. The adjusted high achievement ratios, however, are significantly less than one, indicating that girls are only 0.34 to 0.81 times as likely as boys to be represented in the top 5 percent of the achievement distribution. The adjusted values of AR therefore reveal a significant underrepresentation of young women among students with the highest scores.

These results provide little support for the hypothesis that gender differences in either average performance or representation among the top performers on math and science achievement tests can be explained by gender differences in individual and familial influences. This is especially true for the estimated high achievement ratio. Note that the objective of the statistical models is to partial out gender differences that are due to unequal distributions of the individual and familial covariates between males and females. We interpret our results to mean that equality on all of the covariates would lead to significantly lower odds of female representation among top performers than is currently observed. This is because female students have a more favorable distribution than male students on at least some of the covariates that significantly influence high achievement. From this analysis, however, we do not know the consequence of controlling for particular explanatory factors. It would, for example, be incorrect to assume that equalizing the gender distribution on each type of explanatory factor uniformly depresses the adjusted *AR* relative to the unadjusted value.

To measure the influence of each set of explanatory variables on the estimated gender gap in the odds of representation among top achievers, we use the method of decomposition introduced by Xie and Shauman (1998) and explained in Appendix B. With this method, we try to answer the following counterfactual question: How would the estimated gender gap be changed if the distribution of a particular set of variables were unrelated to gender—that is, if we imposed gender equity for the set of characteristics? We present the results of the exercise in Appendix Table D2.g. The decomposition analysis supports some of the hypothesized explanations for gender differences in achievement but refutes others. The results for math and science achievement are parallel except that the magnitude of the estimated effects tends to be smaller for science. The potential explanatory power of family of origin influences and student attitudes about math/science is noticeable. In contrast, background characteristics, attitudes about dating, expectations about family and work, and high school course participation and performance do not explain gender differences in high math and science achievement.

One particularly important finding of the decomposition analysis is the rejection of the course participation hypothesis for this cohort of students. The values of the high and low estimates for high school math/science course participation and grades are uniformly negative and relatively large for both math and science achievement at grades 10 and 12. This means that accounting for gender differences in course participation and grades actually increases, rather than decreases, the estimated gender gap in the odds of high achievement. As shown in Appendix Table D2.c, math and science course participation patterns are similar between boys and girls, but girls receive better grades than boys in these courses. Specifically, there are no significant gender differences in the proportion of high school seniors who had taken advanced college preparatory math and science courses such as trigonometry, precalculus, calculus, and advanced chemistry. Female high school seniors were more likely than males to have taken biology, chemistry, and advanced biology, but they were less likely to have taken physics. One area of girls' disadvantage was their relatively lower likelihood to have taken science and math courses through their senior year of high school.

Conclusion

The primary conclusion of this chapter is that gender differences in average achievement in math and science are small in magnitude. This statement is especially true for math achievement. This finding is not new but it reinforces the picture of gender differences established by previous research. Gender differences in math are especially small among the most recent cohorts of students. Compared to gender differences in average math achievement, the gap between males and females in science achievement appears to be both larger in magnitude and more stable across cohorts. Although mean differences are relatively slight, the greater variability of achievement scores among males than among females results in a significant underrepresentation of women among the highest achievers.

Explanations of the underrepresentation of women in postsecondary S/E education and in the S/E labor force often focus on the causal influence of gender differences in science and math achievement. On the basis of our results, we expect little to be gained by accounting for gender differences in average achievement, since they are very small. We see more promise in the explanatory power of the gender gap in the representation in the upper tail of the achievement distribution. If very high math and science achievement is a prerequisite to postsecondary education and a career in an S/E field, then the underrepresentation of women among the highest achievers during high school may help explain the underrepresentation of women later in the S/E trajectory. While we established in this chapter the extent and character of gender differences in math and science achievement, the question of the practical significance of these achievement differences is addressed in the chapters that follow.

The second important conclusion that we draw from the statistical analyses presented in this chapter is that gender differences in math and science achievement cannot be explained by the individual and familial influences that we examine. On the contrary, we find that controlling for the complete set of individual and familial explanatory factors increases, rather than decreases, the estimated gender gap both in mean math and science achievement and in the odds that a student is among the top 5 percent of the achievement distribution. There are many other factors that are unaccounted for in this study that have been hypothesized to contribute to gender differences in math and science. They include gender differences in the biological functioning of the brain, social influences in school, and the socializing influences of peers, teachers, counselors, and parents. The limited scope of our analysis precludes us from making any statements about these and other potential causes of gender differences in math and science achievement. However, our results clearly support the conclusion that the observed gender gaps in math and science achievement cannot be explained by differences in the individual and familial influences we have included in our analysis.

CHAPTER THREE

Expectation of a Science/Engineering College Major

One important finding in Chapter 2 refutes a widely held belief that girls lag behind boys in math and science course participation and performance in high school. In other words, we do not find behavioral differences between girls and boys in the early stages of the life course that would set them apart vis-à-vis an S/E career. There may be, however, social psychological gender differences that are not manifested in course-taking behavior in high school but strongly influence S/E participation in subsequent stages of the life course. In this chapter we examine gender differences in an influential social psychological factor: the expectation of pursuing an S/E major in college. An implicit assumption motivating this analysis is that the development of an S/E career involves first the formation of an interest in such a career and then the realization of that interest. As we will demonstrate, there are significant gender differences in aspirations for S/E postsecondary education among high school students. We need to ask why this is the case and what are the consequences. We attempt to address the "why" question in this chapter and leave the "so what" question to Chapter 4.

The transition from high school to college has been identified as the point at which both the largest proportion of students leave the S/E educational trajectory and the exit rates of women exceed those of men by the largest margin (Berryman 1983; Hilton and Lee 1988; OTA 1989; Xie 1996). Examining the decisions that students make at this juncture in the S/E educational trajectory is therefore critical to the study of gender differences in S/E education. Many studies of gender differences in the choice of a college major focus on students' behavior once they are already enrolled in college (Ware and Lee 1988; Ware, Steckler, and Leserman 1985). The choice of a college major is, however, a process that begins before entry into college. Adolescents often think seriously about their future educational and occupational options and gradually develop expectations about whether they will go to college and what major topic of study they will pursue.

Educational statistics show that since the mid-1980s female high school students have been more likely than their male classmates to expect to attend college and to attain a bachelor's degree (Bae et al. 2000; NSF 1994). Since young women are more likely than young men to go to college, the source of women's underrepresentation among S/E degree holders must lie in gender segregation of college majors: girls are less likely than boys to major in science and engineering. This segregation is likely the combined result of a gender gap in S/E interests, in the level of support and encouragement of S/E interests, and in the likelihood of acting on one's S/E interests. Past research shows that female high school students are less interested than male students in S/E education and S/E careers (Bae et al. 2000; Hilton and Lee 1988; NSF 1994, 1996, 1999, 2000) and that they are less likely to be exposed to positive role models or to be encouraged to pursue S/E education by parents, teachers, and counselors (Casserly and Rock 1985; Eccles et al. 1985; Ware and Lee 1988). Furthermore, among those high school students who do expect to pursue higher education in S/E, young women are less likely than young men to realize their expectations (Hilton and Lee 1988; Ware, Steckler, and Leserman 1985).

Although the underrepresentation of women in S/E college majors is well documented (NSF 1994, 1996, 1999, 2000; OTA 1989), few studies measure gender differences in the likelihood that high school students expect to major in S/E fields or assess the link between such expectations and the actual pursuit of an S/E major (Hilton and Lee 1988; OTA 1989; Ware, Steckler, and Leserman 1985). Even fewer studies attempt to develop a causal explanation of gender differences in the expectation of an S/E college major. In this chapter we focus on measuring and explaining gender differences in educational expectations among high school seniors. We use data from the NELS second follow-up to analyze the effects of specific individual and familial influences on the likelihood that a student expects to attend college and pursue an S/E major.

Gender Differences in Educational Expectations

Students' expectations about their intended college major are unstable through the high school years (OTA 1989). Indeed, Lee (cited in OTA 1989) found that more than half of the high school sophomores who said they intended to major in S/E shifted their expectations to a non-S/E field by the time they were seniors. Yet, despite their fluidity, students' expectations about their college major do have significant predictive power: students who expect to major in S/E are much more likely actually to pursue an S/E major than are students without S/E expectations (as will be shown in Chapter 4). We focus our analysis on the educational expectations of students in their senior year of high school, the end point of the precollege period of vacillating expectations. The senior year of high school is an important point of transition in the educational trajectory. It is a time when students are making decisions about future career possibilities, whether or not they will go to college and, if so, how they will use college to prepare for the future. Thoughts about family formation and work become increasingly salient to students as they make the transition to adulthood. The senior year of high school is also a time when individual students feel pressure from family, friends, teachers, and counselors to formalize their thoughts about the future. Since this point in the life course is relatively close to the future about which they are being asked, their responses to survey questions about their intentions are likely to be more realistic than those expressed earlier in the life course.

Students' expectations about their college major can be decomposed into two educational components: (1) their expectations about college attendance and (2) their expectations about their major field of study if they enter college. These two educational components are nested. For students who do not expect to go to college, expectations about an undergraduate major are undefined. In other words, the question of a college major is simply irrelevant to those who do not expect to go to college. More formally, the probability that a student expects to pursue an S/E major is expressed as

(3.1) $P(S/E, C) = P(C) \times P(S/E \mid C),$

where *S/E* denotes the expectation of an S/E college major and *C* denotes the expectation of college attendance. In this equation, $P(S/E, C)$ represents the unconditional joint probability that a student expects to pursue an S/E major in college; $P(C)$ denotes the probability that a student expects to go to college; and $P(S/E \mid C)$ denotes the probability that a student expects to major in an S/E field conditional on the expectation of college attendance. The above equation highlights the fact that the magnitude of gender differences in the likelihood of expecting to major in S/E depends on gender disparities in college attendance expectations as well as in the choice of college major.[1] Furthermore, although these educational expectations are formed in tandem, their determinants are likely to be quite different. In this analysis, therefore, we partition students' expectations about college attendance from their intentions to major in an S/E versus non-S/E subject and examine separately each component expectation.

We use data from the NELS second follow-up, conducted in 1992, to measure the educational expectations of high school seniors. Students were asked if they expected to attend college and in which field they expected to major. Expectation of college enrollment is assessed by the question, "How far in school do you think you will get?" We dichotomized the responses to this question, with positive responses (i.e., the student expected to complete a college degree) coded 1.[2] This is a conservative measure of student expectations of college *attendance* since it actually measures the expectation of college *completion*. We prefer this conservative measure since it clearly distinguishes those with high educational expectations from others. Throughout this chapter we will refer to this variable as the expectation of college attendance. Students were also asked to respond to the question, "Which of these fields are you most likely to study in college?" We dichotomized responses to this question, contrasting whether or not a student expected to major in an S/E field of study (yes = 1). Students who responded that they expected to major in biological science, engineering, mathematical science, or physical science were coded as expecting an S/E major. Respondents who indicated any of the other fields of study were coded as expecting a non-S/E major.[3] The sample of students we use for this analysis includes 12,784 high school seniors enrolled in 1992.[4]

Table 3.1 presents the observed unconditional probability of the expectation of pursuing an S/E college major, $P(S/E, C)$, as well as the component probabilities, $P(C)$ and $P(S/E \mid C)$, separately for males and females of the NELS cohort in 1992. We use the female-to-male ratio of these probabilities to measure gender differences and present the female-to-male odds ratio to facilitate comparison of these descriptive results with the multivariate results presented later in this chapter. In the last row, we observe that girls are less than half as likely as boys (0.08 versus 0.19) to express an interest in pursuing an S/E major in college. According to the descriptive statistics shown in Table 3.1, this gender gap is clearly driven by the significant gender disparity in the proportion of college-bound students expecting to choose an S/E major, for young women are slightly more likely than young men to expect to enroll in and complete college. Among this cohort of students, the probability that a female high school senior expects to complete college is 0.70 whereas it is 0.64 for male seniors. This difference translates into a female-to-male ratio of 1.09, indicating that females are 9 percent more likely than male high school se-

Table 3.1 Observed probabilities of the expectation of college attendance, the expectation of pursuing an S/E major conditional on college attendance, and the unconditional expectation of pursuing an S/E major by gender

Expectation	Females	Males	Female-to-male ratio of probabilities	Female-to-male odds ratio
Expecting to go to college, $P(C)$	0.70	0.64	1.09	1.29
Expecting an S/E major, conditional on college attendance, $P(S/E \mid C)$	0.12	0.30	0.39	0.31
Expecting to pursue an S/E major in college, $P(S/E, C)$	0.08	0.19	0.42	0.37

Source: NELS Second Follow-up, 1992.

Note: S/E denotes the expectation of an S/E college major and C denotes the expectation of college attendance. The unconditional probability of expecting to major in an S/E field is the product of the component probabilities: $P(S/E, C) = P(S/E \mid C) \times P(C)$. Total unweighted sample size is 12,784, including 6,226 male and 6,558 female students.

niors to expect to attend and complete college. In contrast, among female seniors who do plan to complete a college degree, the probability of expecting to major in an S/E field is 0.12. This probability is 60 percent less than the probability of 0.30 among males who expect to complete college. If males and females in this cohort of high school seniors were equally likely to expect to attend college, the gender gap in the unconditional probability of the expectation of pursuing an S/E college major would be slightly larger than what is observed. Young women clearly are more likely than men to aspire to higher education, but they are much less likely than young men to aspire to higher education in S/E.

Explaining Gender Differences in Educational Expectations

In this analysis we investigate the degree to which gender differences in S/E educational expectations can be explained by the individual and familial influences we introduced in Chapter 2: individual background variables, family of origin influences, students' own family expectations and attitudes, students' attitudes about math, and high school math course participation and grades. In addition, we investigate the role of math and science achievement in producing gender disparities in educational expectations. The sex-specific distributions of the individual and familial covariates are presented in Appendix Table D3.a. We expect many of the individual and familial factors to have distinct effects on gender differences in students' expectations about college enrollment and whether they will pursue an S/E or a non-S/E major.

As discussed in Chapter 2, achievement in math and science is commonly thought to influence participation in the S/E educational trajectory. Outstanding achievement is believed to indicate the high level of competence necessary for successful completion of postsecondary education in the fields of math, science, and engineering. The influence of achievement on participation is manifest at both the individual and the structural levels. At the individual level, achievement affects one's motivation for further participation as well as one's confidence in personal prospects for success in the S/E educational and career track. For most students, high achievement at least leaves open the option of further education and employment in the S/E fields, whereas low achievement is usually regarded as a sign that the S/E career trajectory is not an option. At the structural level, access to S/E education, especially at the postsecondary level, is often predicated upon relatively high achievement. Furthermore, high achievement attracts the attention and, perhaps more importantly, garners the support of the gatekeepers of the S/E educational trajectory.

We have established, in Chapter 2, the existence but small magnitude of the gender gap in average math and science achievement and relatively larger differences in the representation of male and female students among the top 5 percent of the distributions of achievement scores. In this chapter, we begin to investigate the practical significance of these achievement differences. We expect that math and science achievement test scores are positively related to the likelihood that a student expects to enter college as well as to the likelihood that a student chooses an S/E college major given their expectation of college enrollment. We further hypothesize that membership among the highest achievers positively predicts the choice of an S/E college major among students who expect to attend college. Note that controlling for girls' relative disadvantage on the measures of achievement is likely to increase the female advantage in students' expectations for college attendance and to decrease the male advantage in the expectation of an S/E major. Furthermore, since the gender gaps in average achievement are smaller in magnitude than those in top performance, the consideration of top performance may have greater power in explaining gender differences in the probability that a student expects to pursue an S/E college major. As in Chapter 2, we operationalize math and science achievement as scores on the standardized tests administered by NELS.[5] We measure high achievement with dummy variables indicating whether or not a student was in the top 5 percent of the distributions of math and science scores, and we include this indicator only in the analysis predicting the choice of an S/E major given the expectation of college enrollment.

Family of origin characteristics affect whether a student expects to enroll in college as well as his or her choice of college major. Measures of socioeconomic status, such as parental income and educational attainment, have proven to be strong predictors of educational aspirations (Hauser, Tsai, and Sewell 1983; Sewell, Haller, and Portes 1969; Sewell and Hauser 1975). Highly educated parents are more likely to expect their children to go to college and to be able to afford the expense of their children's higher education. Furthermore, research shows that parental education has an especially strong effect on the participation, achievement, and persistence of women in S/E education (Berryman 1983; Ware and Lee 1988; Ware, Steckler, and Leserman 1985). Net of socioeconomic status, parents' expectations and overt support may also exert independent influences on the educational expectations and behavior of their children, particularly for girls (Eccles, Jacobs, and Harold 1990; Jacobs and Eccles 1992; Ware and Lee 1988). In our analysis we include the measures of family income, mothers' and fathers' educational attainment, parents' expectations for their child's educational attainment, and family computer ownership described in Chapter 2.[6]

Students' plans for their future education and careers are informed by their expectations for their other social roles. Anticipated family roles and responsibilities play a particularly central part in future planning and can strongly influence students' educational expectations. Research shows that young women expect to experience conflict between career and family and that the perceived incompatibility between an S/E career and family life is an important barrier to the involvement of young women in S/E education (Matyas 1985; McLure and Piel 1978; Seymour and Hewitt 1997). We measure students' orientation toward their future family roles with variables measuring the importance they place on dating, the ages at which they expected to enter marriage and parenthood, and the family-work attitude scale. All of these variables are described in Chapter 2. In our sample of high school students, there are no significant differences in student attitudes toward dating, but there are significant gender differences in attitudes and expectations about future family roles. Young women are more likely than men to view their familial roles as the most important aspect of their future lives and to expect to marry and start having children at younger ages than men (see Appendix Table D3.a).

Students' attitudes about math and their participation in high school math courses are also central to the formation of educational expectations, especially those concerning the choice between S/E and non-S/E college majors (Chipman and Wilson 1985; Ware and Lee 1988). Positive attitudes about math increase the likelihood that a student will expect to major in an S/E field. As we reviewed in Chapter 2, however, the literature shows girls are less likely than boys to hold positive attitudes toward math and are less likely to regard math as a subject that will be useful in their future. Gender differences in attitudes toward math thus may contribute to the observed gender differences in the likelihood that a student expects to major in S/E. In our analysis, we use attitudinal measures recorded when the students were in grade 10. Among the students in our sample, young women are less likely than young men to agree with the statements, "Math is one of my best subjects," "I have always done well in math," and "I get good marks in math."

Since participation and performance in high school math courses indicate a student's preparation for college and for an S/E undergraduate major, these characteristics are important predictors of expected postsecondary educational choices. We derive three variables from the NELS transcript data to measure course participation and performance: (1) a categorical indicator of the year during which students took their final high school math course, (2) a dichotomous variable indicating whether or not a student had participated in any advanced math courses during high school, and (3) the average grade from math courses.[7] The first and the third variables were used in Chapter 2. Codebook B (posted at www.yuxie.com) presents the comprehensive list of the program codes and titles for all high school mathematics courses and highlights those courses considered "advanced."[8] Given the finding in Chapter 2 of small to nil gender differences in precollege math and science course participation and performance (also see Bae et al. 2000; NSF 1999), however, we do not expect these variables to explain much of the gender gap in the expectation of an S/E college major. Indeed, the descriptive statistics reveal a small female disadvantage in course participation and a female advantage in course grades (see Appendix Table D3.a).

Methods

For this analysis, we make the simplifying assumption that the process of choosing a college major can be decomposed into the two sequential decisions represented in equation 3.1: students first decide whether or not they will pursue postsecondary education; if they expect to attend a postsecondary school, they then decide whether to major in an S/E or a non-S/E field. Under this assumption, we model the two component probabilities (i.e., $P(C)$ and $P(S/E \mid C)$) using separate logit models. However, this methodology imposes a strong behavioral assumption that distills the complex processes by which expectations about postsecondary education are formed. For example, the two decisions that we assume to be independent and sequential are, in reality, likely to be considered simultaneously. More complex operationalizations of this process that account for the correlation between the decision to enroll in college and the choice of major suggest that the potential simultaneity does not seriously bias the results (see Xie 1989, Chapter 6).

Given our simplifying assumption, we analyze the effects of individual and familial influences on the students' educational expectations using two sequential logit models. The first logit model assesses the effects of the individual and familial influences on gender differences in the likelihood that a student expects to attend college. With the same notation as equation 3.1, the first logit can be expressed as the natural logarithm of:

$$(3.2) \qquad O_1 = P(C)/[1 - P(C)],$$

where O_1 is the odds of expecting to attend and complete college. The second logit model is applied only to those students who expect to enroll in college and is used to assess the influence of individual and familial factors on gender differences in the probability of expecting to major in an S/E field. Mathematically, the second logit can be written as the natural logarithm of the following odds:

$$(3.3) \qquad O_2 = P(S/E \mid C)/[1 - P(S/E \mid C)].$$

For each logit, we estimate a series of hierarchical, nested models. In each model we are primarily concerned with the estimated effect of sex, which is easily interpretable as the female-to-male odds ratio for an educational expectation through the simple transformation $\exp(b_{sex})$. For each dependent variable, we start by estimating a baseline model that includes sex as the sole covariate. We then sequentially add the sets of explanatory variables representing the distinct individual and familial influences and observe the change in the estimated effect of sex resulting from each addition. The coefficient of sex in each of these models is an estimate of the gender difference after controlling for the included explanatory variables. In this way, we assess the power of each set of independent variables to account for gender differences in the likelihood that students expect to attend college and in the likelihood that they expect to major in an S/E field upon entering college.

Results

The results of the explanatory analysis are presented in Table 3.2. Panel A of this table summarizes the results of the logit models with logged O_1 as the dependent variable, predicting the expectation of attending college; Panel B summarizes the results for the logit models with logged O_2 as the dependent variable, predicting the expectation of pursuing an S/E major among those who expect to go to college. Within a panel, each row of the table presents the variables included in a particular model and the estimated female-to-male odds ratio from the model. For example, the first row of each panel represents the simplest model specification, in which sex is the only independent variable. The estimated female-to-male odds ratios from these base-

Table 3.2 Influence of other covariates on the estimated female-to-male odds ratio in logit models for the probability of expecting to attend college and the probability of expecting to major in an S/E field among those expecting to go to college

Model description	Female-to-male odds ratio
Panel A: Probability of expecting to attend college (n = 12,784)	
(A0): Sex	1.29***
(A1): (A0) + Race + high school program	1.29***
(A2): (A1) + Math and science achievement	1.47***
(A3): (A2) + Family of origin influences	1.59***
(A4): (A3) + Own family expectations/attitudes	1.73***
(A5): (A4) + Math attitudes	1.74***
(A6): (A5) + High school math course participation and grades	1.69***
Panel B: Probability of expecting to major in S/E (n = 8,918)	
(B0): Sex	0.31***
(B1): (B0) + Race + high school program	0.31***
(B2): (B1) + Math and science achievement	0.34***
(B3): (B2) + Math and science achievement high performance	0.34***
(B4): (B3) + Family of origin influences	0.33***
(B5): (B4) + Own family expectations/attitudes	0.34***
(B6): (B5) + Math attitudes	0.35***
(B7): (B6) + High school math course participation and grades	0.34***

Source: NELS Second Follow-up, 1992.

Note: "Family of origin influences," "Own family expectations and attitudes," and "High school math course participation and grades" represent clusters of additive variables, as shown in Appendix Table D3.a.

$*p < .05$, $**p < .01$, $***p < .001$ (two-tailed test).

line models measure the observed gender differences, and the results reproduce the observed odds ratios presented in the final column of Table 3.1. Models A6 and B7 include all the individual and familial factors, yielding the estimated female-to-male odds ratios net of all of the covariates. The direction and the magnitude of change in the odds ratio across the successive rows of a panel indicate whether and to what degree gender differences in each educational expectation can be explained by the individual and familial influences introduced into a given model. The estimated coefficients for the final logit models (Models A6 and B7) are presented in Appendix Table D3.b.

These results show very clearly that not only does gender have distinctly different relationships with the two educational expectations, but also that the control of individual and familial factors has distinct effects on each relationship. Gender differences in the probability of expecting to attend college favor women, and controlling for individual and familial influences significantly increases this gender gap. The estimated female-to-male odds ratio increases from 1.29 to 1.69 between the baseline of Model A0 and the full model of Model A6. The value of the odds ratio from Model A6 suggests that, if male and female high school seniors were equally distributed on all of the covariates, the odds of expecting to attend college (O_1) would be 69 percent greater among women than among men. That is to say, girls are more likely than boys to expect to complete college despite their being less likely to have the characteristics and the experiences associated with high educational expectations. Equalizing the distribution of these characteristics and experiences would increase girls' already higher probability of expecting to attend college.

In contrast to gender differences in the expectation of college attendance, the gender gap in the conditional probability of expecting to major in S/E significantly favors men, and controlling for individual and familial influences tends to decrease the gender gap. The overall decrease in the effect of gender, however, is quite small, so that even when all of the covariates are included in Model B7, the estimated female-to-male odds ratio remains significantly less than one, meaning that women are significantly less likely than young men to expect to pursue an S/E major. Among students who expect to attend college, the unadjusted disparity (Model B0) indicates that women's odds of expecting to major in S/E are 0.31 as high as those of men. After controlling for the unequal distribution of men and women on all of the individual and familial covariates in Model B7, this ratio goes up only slightly to 0.34. These results show that the gender differentials in the distributions of personal and familial characteristics do not account for much of the gender gap in the choice of an S/E major among college-bound students.

Table 3.2 shows that the incremental addition of covariates does not explain much of the gender disparity in the expectation of an S/E major. We further explore whether any single explanatory factor can account for a significant part of the gender disparity using a method of decomposition (Xie and Shauman 1998; Appendix B). The decomposition results presented in Appendix Table D3.c reveal that none of the individual or familial influences has significant power to explain gender differences in the likelihood that a college-bound student expects to pursue an S/E major. The most promising explanatory factors are the ordinary math and science achievement and math attitudes, each of which may explain 0.02–0.03 of the gender gap (in terms of the odds ratio scale). Surprisingly, top performance in math and science does not explain the gender gap in postsecondary S/E educational expectations. Controlling for course participation and grades has the potential to increase, rather than reduce, the gender gap in the expectation of an S/E college major. The role of the variables measuring family of origin influences and own family expectations and attitudes is negligible.

Conclusion

In this chapter we have examined gender differences at a single point in the S/E educational trajectory: the senior year of high school. At this point in the educational process, the expectation of college attendance and concentration in an S/E field of study may be a student's first expressed intention to participate in the S/E educational trajectory. We have shown that at this early point in the trajectory gender differences are large, and that the individual and familial factors we include do not account for much of the disparity.

In this chapter, we have studied gender differences in the expectation of an S/E college major in terms of gender differences in two component educational expectations: (1) the expectation of college attendance and (2) the expectation of pursuing an S/E major given college attendance. It is, however, the combination of these two component expectations that is most relevant to the study of gender differences in the S/E educational trajectory, since it is their product that describes the supply of high school seniors who expect to pursue an S/E college major. To formalize the implications of our empirical results for the analysis of gender differences in the choice of an S/E college major, we calculated the predicted unconditional probability of expected participation in S/E postsecondary education after assigning equal values to males and females for all the individual and familial influences included in Models A6 and B7.[9] This exercise predicts the female-to-male ratio of the probability of pursuing an S/E college major among *all* high school seniors to be 0.45, in contrast to the observed ratio of 0.42. This result shows that equalizing the individual and familial characteristics of male and female high school students will not close the gender gap in the probability of expecting to pursue an S/E college major. In fact, consideration of these variables does little to the observed gender difference.

The significant gender gap in the predicted probability of the expectation of an S/E major is due to the relatively greater tendency among young college-bound men to expect to major in an S/E field. This gender gap is not explained by the individual and familial influences that we have examined in this chapter, since they are shown to reduce the observed female-to-male odds ratio by only 3 points. An important conclusion of this analysis is that the sex disparity in the interest in postsecondary S/E education is not explained by sex differences in math and science achievement. Although gender differences in average math and science achievement levels are found to have the greatest potential explanatory power of all of the covariates we considered, the proportion of the gender gap that can be accounted for by achievement differences is extremely small. Furthermore, contrary to our prediction, female underrepresentation among the very best performers on math and science achievement tests does not explain the dearth of young women who expect to pursue an S/E major. These two findings lead us to conclude that gender differences in expected participation in S/E education cannot be attributed to gender differences in academic achievement. Given this, we suspect that gender differences at later points in the S/E career trajectory will be, at most, weakly associated with achievement differences.

Although students' expectations about their intended college major are notoriously fluid, the underrepresentation of women among students who expect to major in S/E fields at the end of high school is clear and undisputable. This large gender disparity early in the life course may set the stage for the underrepresentation of women in the rest of the S/E trajectory. The analysis presented in this chapter therefore addresses a source of the selectivity bias that plagues much of the extant research on women in S/E careers. Studies that focus on participation disparities later in the S/E educational and career trajectory are not able to account for the fact that gender differences in participation appear to begin very early in the life course. So far, our collective knowledge is quite limited as to why the gender differences emerge so early (see Marini and Brinton 1984; Xie and Shauman 1997). In the next chapter we will assess the extent to which gender differences later in the S/E educational trajectory can be attributed to the gender differences in educational expectations at the end of high school.

CHAPTER FOUR

Attainment of a Science/Engineering Baccalaureate

Two important findings emerged in Chapters 2 and 3. First, gender differences in math and science achievement are not large except at the highest levels of achievement, where women are significantly underrepresented. Second, young women are far less likely than young men to be interested in pursuing the S/E educational trajectory in college: if all students realize their expectations, in the aggregate, men would outnumber women by more than two to one among S/E college majors. In this chapter, we turn our attention from expectations to behaviors and focus on gender differences in the attainment of a bachelor's degree in science/engineering.

There are many reasons an expectation of S/E degree attainment may not be realized later in the life course. In the literature this failure is commonly referred to as "leaking," or attrition, from the S/E "pipeline." The acceptance and expectation of high levels of attrition are structured into the organization of S/E majors in most colleges and universities. For example, the required introductory courses—called "weeder" or "gatekeeper" courses—are often extremely competitive. They utilize curve-grading and other means to separate talented students from the rest of the pack and serve as institutional hurdles that restrict access to S/E degrees. As a result, the rates of attrition from S/E majors are higher than those in social science or humanities disciplines, and the rates of transfer to S/E majors are modest (Seymour and Hewitt 1997). Many students who once expected to attain an S/E bachelor's degree abandon their goal along the way. Although the gap between expectation and attainment is large for all students, previous research shows that women defect from their intention to major in S/E at disproportionately high rates (Hilton and Lee 1988; Oakes 1990; Seymour and Hewitt 1997).

Attainment of a bachelor's degree in an S/E field is an educational outcome that has particular relevance for the S/E career trajectory. For scientists and engineers who pursue research careers, a bachelor's degree in an S/E field is a necessary step toward advanced training and a doctoral degree. For most engineers and some scientists, an S/E bachelor's degree serves as a terminal degree and as such provides the necessary credential for working in applied settings, such as in industry. Indeed, as we discussed in Chapter 1, according to the supply-based definition, holding an S/E bachelor's degree is a defining criterion for inclusion in the scientist/engineer population. The gender gap in the likelihood of attaining an S/E bachelor's degree is large (Berryman 1983; Xie 1996). Knowing the underlying reasons for this gap is essential to understanding why women are underrepresented in the S/E labor force. So far, our knowledge of the causal factors that contribute to the gender gap in attaining an S/E bachelor's degree is limited.

In this chapter we examine the educational paths taken by male and female students to a bachelor's degree in an S/E field. We focus on transitions that students make between an S/E major and a non-S/E major, while acknowledging that in doing so we ignore the occurrence of "internal resettlement" or transitions among S/E majors (Seymour and Hewitt 1997). Our statistical analyses are based on longitudinal data from the HSBSo.[1] We trace the educational experiences of the survey respondents during the six years that followed their high school graduation in 1982, as many of them went to college, chose a college major in S/E, and attained a bachelor's degree in S/E. In this cohort, 24 percent of the students (for both men and women) had earned a bachelor's degree by 1988, six years after they graduated from high school. Of all degrees earned, 24 percent were in S/E fields. Of all the S/E bachelor's degrees earned, 32 percent were conferred to female members of this cohort, producing a large two-to-one gender gap in S/E degree attainment favoring men over women.

Educational Paths to an S/E Baccalaureate

At the highest level of abstraction, an educational path is composed of a series of transitions leading across educational states from an educational origin to an educational outcome. Any single educational outcome may theoretically be attained through many different paths. The number of feasible paths, however, may depend on the nature of the educational outcome. When an outcome is attainable by only a few pathways, the process of attainment is considered a highly structured one. In contrast, outcomes that can be attained through many different paths are considered relatively "open" or accessible. Regardless of the number of possible routes available, there are usually "typical or most frequently traveled pathways" (Kerckhoff 1996, p. 38) by which a majority of students attain a specific outcome. Less-traveled paths contribute a relatively small proportion of students to the population who attain an educational outcome.

What educational paths lead to the attainment of a bachelor's degree in an S/E field? Based largely on cross-sectional data, previous studies on the topic have been dominated by the "science pipeline" conceptualization, which portrays the S/E educational trajectory as a highly structured process with only one pathway to attainment: the path of early entry and persistence. This emphasis on a singular path has generated a singular explanation of gender differences in S/E degree attainment. The underrepresentation of women among S/E baccalaureates is commonly attributed to lower rates of persistence among women relative to men. Indeed, previous research has mostly focused on gender differences in the rate at which students leak from the S/E educational trajectory (e.g., AAAS 1992a; Alper 1993; Oakes 1990). However, recent studies (Hilton and Lee 1988; Xie 1996) that utilize longitudinal data and dynamic analytic models have identified a less-traveled, but important, tributary path to postsecondary S/E education: entry from non-S/E educational trajectories during the college years. Hilton and Lee (1988) found that students were likely to enter S/E education at nontrivial rates through their sophomore year of college. Xie (1996) found significant gender differences favoring males in the rate of entry into the S/E educational trajectory during the college years but small gender differences in the rate of exit.

The studies by Hilton and Lee (1988) and Xie (1996) identify gender differences in entry rates as a partial explanation of the gender gap in S/E education during college, but they leave unanswered several important questions about the significance of entry as a path to S/E degree attainment. First, these studies identify students who enter S/E majors in college but do not assess their relative contribution to S/E degrees relative to those who followed other potential paths. Second, past research has not distinguished entry (i.e., entering S/E education after never having been involved in an S/E educational state) from reentry (i.e., entering S/E education from a non-S/E educational state after having previous experience in S/E). In this analysis, we disaggregate entry from reentry and assess the relative importance of each of these paths as routes to S/E degree attainment. The third unanswered question concerns the influence of the paths of entry and reentry on gender differences in S/E degree attainment. To the extent that the paths of entry and reentry into S/E educational states are significant routes to S/E degree attainment, we are interested in how much of the gender gap in attaining S/E bachelor's degrees is attributable to gender differences in the probability of following these educational paths.

The probability that an individual attains an S/E bachelor's degree can be decomposed into the set of possible paths that potentially lead to an S/E baccalaureate. Mathematically, let S_t denote an educational state at time t, where t denotes discrete points of observation with T representing the final point of observation, and let $D_T^{S/E}$ denote the educational outcome of attaining a bachelor's degree in an S/E field at time T. The total probability of attaining an S/E degree conditional on educational paths can be expressed as:

$$(4.1) \qquad P(D_T^{S/E}) = \sum_{k=1}^{3} P(S_t = k) \times P(D_T^{S/E} \mid S_t = k).$$

Equation 4.1 identifies the marginal probability of attaining a degree as being equal to the sum of the product of the marginal probability of an origin state and the conditional probability of attaining a degree given the origin state. For convenience, we will refer to the first part—the marginal probability of the origin state—as the distribution component, and the second part—the conditional probability—as the transition component. Three mutually exclusive educational states (k) are defined for this analysis:

1 = Not in college
2 = Enrollment in a non-S/E college major or non-S/E degree attainment
3 = Enrollment in an S/E college major or S/E degree attainment.

For the first time period, the above three states refer to "expected" status, measured when the HSBSo subjects were in their senior year of high school. Time is assumed to be discrete in this analysis and is defined as follows:

$t = 1$, S_1 measures educational expectations in the spring of 1982 (senior high school year)
$t = 2$, S_2 measures educational status in the fall of 1982 (after high school graduation)
$t = 3$, S_3 measures educational status in 1984
$t = 4$, $D_4^{S/E}$ measures educational outcome in 1986–1988.[2]

Note that $D_4^{S/E}$ measures degree attainment in any S/E field. Our operationalization of S/E fields includes all the natural sciences plus engineering and math but excludes all social science fields. See Codebook C (posted at www.yuxie.com) for a list of the specific fields that are included in our operationalization.

Reduced-Form Educational Paths

A reduced-form educational path is the simplest representation of an educational path. It refers to the transition between an educational origin state at $t = 1$ and an educational outcome at $t = T$. A reduced-form educational path ignores the timing and frequency of educational transitions that may occur in between. From the reduced-form perspective, the timing and frequency of intervening transitions between the origin state S_1 and the final outcome state $D_4^{S/E}$ are considered inconsequential (Xie 1996). All attention is paid to the distribution of educational expectation, $P(S_1)$, and to the transition from educational expectation to S/E degree attainment, $P(D_4^{S/E}|S_1)$. This makes intuitive sense. For students who expect to attain an S/E degree in high school, we are interested in the likelihood that they actually realize their plan. For students who did not expect to attain an S/E degree, attainment of an S/E degree is accomplished only by entering into the S/E educational trajectory sometime after high school graduation.

The reduced-form paths to attainment of a bachelor's degree in an S/E field are presented in Figure 4.1. The contributions of the three conditional paths (the probabilities of degree attainment conditional on path) to the marginal probability of S/E degree attainment (the total unconditional probability of degree attainment) are measured by the product of the distribution and transition components of each path: (1) the probability of an educational expectation at $t = 1$ and (2) the probability of degree attainment at $t = 4$ conditional on educational expectation at $t = 1$. Applying the above notation to the paths identified in Figure 4.1, the marginal probability of attaining an S/E bachelor's degree by 1988 is equal to the sum of the probabilities of degree attainment conditional on an educational path, weighted by the probability of taking the educational path:

$$P(D_4^{S/E}) = P(S_1 = 1) \times P(D_4^{S/E} \mid S_1 = 1) \qquad \text{[entry from expectation of no college education]}$$

$$+ P(S_1 = 2) \times P(D_4^{S/E} \mid S_1 = 2) \qquad \text{[entry from expectation of non-S/E major in college]}$$

$$+ P(S_1 = 3) \times P(D_4^{S/E} \mid S_1 = 3) \qquad \text{[persistence in an S/E college major].}$$

As noted earlier, among the HSBSo students, men were about two times more likely than women to earn an S/E baccalaureate by 1988. Figure 4.1 shows that the marginal probability of S/E degree attainment is 0.078 for men and 0.037 for women.[3] Among students who expected no college education, the probability of S/E degree attainment is extremely low: only 0.5 percent of both male and female students. This is not surprising, as this group of students did not plan to enter college upon high school graduation. The statistics reflect the fact that the educational path of entry into S/E from the expectation of no college education is not a well-traveled route to an S/E baccalaureate.

The second reduced-form educational path to S/E degree attainment originates with the expectation of postsecondary education in a non-S/E field of study. Striking gender differences are apparent for both the distribution and the transition components of this path. Women are more likely than men to expect to pursue a non-S/E major in college (0.355 for women versus 0.263 for men). Men, however, are more than twice as likely as women to make the transition from a

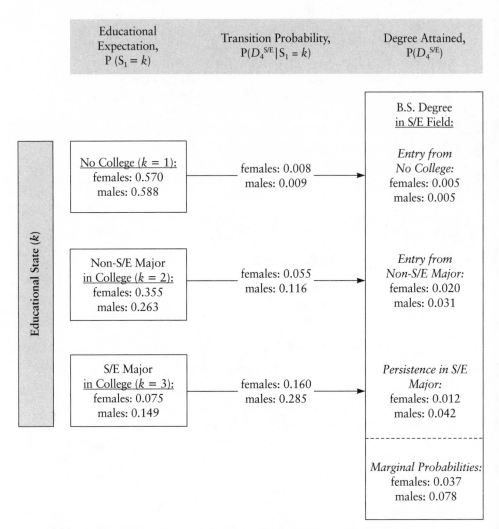

Figure 4.1. Probability of attaining an S/E bachelor's degree by reduced-form paths to degree attainment and gender. *Source:* HSB Sophomore Cohort First Follow-up through Fourth Follow-up, 1982–1992.

non-S/E education expectation to degree attainment in an S/E field (0.116 for men versus 0.055 for women). The product of the two components of this educational path generates a large gender difference in the likelihood of S/E degree attainment that favors men. For this cohort, 3.1 percent of men and 2.0 percent of women expected to major in a non-S/E field in high school but went on to attain a bachelor's degree in an S/E field. It is important to note that the gender gap in the probability of S/E degree attainment via the path of entry from a non-S/E education expectation would be greater *if* male and female students were equally distributed at the origin of this educational path. That is, the higher relative representation of women among students who expect a non-S/E major dampens the effect of the relatively low female rate of transition from this path into S/E.

The final route to S/E degree attainment is the path of persistence. Individuals pursuing this path expressed the expectation of pursuing S/E postsecondary education in high school and ultimately attained an S/E degree within six years. Gender differences are evident for both the distribution and the transition components of this path. Women are half as likely as men to express the expectation of entering the S/E educational trajectory (0.149 for men versus 0.075 for women). Of those students who expressed this expectation, women are about a third less likely than men to realize it by attaining an S/E bachelor's degree (0.285 for men versus 0.160 for women). Compounding the gender differences from these two sources, the gender disparity in attaining an S/E degree through this path is large: 4.2 percent of all men versus 1.2 percent of all women. Gender differences in the path of persistence are clearly an important source of the gender disparity in S/E baccalaureates. In fact, about three-fourths of the gender difference in attaining an S/E degree (0.078 for men versus 0.037 for women) can be attributed to the persistence path alone. In this sense, there is some justification for the focus in the past literature on gender differences in attrition from the science pipeline.

It is also clear from the above analysis, however, that there are gender differences in the educational paths that students are most likely to follow to attain an S/E degree. Persistence is the route most often traveled by male S/E baccalaureates, as it accounts for over half of S/E degree attainment among men (0.042/0.078 = 54 percent). In contrast, only 32 percent of women S/E baccalaureates followed the persistence path to degree attainment (0.012/0.037 = 32 percent).

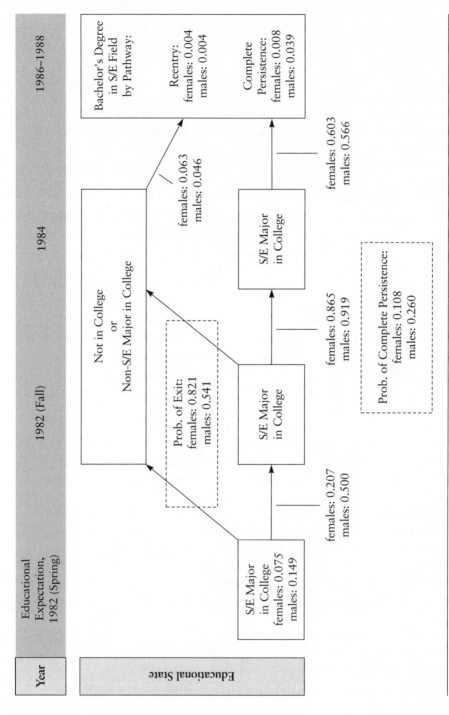

Figure 4.2. Probability pathways from expectation of an S/E major to S/E degree attainment by gender. *Source:* HSB Sophomore Cohort First Follow-up through Fourth Follow-up, 1982–1992.

Instead, for women the most frequently traveled path is entry from non-S/E educational states, which accounts for more than half of all women who eventually attain an S/E baccalaureate (0.020/0.037 = 54 percent).

The reduced-form analysis shows that women are less likely than men to persist in the S/E educational trajectory. This reduced-form path, however, infers persistence from observation of the origin and destination educational states only. We do not know whether these differences are due to differential attrition alone or to differential attrition plus differential reentry, with reentry defined as first exiting from and then returning to the S/E educational trajectory. To answer this question, we further decompose the reduced-form persistence path into its component educational paths.

Detailed Educational Paths of Reentry and Complete Persistence
Reduced-form paths can be further decomposed into detailed paths comprising of a number of component transitions that link the origin and outcome states; the number of component parts of an educational path is determined primarily by the number of times educational status is observed. Decomposing an educational path into a set of component parts can reveal the specific transition or set of transitions that have the most influence on the probability of attaining an S/E degree.

In the reduced form, if a student expected to enroll in an S/E field of study in high school and then attained an S/E bachelor's degree by 1988, he/she is assumed to have traveled the path of persistence. However, persistence is only one of the many paths that may connect S/E educational expectation in 1982 with S/E degree attainment in 1988. By observing educational statuses at intervening points in the educational trajectory, we can decompose the path of apparent persistence into two distinct paths: the path of "reentry" and the path of "complete persistence." Figure 4.2 illustrates the decomposition. The path of reentry to S/E consists of three components: (1) the expectation of an S/E college major ($t = 1$), (2) an exit from the S/E educational trajectory—a transition from an S/E educational state to a non-S/E educational state at some point between 1982 and 1984 ($t = 2, 3$), and (3) reentry into the S/E educational trajectory so as to attain an S/E bachelor's degree by 1988 ($t = 4$).

In addition to specifying the path of reentry, we break the complete persistence path into time- and sex-specific component probabilities to determine where in the persistence chain the large gender gap is generated: (1) the probability of persistence in S/E from high school to college, (2) the probability of persistence in S/E education during college, and (3) the probability of persistence to S/E degree attainment. The probability of degree attainment via the path of persistence is equal to the sum of the probability of degree attainment via the path of reentry and the probability of degree attainment via the path of complete persistence:

$P(S_1 = 3) \times P(D_4^{S/E} | S_1 = 3)$ Reentry + Complete persistence

$= P(S_1 = 3)$ [expectation of an S/E major]

$\times P(S_2 \neq 3 \cup S_3 \neq 3 | S_1 = 3)$ [exit from an S/E major]

$\times P(D_4^{S/E} | S_1 = 3 \cap (S_2 \neq 3 \cup S_3 \neq 3))$ [reentry after exit from S/E major]

$+ P(S_1 = 3)$ [expectation of an S/E major]

$\times P(S_2 = 3 | S_1 = 3)$ [persistence from high school to college]

$\times P(S_3 = 3 | S_1 = 3 \cap S_2 = 3)$ [persistence during college]

$\times P(D_4^{S/E} | S_1 = 3 \cap S_2 = 3 \cap S_3 = 3)$ [persistence to bachelor's degree],

where the symbols $\cup$ and $\cap$ represent "or" and "and," respectively. Gender differences in the component parts of the paths of reentry and complete persistence are presented in Figure 4.2. The contribution of the path of reentry to the marginal probability of S/E degree attainment is relatively small. During the transition from high school to college, the rate of exit from the S/E educational trajectory is generally large, and it is about 50 percent greater among women than among men (0.82 versus 0.54). However, women's higher exit rate is counterbalanced by their higher rate of reentering and earning a bachelor's degree in S/E. As a result, there is no gender gap in attaining an S/E degree via the reentry path.

Given the low likelihood of reentry for both male and female students, it follows that much of the disparity in the persistence path lies in differential attrition—hence in the path of complete persistence. Indeed, complete persistence is observed among 3.9 percent of all male students, but this educational path is followed by only 0.8 percent of all female students. Detailed analysis of the path of complete persistence reveals the temporal location of gender differences in the S/E educational trajectory: most of the gender differences are generated by the combination of gender differences in the distribution of the educational expectation and the significant gender disparity in the probability of persistence in S/E education from high school to college enrollment. Men are 2.4 times more likely than women to persist in the S/E educational trajectory during the transition from high school to college. During college, however, gender differences in the probability of persistence in an S/E field of study narrow and then reverse. The percentage of students who were in an S/E college major in 1982 ($t = 2$) and persisted in S/E education in 1984 ($t = 3$) is only slightly lower for women (at 86.5 percent, versus 91.9 percent for men). The rate of transition from majoring in an S/E field in 1984 ($t = 3$) to later S/E degree attainment ($t = 4$) is slightly higher among women (60 percent) than among men (57 percent).

This detailed analysis of the path of complete persistence leads us to conclude that during college women are as likely as men, if not more likely, to persist in S/E education. Significant gender differences in the S/E educational trajectory occur prior to, and upon, college entry—namely, during the formation of educational aspirations and in the transition from high school to college enrollment.

Detailed Educational Paths of Entry

The reduced-form path of entry from the expectation of a non-S/E major in Figure 4.1 considers only entry into the S/E educational trajectory at some point but ignores the exact timing of entry. As Hilton and Lee (1988) suggest, however, the probability of entry may be greatest early in the educational trajectory. In addition, the probability of S/E degree attainment is likely to be affected by the timing of entry into the S/E trajectory. In this section, we attempt to understand the paths by which students who expected to pursue a non-S/E college education in high school later enter the S/E educational trajectory.

We consider three possible educational paths students may follow from the original expectation of a non-S/E college major to degree attainment in an S/E field. These paths focus only on single transitions from non-S/E to S/E educational states. Many other educational paths connect this origin-destination dyad, including paths consisting of multiple transitions between non-S/E and S/E educational states and transitions that encompass movement out of college enrollment. Given the very small proportion of S/E bachelor's degrees earned by students who followed these more complex educational paths, we do not consider them in our analysis. Figure 4.3 presents each of the paths we examine. The path of early entry, presented in Panel A, is followed by students who expected to pursue a non-S/E college major in high school ($t = 1$) but actually enrolled in an S/E major field of study when they first entered college in the fall of 1982 ($t = 2$) and then persisted in the S/E educational trajectory to attain an S/E bachelor's degree. Students could also enter the S/E educational trajectory after majoring in a non-S/E field for some time. Panel B presents the path of mid-college entry. This path is followed by students who expected to enroll (at $t = 1$) and actually enrolled (at $t = 2$) in non-S/E higher education but switched to an S/E major field by 1984 ($t = 3$). Panel C illustrates the path of late entry—the path that leads to S/E degree attainment following entry into S/E education sometime after 1984 ($t = 4$).

The path-specific probabilities of degree attainment indicate that S/E degree attainment via the path of entry is dominated by early entrants. Among all the students who entered the S/E educational trajectory and attained an S/E bachelor's degree, 84 percent (0.026/0.031) of male students and 75 percent (0.015/0.020) of female students took the path of early entry. In addition, we observe the largest gender gap in the attainment of an S/E degree via the path of early entry (0.026 for men versus 0.015 for women). This path appears to be important for two reasons. First, among high school seniors who expected to pursue a non-S/E college major, the rates of transition to S/E majors upon entering college are high relative to the entry rates later in the educational trajectory. Second, the rates differ substantially by gender (0.188 for men versus 0.091 for women). In contrast, the paths of mid-college and late entry contribute very few students to the pool of S/E baccalaureates and do not differ significantly by gender.

Contributions of Educational Paths to the Gender Gap in S/E Degree Attainment

The above analysis shows gender differences in the probability of attaining an S/E degree through many component educational paths.

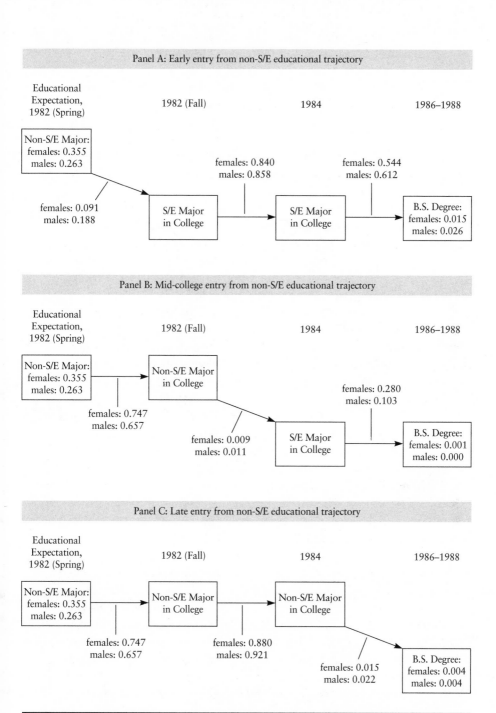

Figure 4.3. Probability pathways from expectation of a non-S/E major to S/E degree attainment by gender. *Source:* HSB Sophomore Cohort First Follow-up through Fourth Follow-up, 1982–1992.

We now attempt to measure the practical importance of the gender differences in these component educational paths to the overall gender gap in S/E degree attainment. Toward this end, we pose the following counterfactual question: How much reduction in the gender disparity in S/E degree attainment would be achieved if there were no gender difference at each point in the paths that lead to S/E degree attainment? To answer this question, we impose gender equity by assigning the male-specific probability to women for each component, either the distribution or the transition component, of the paths to degree attainment. We then observe the effect of the counterfactual gender equity at the component level on the overall gender gap in the marginal probability of attaining an S/E degree. The results of this "equity experiment" are presented in Table 4.1.

Table 4.1 presents the female marginal probability of S/E degree attainment and the percent reduction in the observed gender gap achieved by assigning the male probability to all students. Each line represents the substitution of a different component probability. As a reference, the first line displays women's observed marginal probability of attaining an S/E degree, equal to 0.036. Thus, a hypothetical probability of attaining an S/E degree greater than 0.036 indicates a reduction in the gender gap. The magnitude of the reduction is normalized by comparison with men's observed marginal probability of attaining an S/E degree (0.078). For example, equalizing the gender difference in the proportion of high school students who expected no college education would not explain the gender gap in S/E degree attainment (0.4 percent). Overall, the results of this exercise highlight the critical importance of the transition from high school to college. At this point, gender differences in distribution, entry, and persistence have the most significant effects on gender differences in later S/E degree attainment. What is most notable is that the gender gap in attaining an S/E bachelor's degree would be reduced by 48.9 percent if there were no gender differences in the early entry transition rate into S/E college majors among high school seniors with non-S/E educational expectations. Another important source of the gender gap in S/E graduation is the rate of persistence in the S/E educational track from high school to college: imposing on female students the male rate of persistence in S/E from high school to college accounts for 27.5 percent of the gender gap in S/E degree attainment.

Table 4.1 Female students' probability of S/E degree attainment by 1988 if men's component distribution/transition probability is substituted for women's

Component probability of men substituted for women	Probability of S/E degree attainment for women	Percentage of gender gap explained
No substitution (observed)	0.036	0.0
Entry from no college expectation:		
Distribution	0.036	0.4
Transition to S/E degree	0.036	0.6
Entry from non-S/E expectation:		
Distribution	0.035	−12.0
Early entry to S/E degree	0.058	48.9
Mid-college entry to S/E degree	0.040	3.7
Late entry to S/E degree	0.039	3.3
Complete persistence from S/E expectation:		
Distribution	0.048	28.1
Persistence in S/E from high school to college	0.048	27.5
Persistence in S/E during college	0.037	1.2
Persistence in S/E to bachelor's degree	0.036	−1.2
Reentry after exit from S/E expectation:		
Exit from S/E major	0.035	−3.2
Transition to S/E degree after exit from S/E	0.035	−2.5

Source: HSB Sophomore Cohort First Follow-up through Fourth Follow-up, 1982–1992.
Note: Men's overall probability of attaining an S/E bachelor's degree is 0.083. See Figure 4.1 for definition of component probabilities.

Gender differences in the distribution of the S/E educational expectation before entry into college also significantly influence the underrepresentation of women among S/E baccalaureates.[4] If the same proportion of women as men planned to pursue an S/E education prior to college, the gender gap in S/E bachelor's degree attainment would be reduced by 28.1 percent. Note that young women are more likely than young men to expect to pursue a non-S/E college major. Equalizing the proportion of men and women who have this expectation would widen the gender gap in degree attainment by 12.0 percent.

The other components of the complete persistence path have negligible effects on the gender gap in S/E degree attainment. Most significantly, assuming gender equality in the rates of attrition from the S/E educational trajectory after college enrollment does not significantly increase the probability of S/E degree attainment for women.

Explaining the Gender Gap in Attainment of an S/E Baccalaureate

The analysis of educational paths reveals that the transition from high school to college is a particularly significant juncture in the pursuit of an S/E bachelor's degree. The probability of attaining an S/E bachelor's degree is highest among individuals who either persist in or newly enter the S/E educational trajectory at this stage. In addition, since it is at this early point in the educational trajectory that gender differences in the rates of persistence and entry are the greatest, the transition from high school to college is also very consequential for gender differences in rates of S/E degree attainment. Identifying the factors that influence the educational choices made by male and female students at the transition from high school to college is therefore critical to understanding the causes of gender differences in the supply of S/E baccalaureates.

In an attempt to explain the gender gap in S/E degree attainment, we investigate the influence of a set of individual and familial characteristics of the HSBSo students on the two educational outcomes in the undergraduate S/E educational trajectory we have identified as most consequential: (1) the choice of an S/E college major upon entering college and (2) the attainment of an S/E bachelor's degree. Our goal for this analysis is to measure the extent to which gender differences in these educational outcomes are explained by selected individual and familial characteristics commonly assumed to influence S/E education. To do this we use a modeling strategy similar to that of Chapter 3 in which we estimate a series of hierarchical logit models separately for the two educational outcomes. The simplest model includes only the effect of sex, and each successive model in the hierarchy incorporates a new covariate or set of covariates. As explained in Chapter 1, this strategy allows us to examine the degree to which the effect of sex (i.e., b_{sex}) is changed by the addition of new variables to the model.

Influences on College Enrollment and Selection of S/E Major in College

We examine the transition from high school to college as two nested educational decisions: students first decide whether or not to enroll in college, and then they decide what major field of study to pursue. This conceptualization is justified for two reasons. First, since women are more likely than men to attend college, the underrepresentation of women in S/E college majors is the outcome of gender differences in the choice of major field, not college enrollment. Second, the influence of the independent variables may differ for the two educational outcomes. Separating the process of majoring in an S/E major in college into two sequential decisions therefore allows us to gauge more precisely the degree to which gender differences are explained. The logit analysis of college enrollment is based on a sample of 6,728 students who could potentially enroll in college in the fall of 1982. The analysis of college major is based on the subset of 4,210 students who actually enrolled in a postsecondary institution in 1982.

We examine how the transition from high school to college is influenced by the same four types of independent variables used in Chapter 3: individual background characteristics, family of origin influences, students' own family expectations and attitudes, and high school math grades and participation. The individual background characteristics include students' educational expectation in Spring 1982, their high school program, and their math achievement. Since our earlier analysis has shown large gender differences not in average math achievement but in high math achievement, we also add a dummy variable indicating whether a student scored in the top 5 percentile on the math test in Spring 1982. Measures of family of origin influences include the educational attainment of both mother and father and the parents' expectations for the student's educational attainment.[5] Students' views about their future family status and roles are measured using three variables: the age at which they expect to marry for the first time, the number of children they expect to have during their lifetime, and the attitude scale contrasting their family and work orientations.[6] To investigate the influence of prior educational experiences on gender differences, we include three measures of participation and performance in high school mathematics courses: the students' mean math course grade, an indicator of participation in advanced math courses, and a variable measuring the final grade during which students took their last math class.[7] The coding of all of these variables parallels that of the variables used for the analysis of the NELS data and is described in Chapters 2 and 3. The distributions of the independent variables by gender are presented in Appendix Table D4.a.

The results of the multivariate analysis of the transition from high school to college are presented in Table 4.2. Panel A of the table summarizes the results of the logit model for the likelihood of enrolling in college; Panel B summarizes the results of the logit model for the likelihood of selecting an S/E college major conditional on enrolling in college. Each panel presents a series of hierarchical logit models and

Table 4.2 Influence of other covariates on the estimated female-to-male odds ratio in logit models for the probability of enrolling in college and the probability of selecting an S/E major among those who enroll in college in the fall of 1982

Model description	Female-to-male odds ratio
Panel A: Probability of enrolling in college in 1982 (n = 6,728)	
(A0): Sex	1.27***
(A1): (A0) + Educational expectations, spring 1982	1.31***
(A2): (A1) + High school program	1.30**
(A3): (A2) + Math achievement	1.49***
(A4): (A3) + Family of origin influences	1.50***
(A5): (A4) + Own family expectations and attitudes	1.67***
(A6): (A5) + High school math course participation and grades	1.63***
Panel B: Probability of selecting an S/E college major in 1982 (n = 4,210)	
(B0): Sex	0.27***
(B1): (B0) + Educational expectations, spring 1982	0.31***
(B2): (B1) + High school program	0.30***
(B3): (B2) + Math achievement	0.36***
(B4): (B3) + Math achievement high performance	0.36***
(B5): (B4) + Family of origin influences	0.36***
(B6): (B5) + Own family expectations and attitudes	0.36***
(B7): (B6) + High school math course participation and grades	0.34***

Source: HSB Sophomore Cohort First Follow-up through Fourth Follow-up, 1982–1992.

Note: "Family of origin influences," "Own family expectations and attitudes," and "High school math course participation and grades" represent clusters of additive variables, as shown in Appendix Table D4.b.

*$p < .05$, **$p < .01$, ***$p < .001$ (two-tailed test).

the associated female-to-male odds ratios of college enrollment and selection of an S/E major. Estimated coefficients for the final models (Models A6 and B7) are presented in Appendix Table D4.b.

Model A0 is the simplest model specification. Since this model includes only the effect of sex and no other covariates, it estimates the raw gender gap in the likelihood of enrolling in college. The estimated female-to-male ratio in the odds of college enrollment from this model reflects the fact that observed gender differences in college enrollment significantly favor women: young women are 27 percent more likely than young men to enroll in college following graduation from high school. Furthermore, controlling for the other covariates in subsequent models in Panel A tends to further exacerbate the gender gap in favor of female students. The estimated female-to-male odds ratio from Model A6 indicates that if the distributions of the independent variables were the same for men and women, the odds of enrolling in college would be 63 percent greater among women than among men. Clearly, the gender gap in S/E baccalaureates is *not* the result of gender differences in enrollment.

In stark contrast to the gender gap in college enrollment, the gender gap in choice of an S/E college major significantly favors men. The observed sex difference in the likelihood of majoring in S/E among those students who enrolled in college is measured by Model B0, which shows that women's odds of selecting an S/E major are only 27 percent as high as the odds for men. The subsequent inclusion of the additional independent variables in Models B1 through B7 tends to narrow the gender gap, but the change in the female-to-male odds ratio is slight even after controlling for all the covariates. The estimated female-to-male odds ratio from Model B7 indicates that young women in college are only 0.34 times as likely as men to select an S/E major even after accounting for gender differences in all the individual and familial factors considered.

The small increase in the estimated female-to-male odds ratio of selecting an S/E college major between Models B0 and B7 attests to the relatively low explanatory power of all the covariates in the complete model. The results of the decomposition analysis (see Appendix Table D4.c) reinforce this conclusion: none of the explanatory factors has significant power in explaining sex differences in the likelihood that a student who enrolls in college chooses to pursue an S/E major. The upper bound of the increase in the female-to-male odds ratio attributable to any single explanatory factor is 0.05. The most important explanatory factor is students' educational expectation in high school, with both "low" and "high" estimates at 0.04.

Influences on S/E Degree Attainment

We examine degree attainment as the combination of two nested educational achievements: the attainment of a bachelor's degree, and among those students who earn a baccalaureate, the attainment of an S/E degree. Our justification for this conceptualization parallels our argument for the analysis of the transition from high school to college. First, since women are as likely as men to earn a bachelor's degree, the underrepresentation of women among those who hold an S/E baccalaureate is not due to sex differences in the attainment of a four-year college degree per se but in the type of degrees attained. Second, these two educational achievements may be influenced differently by the set of explanatory factors we include in our analysis. The logit analysis of degree attainment is based on the complete sample of 6,728 students who graduated from high school in the fall of 1982. The analysis of degree attainment in an S/E field is based on the subset of 1,883 students who earned a bachelor's degree in any field by 1988.

We examine how sex differences in degree attainment are influenced by four types of independent variables: individual background characteristics, high school math grades and participation, students' own family status and attitudes, and college grade-point average (GPA) and course grades. The variables measuring background characteristics and high school math grades and participation are identical to those used in the earlier analysis except that we substitute college major in the fall of 1982 for educational expectations expressed during the spring of 1982. Students' family status in 1984 is captured by variables measuring marital and parental status. Marital status is measured as a binary variable contrasting currently married (coded one) with currently unmarried. Parental status is also a dichotomous variable that contrasts those who have children with those who do not have children in 1984. In addition, we include the family vs. work attitude scale measured in 1984. Academic performance in college as of 1984 is measured with two variables: cumulative college grade-point average and a scale of college grades that contrasts performance in S/E courses with performance in non-S/E courses.[8] See Appendix

Table 4.3 Influence of other covariates on the estimated female-to-male odds ratio in logit models for the probability of earning a bachelor's degree and the probability of earning an S/E degree among those who earn a bachelor's degree by 1988

Model description	Female-to-male odds ratio
Panel A: Probability of earning a bachelor's degree (n = 6,728)	
(A0): Sex	1.05
(A1): (A0) + College major, fall 1982	0.98
(A2): (A1) + High school program	0.94
(A3): (A2) + Math achievement	1.23*
(A4): (A3) + High school math course participation and grades	1.08
(A5): (A4) + Own family status and attitudes	1.16
(A6): (A5) + College GPA	1.03
Panel B: Probability of earning an S/E bachelor's degree (n = 1,883)	
(B0) Sex	0.35***
(B1): (B0) + College major, fall 1982	0.57*
(B2): (B1) + High school program	0.55*
(B3): (B2) + Math achievement	0.61*
(B4): (B3) + Math achievement high performance	0.62
(B5): (B4) + High school math course participation and grades	0.52*
(B6): (B5) + Own family status and attitudes	0.52*
(B7): (B6) + College GPA and course grade scale	0.49**

Source: HSB Sophomore Cohort First Follow-up through Fourth Follow-up, 1982–1992.
Note: "High school math course participation and grades" and "Own family status and attitudes" represent clusters of additive variables, as shown in Appendix Table D4.d.
*$p < .05$, **$p < .01$, ***$p < .001$ (two-tailed test).

Table D4.a for the definition and sex-specific distribution of each of these variables.

The results of the multivariate analysis of degree attainment are presented in Table 4.3. Panel A of this table summarizes the results of the logit analysis of gender differences in the likelihood of earning a bachelor's degree in any field, and Panel B presents the results of the logit analysis of gender differences in the likelihood that an earned baccalaureate is in an S/E field. The estimated coefficients of all explanatory factors included in the final models (Models A6 and B7) are presented in Appendix Table D4.d.

The estimated female-to-male odds ratio from the baseline model, Model A0, shows that men and women are about equally likely to earn a bachelor's degree. Adding college major and high school program in Models A1 and A2 does not change this basic pattern. However, controlling for math achievement in Model A3 causes the female-to-male odds ratio to increase in magnitude and significance. This change in the estimated effect of sex reveals that if women and men achieved equally on standardized tests of mathematics ability, women would be about 23 percent more likely than men to earn a bachelor's degree. Controlling for the remaining covariates in Models A4 through A6, however, reduces the female-to-male odds ratio of degree attainment to insignificance. This result means that there is no gender difference in degree attainment if all the covariates are equally distributed between men and women.

Although young men and women are equally likely to earn a baccalaureate, they earn their degrees in distinctly different fields. According to the estimated female-to-male odds ratio from Model B0, women's odds of earning an S/E baccalaureate are only a third as high as men's. The estimated magnitude of the female-to-male odds ratio markedly increases toward 1 as we add 1982 college major in Model B1. The estimated gender difference becomes insignificant after the addition of high math performance in Model B4, indicating that much of the gender disparity is explained by gender differences in the background characteristics included in Model B4. Adding the other sets of explanatory factors in Models B5 through B7, however, causes the female-to-male odds ratio of S/E degree attainment to regain statistical significance. Clearly, these results show that the gender gap in S/E degree attainment is not explained by gender differences in high school math course participation and grades, family status and attitudes, and college grades. On the contrary, equalizing the existing gender differences on these factors would exacerbate the gender gap in S/E degree attainment. After controlling for all of the individual and familial influences, the odds of earning an S/E bachelor's degree among women are estimated to be half the odds for men.

We further conducted a decomposition analysis to ascertain the explanatory power of each group of independent variables included in the final model of S/E degree attainment (see Appendix Table D4.e). We report three main findings from the decomposition analysis. First, background characteristics are important. Gender differences in college major in the fall of 1982, math achievement, and math high performance are shown to have the largest potential effect on the gender gap in S/E degree attainment. In particular, the large positive values of both the low and high estimates of 1982 college major (at 0.11 and 0.22) attest to the fact that gender differences in early involvement in the S/E educational trajectory have a significant impact on gender differences in eventual S/E degree attainment. Although the high estimates of both mathematics achievement measures are positive and moderately large, the small low estimates suggest that, controlling for the other explanatory factors, the gender gap in math achievement may have little to no power in explaining the gender gap in S/E degree attainment. Second, high school program, high school math course participation and grades, and college GPA and course grade scale clearly hold no power to explain the gender gap in S/E degree attainment. Their high and low estimates are negative, meaning that controlling for these explanatory factors only has the potential to widen the gender gap in S/E degree attainment. Third, the potential influence of the students' own family status and attitudes on the estimated gender gap in S/E degree attainment is limited, and the results do not clearly indicate the direction of the influence.

Conclusion

The analysis presented in this chapter identifies the "most frequently traveled pathways" to the attainment of a bachelor's degree in an S/E field. Previous research has generally assumed that a single pathway leads to S/E degree attainment: persistence in the science pipeline. By measuring empirically the prevalence of multiple possible paths to the attainment of an S/E bachelor's degree, we find that there are two most frequently traveled pathways: (1) complete persistence in the S/E educational trajectory from high school to degree attainment and (2) entry from the non-S/E college educational trajectory. In addition, we find gender differences in the composition of students who travel each of these paths: the majority of male S/E baccalaureates have taken the path of complete persistence, whereas most female S/E baccalaureates entered the S/E educational trajectory during college, after starting on the non-S/E educational track. Decomposition of the path of entry from the non-S/E track reveals that entry into S/E education is most likely to occur at the transition from high school to college.

The significance of an alternative to the persistence path to S/E degree attainment indicates that the S/E educational trajectory is not as highly structured as has been assumed previously. The S/E educational trajectory is far from open, however. The paths of complete persistence and early entry from the non-S/E track carry the overwhelming majority of students to S/E degree attainment. The relatively large contribution of the path of early entry from the non-S/E track is driven less by the rate of transition from non-S/E to S/E education than by the large supply of high school students who expected to have a non-S/E college education. This is especially true for women. The critical importance of the early transition indicates that the structure of S/E education is such that a shift from the non-S/E track to the S/E track should be made early in college and that S/E students need to stay on the S/E track for an extended time to attain S/E degrees.

The significance of early involvement in the S/E educational trajectory is reinforced by the results of the multivariate analysis of gender differences in S/E education. Students' educational expectation in high school is the most important single factor explaining gender differences in the likelihood of majoring in S/E in college. Similarly, the major they declare early in their college career holds the greatest power for explaining gender differences in the S/E degree attainment. Our analysis has shown that the potential explanatory power of early involvement is still limited, however, and that none of the other individual and familial variables we include in our analysis is found to have a significant influence on sex differences in S/E degree attainment. Our attempt to explain the gender difference in the choice of an S/E college major is largely unsuccessful, but we were able to explain a sizable portion of the observed gender disparity in the likelihood of earning an S/E baccalaureate.

Our results have an important implication for the potential role of gender differences in mathematics achievement in causing gender differences in S/E education and degree attainment. There is little doubt that mathematics achievement is strongly associated with participation in S/E college majors and the attainment of an S/E degree. The results of this analysis, however, lead us to conclude that mathematics achievement per se does not explain the *gender differences* in S/E educational and degree attainment at the undergraduate level. Although discovering the causes of persistent sex differences in mathematics achievement is worthy of further research, we should not expect this line of research to provide a full explanation for gender differences in S/E education.

CHAPTER FIVE

Career Paths after a Science/Engineering Baccalaureate

The preceding chapters have documented persistent gender gaps in mathematics and science achievement (Chapter 2), aspirations for obtaining a science/engineering (S/E) education (Chapter 3), and the likelihood of obtaining a bachelor's degree in S/E (Chapter 4). The gender differences in these outcomes, however, are smaller in magnitude than the observed gender disparities in the S/E labor force. For example, women accounted for roughly 17 percent of S/E personnel aged 25–34 with a bachelor's degree in 1980. In contrast, the proportion of women among recipients of S/E bachelor's degrees rose to well above 25 percent from 1978 onward (see Tables 7.1 and 7.2 in Chapter 7). While we resist the conventional "pipeline" conceptualization, we acknowledge the very close relationship between acquiring educational credentials in science/engineering and working as a scientist/engineer. That the gender gap in S/E labor force participation is greater than the gender gap in the S/E educational trajectory suggests that women face more significant barriers to becoming scientists/engineers than do men with comparable educational credentials.

Indeed, Xie (1996) shows that eliminating gender differences in the attainment of S/E educational credentials would narrow only slightly the gender gap in participation in S/E occupations. Most of the gender gap in S/E labor force participation instead results from gender differences in the *utilization* of S/E education among those who have attained it. Attainment of an S/E bachelor's degree is an intermediate step in the process of becoming a scientist/engineer that by itself does not guarantee participation in an S/E occupation. Given that women are a significantly smaller proportion of the S/E labor force than they are of S/E baccalaureates, investigating gender differences in the transition from an S/E bachelor's degree to further participation in S/E is particularly important. This transition appears to rival the transition from high school to college (see Chapter 4) as a point in the S/E career trajectory where the participation rates of women fall dramatically in comparison with those of men. The career transitions following the completion of a bachelor's degree in S/E may exacerbate the already large gender differences observed in earlier educational processes.

In this chapter, we examine gender differences in the career paths individuals take upon completing a bachelor's degree in S/E. The analyses are conditional in the sense that gender differences in the educational process prior to obtaining an S/E bachelor's degree are treated as given (and indeed are analyzed in preceding chapters). We investigate gender differences among recent college graduates with an S/E bachelor's degree in their likelihood of pursuing S/E graduate education if they enter graduate school and in their likelihood of working in S/E occupations if they enter the labor force. Because the marketability of an S/E bachelor's degree, in terms of the career options it opens, varies across the different fields of science, we control for field of S/E degree in our analysis. We also study the differential influence of family status on the career transitions of male and female S/E baccalaureates.

Career Transitions following a Bachelor's Degree in S/E

Upon completing an S/E bachelor's degree, graduates are faced with choices about how to use the significant human capital they have accumulated. Their career options can be characterized as falling into one of the following categories: (1) going to graduate school to study S/E, (2) going to graduate school in a non-S/E field, (3) entering the labor force and working in an S/E occupation, (4) working in a non-S/E occupation, or (5) neither going to graduate school nor working. These five states are depicted in Figure 5.1.

There are two ways to conceptualize the career choices open to those graduating with an S/E bachelor's degree. One gives priority in the career decision process to whether college graduates wish to go on to graduate school or to work in the labor force. Those who choose to pursue graduate education then decide whether to major in an S/E or a non-S/E field (State 1 versus State 2). Similarly, those who enter the labor force have the option of working in an S/E or a non-S/E occupation (State 3 and State 4). This conceptualization is represented in Figure 5.2a.

A second conceptualization of the decision process emphasizes the decision between an S/E career versus a non-S/E career. The decision to pursue an S/E career necessitates the choice between an S/E career that requires advanced education (i.e., State 1) and an S/E career requiring only a bachelor's degree (i.e., State 3). Similarly, those who choose to pursue a non-S/E career further decide if they want the type of career that requires an advanced degree or one for which their bachelor's degree is adequate (i.e., State 2 versus State 4). This conceptualization is represented by Figure 5.2b. Note that, in both conceptualizations, State 5 is the residual category, denoting the outcome state for those who enter neither graduate school nor the labor market.

In the analysis for this chapter, we primarily rely on the conceptual model of Figure 5.2a. This choice is based on our belief that further investment in graduate education is costly and is likely to override individuals' preferences for S/E versus non-S/E careers. We therefore assume that individuals first choose whether or not to invest in further education and then decide between S/E and non-S/E options.[1] In the

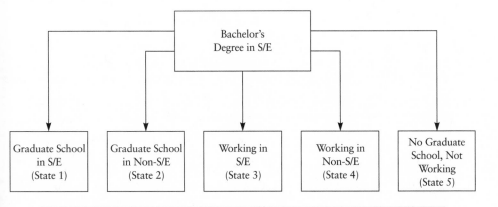

Figure 5.1. Career paths of S/E baccalaureates

statistical analyses that follow, we treat these five outcome states as mutually exclusive, although we recognize that they may overlap in reality. For instance, it is common for graduate students to support their continuing education through academic jobs, such as research and teaching assistantships, or through part-time employment outside of universities. However, we consider such employment secondary to graduate training and give priority to graduate school enrollment status over employment status when assessing career transitions.

Measuring Gender Differences in Career Transitions following a Bachelor's Degree

To study career transitions following graduation with a bachelor's degree in S/E, we analyze data from two sources: (1) the Baccalaureate and Beyond Longitudinal Study (B&B) first follow-up, conducted in 1994, and (2) the New Entrants Surveys (NES) that were conducted by the National Science Foundation in 1978 and 1979 and then biannually from 1980 to 1988. B&B is a longitudinal study of the cohort of college graduates who received their bachelor's degrees during the 1992–93 academic year (Green et al. 1996). Respondents to the B&B survey were first interviewed as part of the 1993 National Postsecondary Student Aid Study and were reinterviewed in the summer and

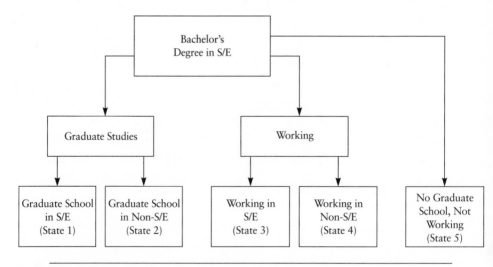

Figure 5.2a. Conceptualization of career paths

fall of 1994 as part of the B&B first follow-up study. After weighting, the sample is representative of the population of U.S. students who completed an S/E bachelor's degree in 1992–93. Our analytical sample consists of 2,086 individuals for whom we have valid information about enrollment, employment, degree and major fields of graduate study, and family status. The NES study is a survey of recent college graduates who had earned either a bachelor's or a master's degree. NES employed a multistage sampling procedure that resulted in disproportionate sampling by major. We handle this feature of the dataset by using a weight that adjusts for the disproportionate sampling as well as disproportionate nonresponses. Furthermore, we break down the descriptive results by major and include major as a covariate in multivariate analyses. Our analytical sample from NES consists of all individuals who earned a bachelor's degree in any S/E field two years prior to the survey date. The data were pooled from the NES surveys in years 1978, 1979, 1980, 1982, 1984, 1986, and 1988. See Appendix A for a detailed description of these data sources.

Outcome Variable

The outcome variable for this analysis is the career choice of each S/E baccalaureate, observed one year after bachelor's degree attainment for the B&B respondents and two years after bachelor's degree attain-

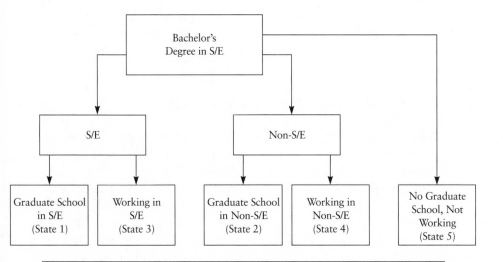

Figure 5.2b. Alternative conceptualization of career paths

ment for the NES respondents. Career outcome is assessed on the basis of self-reported employment, degree attainment, and enrollment status. As stated earlier, we define five outcome states: (1) attending graduate school in an S/E field, (2) attending graduate school in a non-S/E field, (3) working in an S/E field, (4) working in a non-S/E field, and (5) neither in graduate school nor working. Note that by design the outcome variable distinguishes between S/E and non-S/E fields only and thus does not identify individuals who switch between different S/E fields.

Outcome States 1 and 2 include all those who report being currently enrolled in a graduate program for at least part-time credit or who have attained either a master's or a doctorate degree. Individuals meeting one of these criteria are classified as being in graduate school even if employment is also reported. The B&B study collected detailed information about respondents' graduate school experiences. From responses to questions about enrollment status, degree attainment, and majors, we are able to identify B&B respondents who went on to graduate education either in an S/E or a non-S/E field. That is, we can distinguish the B&B respondents who made the transition to State 1 from those who entered State 2. Respondents who reported enrollment or degree attainment in S/E are coded as having entered State 1. Enrollment or degree attainment in all other fields is coded as entrance into State 2. Codebook E (posted on www.yuxie.com) lists detailed major codes identified as S/E. The B&B instrument, however, did not collect information about occupation fields that is sufficiently detailed to enable us to distinguish respondents who were employed in S/E occupations from those who were employed in non-S/E occupations. For this reason, we are not able to distinguish States 3 and 4 and therefore collapse them into a single category for our analysis. Respondents are considered to have entered State 3 or 4 if they have attained no more formal education than a bachelor's degree, report being currently out of school, and are working at least part-time.

While the B&B study collected better educational data than occupational data, the converse is true for the NES dataset. The occupational measures in NES were detailed enough for us to identify respondents who worked in S/E occupations versus those who worked in non-S/E occupations. That is, we can distinguish between States 3 and 4. Codebook F (posted on www.yuxie.com) lists the S/E occupational categories. NES, however, lacks sufficiently detailed information on field of enrollment and degree attainment for us to separate

S/E majors from non-S/E majors among the respondents who went on to graduate education. This data restriction forces us to treat States 1 and 2 as a single collapsed category in statistical analyses of the NES data. For both B&B and NES, respondents are classified as having made the transition to State 5 if they are not currently enrolled in school, have not achieved an advanced degree, and are not currently working at least part-time.

Not knowing the distribution of respondents across the full classification of the states within a single dataset undoubtedly limits our ability to draw firm conclusions. By capitalizing on the complementary structures of the two datasets, however, our analysis provides a composite picture of the career development process. B&B provides information on transitions into four transition outcomes: States 1, 2, 3 *or* 4, and 5. Similarly, NES provides information on transitions into four outcomes: States 1 *or* 2, 3, 4, and 5. If career transitions upon graduation with an S/E bachelor's degree can be conceptualized according to the model presented in Figure 5.2a, each of these two datasets allows us to understand four key component transitions. Using both the B&B and NES datasets, we study the likelihood that a college graduate does *not* exit both the educational and occupational trajectories, and then the likelihood that he or she enters graduate school versus the labor force. We then focus on those B&B respondents who made the transition to graduate school and examine gender differences in the likelihood of making the transition to S/E versus non-S/E graduate education. Similarly, we analyze the NES respondents who made the transition to work to model the likelihood of transitioning to S/E versus non-S/E employment. Needless to say, this is a compromise that at best can provide only an approximation of the true career development process. This composite approach rests on two assumptions: (1) the transition process is stable during the period examined and (2) all the measures are comparable between B&B and NES. We attend to the first assumption by testing interactions between survey year and other covariates in our analysis of the NES data and to the second assumption by maximizing the comparability of measures across the datasets.

S/E Major

Respondents in both B&B and NES were asked to classify their undergraduate degree according to a list of over one hundred degree areas. We recoded these detailed categories of degree areas into five

Table 5.1 Outcome distribution of B&B respondents by S/E major, family status, and gender

| | Postbaccalaureate state | | | | | | | | Sample size (n) | |
| | Graduate school in an S/E field (State 1) | | Graduate school in a non-S/E field (State 2) | | Working (States 3 or 4) | | Not in graduate school, not working (State 5) | | | |
	Women	Men	Women	Men	Women	Men	Women	Men	Women	Men
Total (%)	9.94	14.92	12.02	8.19	74.44	73.95	3.60	2.94	(709)	(1,377)
Undergraduate S/E major (%)										
Biological	6.66	9.69	16.55	15.71	71.65	70.69	5.15	3.91	(379)	(418)
Engineering	19.54	15.21	1.83	4.88	74.68	77.23	3.95	2.68	(88)	(602)
Mathematical	7.44	12.78	6.37	5.00	85.00	80.22	1.19	2.01	(182)	(236)
Physical	23.57	37.52	19.44	5.19	55.81	54.47	1.19	2.82	(60)	(121)
Family status (%)										
Single	12.36	15.67	13.69	9.43	71.21	72.24	2.73	2.66	(543)	(1,054)
Married without children	4.15	11.44	6.54	3.70	88.66	81.32	0.65	3.54	(94)	(194)
Married with children	0.00	14.00	7.21	5.07	78.61	76.75	14.18	4.18	(72)	(129)

Note: Data are from Baccalaureate and Beyond Longitudinal Study First Follow-up. Entries are weighted and presented as row percentages, except for sample sizes (n) given in the last two columns.

broad fields: (1) biological science, (2) engineering, (3) mathematical science (which includes computer science and statistics), (4) physical science, and (5) non-S/E. Respondents who had attained non-S/E bachelor's degrees are excluded from our analysis. See Codebooks E and F (posted at www.yuxie.com) for details on the S/E field codes.

Family Status

We use self-reported marital and parental statuses to classify NES and B&B respondents according to a three-category family status variable. Respondents are categorized as single, married with no children, or married with children. In preliminary analysis, we separated out divorced and separated respondents as a fourth category. We found, however, that their behavior is very similar to that of single respondents for both sexes. Therefore, for the final analysis reported below, the category of divorced and separated is collapsed with the single category.

Describing Gender Differences in Career Transitions

Table 5.1 presents, separately for men and women, the outcome distribution of the B&B respondents by S/E major and family status. We present these results with two caveats. First, some of the percentages presented are based on small sample sizes, so that differences that appear large may not be statistically significant. Second, these are bivariate statistics and as such may mask underlying multivariate relationships. We address these two shortcomings with our multivariate analyses presented in the next section.

Several findings emerge from the descriptive statistics. First, both male and female graduates with a bachelor's degree in physical science are very likely to continue graduate education in S/E, although there is a substantial sex difference in the percent of students who do: 24 percent of women versus 38 percent of men. Furthermore, female degree recipients in the physical sciences are much more likely than their male counterparts to pursue graduate education in a non-S/E field (19 percent versus 5 percent). Second, a very small portion (between 2 and 6 percent) of graduates with degrees in engineering and mathematical science shift to graduate education in a non-S/E field. This reflects the specialized nature of the training received by undergraduates majoring in engineering and mathematical science. Third, it appears

Table 5.2 Outcome distribution of NES respondents by S/E major, family status, and gender

| | Postbaccalaureate state | | | | | | | | Sample size (n) | |
| | Graduate school (States 1 or 2) | | Working in S/E (State 3) | | Working in non-S/E (State 4) | | Not in graduate school, not working (State 5) | | | |
	Women	Men	Women	Men	Women	Men	Women	Men	Women	Men
Total (%)	33.65	36.37	41.03	49.89	18.88	11.02	6.44	2.72	(5,959)	(19,211)
Undergraduate S/E major (%)										
Biological	38.65	49.65	28.02	28.25	25.39	18.06	7.93	4.04	(1,827)	(2,915)
Engineering	28.93	26.97	60.57	65.12	5.94	6.06	4.55	1.85	(1,471)	(10,512)
Mathematical	21.35	27.72	60.75	59.86	13.50	10.44	4.40	1.98	(1,499)	(2,478)
Physical	42.93	51.26	31.08	30.37	19.23	14.48	6.76	3.89	(1,162)	(3,306)
Family status (%)										
Single	37.97	39.89	39.19	45.85	18.66	11.09	4.18	3.17	(4,153)	(12,661)
Married without children	25.82	32.76	48.31	54.84	19.09	10.70	6.79	1.70	(1,469)	(4,464)
Married with children	13.34	22.15	34.33	64.58	20.61	11.21	31.73	2.06	(337)	(2,086)

Note: Data are from the 1978–1988 New Entrants Surveys. Entries are weighted and presented as row percentages, except for sample sizes (n) given in the last two columns.

that the gender gap for pursuing graduate education in S/E differs substantially by family status, with married women with children transitioning to State 1 at a much lower rate than their male counterparts (0 percent versus 14 percent). In contrast, the gender gap is smaller for unmarried graduates (12 percent versus 16 percent). Finally, the gender gap in the likelihood of exiting both the educational trajectory and the labor force (State 5) appears to exist only for respondents who are married and have children: Fourteen percent of married mothers make the transition to State 5 whereas less than 5 percent of other women and all men choose this path.

The above findings are complemented by the descriptive results from the NES data shown in Table 5.2. Comparing Table 5.2 and Table 5.1, we first observe that the distribution of cases (as indicated by sample sizes for women and men) across S/E majors differs for the two datasets. The difference is largely due to the disproportionate sampling of NES. We also note that the distribution in graduate school (States 1 and 2) is about 13 percentage points higher in NES than in B&B (34–36 percent versus 22–23 percent). Conversely, the distribution of survey respondents in the workforce (States 3 and 4) is about 14 percentage points lower in NES than in B&B. These gaps are partly attributable to the different survey methodologies, particularly the difference in the lag time between the completion of a bachelor's degree and the fielding of the survey, but they may also reflect real trends toward decreased rates of participation in graduate education by S/E bachelor's degree recipients.[2] The proportion of married women with children who exit the educational trajectory and labor force is greater in NES than in B&B (32 versus 14 percent). Again, this could be due to differences both in survey implementation and in real changes over time in the behavior of married women with children.

We now turn to the substantive interpretation of the NES results regarding the transitions to working in S/E occupations (State 3) and working in non-S/E occupations (State 4). Here, differences by field are evident, as smaller proportions of graduates with a degree in the physical or biological sciences (28–31 percent) make the transition to the S/E labor force (i.e., State 3) than those with a degree in engineering and mathematical science (60–65 percent). We can combine transition rates to State 1 (from Table 5.1) and State 3 (from Table 5.2) for an overall assessment of the variation in S/E "retention" by field.[3] By this measure, we observe that engineering retains the highest proportion of its undergraduate talent pool, with about 80 percent in the postbaccalaureate outcome States 1 and 3. Between 55 percent and 73 percent of graduates with a degree in physical science or mathematical science stay on the S/E track by entering either State 1 or State 3, as do 35 to 38 percent of the graduates with a degree in biological science. One interesting contrast between the physical and mathematical sciences is the different channels through which these fields retain such high proportions of their undergraduate majors: for physical science a significant percentage (24 percent of women and 38 percent of men) remains on the S/E track through the pursuit of S/E graduate education; for mathematics the main channel is through working in S/E (at 61 percent for women and 60 percent for men).

While Table 5.2 shows substantial differences by major in the distribution of career outcomes, gender differences within each major are generally small, except that women are more than twice as likely as men to make the transition to State 5 (neither working nor going to graduate school). With few exceptions, the distribution of male and female baccalaureates in States 3 and 4 appears to be similar within each major. However, gender differences become apparent when we break down the outcome state distribution by family status, shown in the bottom panel of Table 5.2. Gender differences in transition rates are present among S/E graduates who are single or married without children, but they are more pronounced among married respondents with children. For example, while 39 percent of single women and 46 percent of single men work in S/E, the contrast is much greater among married respondents with children (34 percent among women versus 65 percent among men). These observations are, however, based on descriptive results and need to be verified by multivariate analyses of the transition probabilities following the completion of a bachelor's degree in S/E. It is to these multivariate results that we now turn.

Explaining Gender Differences in Career Transitions

Although the conceptual framework presented in Figure 5.2a entails five exclusive destination states, the structure of our data constrains our observation to only four states for each dataset. For the B&B data, the two working states (States 3 and 4) are combined; for the NES data, the two graduate school states (States 1 and 2) are combined. This data limitation is reflected in Tables 5.1 and 5.2, where only four transition probabilities are given.

With four mutually exclusive outcomes, the transition probabilities can be captured by three pairs of contrasts (Powers and Xie 2000, pp. 223–252), each contrast being an odds, or the ratio of two probabilities. The logarithm of each of these odds forms the dependent variable for logit regression models. We construct a set of odds (or contrasts) that not only exhausts all observed states but also affords us a convenient way to interpret the data and compare results across the two datasets. Let the destination state be denoted by Y ($Y = 1, 2, 3, 4, 5$) and the probability of transitioning to a particular destination be denoted by $P(Y)$. The first odds of interest, O_1, the odds of entering either graduate school or the labor force, can be expressed as:

$$(5.1) \qquad O_1 = P(Y = 1 \cup 2 \cup 3 \cup 4)/P(Y = 5),$$

where the symbol $\cup$ denotes the union of two or more states. The logarithm of this odds is the dependent variable of the first logit model for both datasets. Using this odds, we model the likelihood that a respondent is either in graduate school or working (States 1 through 4) versus neither (State 5).

After we know the determinants sorting individuals into States 1 through 4 versus State 5, we proceed to model the likelihood that a respondent goes on to graduate school (States 1 or 2) versus the likelihood that he/she works (States 3 or 4), conditional on their not being in State 5. Using the B&B data, we examine the likelihood that a baccalaureate enters graduate school. This leads us to specify odds O_2 as:

$$(5.2) \qquad O_2 = P(Y = 1 \cup 2 \mid 1 \cup 2 \cup 3 \cup 4)/$$
$$P(Y = 3 \cup 4 \mid 1 \cup 2 \cup 3 \cup 4).$$

Conversely, for the NES data, we focus on the likelihood of working by specifying odds O_3 as

$$(5.3) \qquad O_3 = P(Y = 3 \cup 4 \mid 1 \cup 2 \cup 3 \cup 4)/$$
$$P(Y = 1 \cup 2 \mid 1 \cup 2 \cup 3 \cup 4).$$

Needless to say, O_2 and O_3 are redundant in the sense that one is the inverse of the other (i.e., $O_2 \times O_3 = 1$). If we understand the determinants of O_2, we also understand the determinants of O_3. To compare the regression results for O_3 with those for O_2, we only need to invert the estimated coefficients in odds ratios. If the two survey instrumentations were identical and if the determinants of the transition probabilities were truly stable over time, the two datasets should yield the same results subject only to sampling variability.[4]

The redundancy in our analysis of the two datasets ends there. The final models that we estimate differentiate S/E tracks from non-S/E tracks, either among those who continue on to graduate education or among those who work. We use the B&B data to study the relative likelihood of pursuing an S/E graduate education versus a non-S/E education conditional on graduate school enrollment, with odds O_4 defined as

$$(5.4) \qquad O_4 = P(Y = 1 \mid 1 \cup 2)/P(Y = 2 \mid 1 \cup 2).$$

For the NES data, we define odds O_5 as

$$(5.5) \qquad O_5 = P(Y = 3 \mid 3 \cup 4)/P(Y = 4 \mid 3 \cup 4),$$

to model the relative likelihood that a respondent works in S/E versus in non-S/E given that he/she has made the transition to the labor force.

For the B&B data, O_1, O_2, and O_4 exhaust all the possible contrasts among the four observed states. Similarly, O_1, O_3, and O_5 exhaust all the possible contrasts among the outcome states for the NES data. In addition, there is a nested structure to each set of odds, with prior odds defining the conditional population for the odds that follows. Through logit regressions, we model each odds (in logarithm) as a linear function of a vector of covariates including gender, major, family status, and potential interactions between family status and gender. In our multivariate analysis of the NES data, we also include an indicator of survey year. For each dataset, the model specification is parallel across the three nested odds. For each dependent odds, we estimate a series of hierarchical models, with new covariates being added to simpler models. We pay particular attention to the value of the estimated coefficient of sex as we introduce new controls.

The logit regression results from the B&B data are given in Table 5.3. Panel A presents the results of a series of logit regressions for the likelihood that the respondent is either in graduate school or working, with the dependent logit defined as the logarithm of O_1. With sex as the sole independent variable, Model A0 reproduces the aggregate,

Table 5.3 Influence of other covariates on the estimated female-to-male odds ratio in sequential logit models of postbaccalaureate choices among recent graduates (B&B)

Model description	Female-to-male odds ratio
Panel A: Likelihood of either entering graduate school or working (n = 2,086)	
(A0): Sex	0.81
(A1): (A0) + Bachelor's degree major	0.86
(A2): (A1) + Family status	0.86
(A3): (A2) + Sex × (Family status)	
Among those single	1.03
Among those married without children	5.74
Among those married with children	0.30
Panel B: Likelihood of entering graduate school (n = 2,019)	
(B0): Sex	0.94
(B1): (B0) + Bachelor's degree major	0.91
(B2): (B1) + Family status	0.91
(B3): (B2) + Sex × (Family status)	
Among those single	1.02
Among those married without children	0.67
Among those married with children	0.35*
Panel C: Likelihood of pursuing an S/E graduate degree conditional on entering graduate school (n = 506)	
(C0): Sex	0.45**
(C1): (C0) + Bachelor's degree major	0.62
(C2): (C1) + Family status	0.62
(C3): (C2) + Sex × (Family status)	
Among those single	0.77
Among those married (with or without children)	0.11**

Source: Baccalaureate and Beyond Longitudinal Study First Follow-up.

Note: The logit analysis in Panel B is conditional on the dependent variable in Panel A being 1, and the logit analysis in Panel C is conditional on the dependent variable in Panel B being 1. The interaction between sex and family status is statistically significant at $p = .020$ in Panel A, at $p = .062$ in Panel B, and at $p = .038$ in Panel C.

*$p < .05$, **$p < .01$, ***$p < .001$ (two-tailed test).

observed sex difference. The estimated female-to-male odds ratio at 0.81 is not significantly different from 1, meaning that there is no overall significant gender difference in the likelihood of either entering graduate school or working (O_1). We control for bachelor's degree major in Model A1 and for family status in Model A2, but neither has much of an effect on the estimated net gender gap in O_1. In Model A3, we let family status interact with gender and find the interaction to be significant. With the interaction results presented in a way that directly compares women and men by family status, it appears that the odds of going to graduate school or working among married women with children are 0.30 times (i.e., 70 percent less than) the odds for married men with children. However, this gender difference is not statistically significant.[5] Neither are the estimated gender differences for the other two categories of family status. Parameter estimates and their z-ratios for Model A3, as well as for Models B3 and C3, are presented in Appendix Table D5.a.

The logit regression results in Panel B shed light on the gender disparity in the relative odds of entering graduate school versus working, O_2. The bivariate model (Model B0) shows no significant sex difference in O_2. The estimated female-to-male odds ratio bounces between 0.94 in Model B0 and 0.91 in Model B2 but is not statistically different from 1 for these models. However, a gender difference emerges in Model B3, which allows for the interaction between gender and family status (at $p = .062$). The estimates indicate that married women with children are only a third as likely as their male counterparts to enter graduate school. No gender difference is found for respondents who either are unmarried or do not have children.

In Panel C of Table 5.3, we present the results of the logit regression of O_4, the odds of transitioning to an S/E versus a non-S/E field of study, given that a respondent pursues graduate education. In the bivariate model, Model C0, it is shown that women are only 0.45 as likely as men to go to graduate school in S/E. This gender gap is statistically significant, but most of the difference is due to women's concentration in bachelor's majors that have low S/E retention rates at the graduate level.[6] After we control for major in Model C1, the gender gap is no longer statistically significant. The addition of family status in Model C2 does not change the estimated gender gap. In Model C3, we introduce the interaction between gender and family status. Due to the small sample size for this analysis ($n = 506$), there is insufficient information for estimating the interaction effects with the three-category measure of family status. We resolve the difficulty by combining married respondents who have children with those who are married but childless. After collapsing these groups, we observe a significant interaction between gender and marital status. The interaction effects are such that, while there is no gender difference for respondents who are unmarried, the odds of pursuing S/E graduate education among married women is only 0.11 times as high as that of married men.[7]

The NES data, which are pooled across seven years, constitute a much larger sample and consequently yield more statistically significant results than the B&B data. The NES results are summarized in Table 5.4, with all estimated parameters of the final models reported in Appendix Table D5.b. The logit results for the likelihood of either entering graduate school or working versus neither (odds O_1) are presented in Panel A. From the NES data, we find women overall to have a lower O_1 odds than men. The interactive model (A4) reveals that the gender gap is nonexistent for unmarried respondents, fairly large for married respondents without children (with the sex odds ratio at 0.28), but particularly large for married respondents with children (with the sex odds ratio at 0.05 percent).[8] Since the reciprocal of odds O_1 represents the odds of transitioning to State 5, the last estimate indicates that women who are married and have children are 20 times more likely than similar men to leave both education and work.

Panel B of Table 5.4 displays the regression results for the odds that recent S/E baccalaureates begin to work rather than enter graduate school (O_3). The female-to-male odds ratio from Models B1 through B3 show that, net of major, women are more likely to work (i.e., less likely to attend graduate school) than men, and this pattern is unaffected by the control of year and family status. Recall that the inverses of these estimates are comparable to the results in Panel B of Table 5.3. The NES estimates from Models B0 through B3 are congruent in direction and magnitude with those from Models B0 through B2 in B&B, although the B&B results are not statistically significant because of the small B&B sample size. There is a minor disagreement for the interactive model (Model B3 in Table 5.3 and Model B4 in Table 5.4): while the B&B results reveal a significant gender gap among respondents who are married with children, this gender gap is not significant for the NES data (although the point estimates are consistent). As is revealed by the estimated coefficients of Model B4 in Appendix Table D5.b, marriage and parenthood generally tend to push college graduates toward working instead of graduate school.[9]

In Panel C, we present the logit results for the likelihood of working in an S/E occupation versus a non-S/E occupation among those who work (O_5). Model C0 estimates the female-to-male odds ratio to be 0.48 and significantly different from one. However, a large portion of

Table 5.4 Influence of other covariates on the estimated female-to-male odds ratio in sequential logit models of postbaccalaureate choices among recent graduates (NES)

Model description	Female-to-male odds ratio
Panel A: Likelihood of either entering graduate school or working (n = 25,170)	
(A0): Sex	0.41***
(A1): (A0) + Bachelor's degree major	0.48***
(A2): (A1) + Year	0.49***
(A3): (A2) + Family status	0.46***
(A4): (A3) + Sex × (Family status)	
Among those single	0.90
Among those married without children	0.28***
Among those married with children	0.05***
Panel B: Likelihood of working (n = 24,305)	
(B0): Sex	1.06
(B1): (B0) + Bachelor's degree major	1.31***
(B2): (B1) + Year	1.29***
(B3): (B2) + Family status	1.34***
(B4): (B3) + Sex × (Family status)	
Among those single	1.29***
Among those married without children	1.52***
Among those married with children	1.42
Panel C: Likelihood of working in S/E given working (n = 15,861)	
(C0): Sex	0.48***
(C1): (C0) + Bachelor's degree major	0.76***
(C2): (C1) + Year	0.73***
(C3): (C2) + Family status	0.73***
(C4): (C3) + Sex × (Family status)	
Among those single	0.78**
Among those married without children	0.72**
Among those married with children	0.39***

Source: 1978–1988 New Entrants Surveys.

Note: The logit analysis in Panel B is conditional on the dependent variable in Panel A being 1, and the logit analysis in Panel C is conditional on the dependent variable in Panel B being 1. The interaction between sex and family status is statistically significant at $p = .000$ in Panels A and C and at $p = .010$ in Panel B.

$*p < .05, **p < .01, ***p < .001$ (two-tailed test).

this gender gap is due to the sex segregation of undergraduate S/E majors, as the odds ratio jumps to 0.76 after controlling for major in Model C1. The introduction of year and family status in subsequent models has no noticeable influence on the estimated gender gap. Interacting family status with gender, Model C4 reveals the female-to-male odds ratio to be much lower (i.e., representing a larger gender gap) among respondents who are married with children (at 0.39) than among respondents who are either unmarried or married without children (at 0.78 and 0.72, respectively). To understand the gender-specific effects of family status on the likelihood of working in S/E, however, we must combine the estimated effects of family status for men (i.e., the main effect of family status) and the interaction effects (shown in Appendix Table D5.b). For men the estimated effect $(\exp(b))$ of being married with children is greater than one (1.37), indicating that marriage and parenthood push men toward S/E occupations. However, the exponentiated interaction effect for married women with children is significantly smaller than one (0.50), and the combination of these two components represents the estimated effect of family status for women. The results should therefore be interpreted as showing that marriage and parenthood affect women in the opposite direction: they significantly reduce their likelihood of transitioning to S/E occupations relative to the odds of non-S/E employment.

The NES dataset consists of repeated cross-sectional surveys over seven years. In the preceding logit analyses, we have taken a simple approach to studying trends by including a set of dummy variables allowing for additive effects of year. The estimated coefficients of these dummy variables for the final models in Table 5.4 are given in Appendix Table D5.b. Two trends emerge from these estimates. First, the relative likelihood of work versus graduate school increased during the period from 1978 to 1988.[10] Second, among those who worked, the relative likelihood of working in an S/E occupation versus in a non-S/E occupation also increased. To our final NES models (A4, B4, and C4 of Table 5.4), we further added the interaction between gender and year in an effort to examine the trends in gender differences for the three outcome odds. The only statistically significant trend we observe is a narrowing of the gender gap for O_1. In fact, a linear interaction term added to Model A4 fits the data well, with the estimated interaction coefficient being 0.07 (z-ratio of 2.06), suggesting that the gender gap in the odds of being either in graduate school or working is being closed at a rate of 0.07 per year. This result parallels the general trend of women's greater involvement and improved status in the labor force (Spain and Bianchi 1996).

Conclusion

In this chapter, we have examined the gender differences in the career outcomes of graduates who recently attained an S/E bachelor's degree. Career outcomes are conceptualized according to the decision process that prioritizes the choice between entering graduate school or the labor force over the choice of staying in S/E or leaving S/E. We have also analyzed gender differences in the likelihood that a B.S. or B.A. graduate exits from both graduate school and the labor force. Our analyses yield four main findings.

First, a large proportion of the raw gender differences in career outcomes following the completion of an S/E bachelor's degree is attributable to sex segregation among fields of study. This finding can be decomposed into two related empirical patterns. The first is that women are more likely to be found in biological science than in other fields (particularly engineering and physical science). The second is that the college graduates in biological science where women are concentrated are less likely to pursue S/E careers than graduates in other fields where men tend to dominate. When all S/E fields are aggregated, women appear to be less likely than men to pursue S/E. Once we control for major, however, the gap between men and women in their likelihood of pursuing S/E careers is smaller.

One persistent gender gap after the control for major lies in women's lower likelihood to work in S/E occupations. This constitutes our second finding. For all graduates as a whole, women are about one-quarter less likely (in odds) than men to work in S/E occupations, net of field of study differences.

Our third finding is that married women, particularly those who have children, are much more likely to exit from both school and work (i.e., to enter State 5) than are men and women in other family statuses. Related to this, our fourth principal finding is that married female S/E baccalaureates, especially those with children, are much less likely to continue S/E careers than their male counterparts. These interaction effects mainly result from advantages that men gain from marriage, but they also suggest that family responsibilities tend to disadvantage women. These last two findings reflect the gender role differences that characterize American society as a whole: women are more likely to take primary responsibility for household labor whereas men are more likely to participate fully in the labor market.

To explain this disparity, a neoclassic economic model has emerged (e.g., Becker, G. S. 1981), asserting that this gendered division of labor is the result of differential human capital investments by men and women. Given the greater average human capital investments of men relative to women, the economic welfare of a family is maximized when men continue to invest in and fully utilize their human capital in the labor market and women curtail their labor force participation and concentrate on household labor. The case we examine here, however, does not neatly fit the neoclassical model because all respondents in our study have invested heavily in their marketable human capital by completing a bachelor's degree in S/E. We find that, although the married women in our analysis have made substantial human capital investments, they are still less likely than men to take full advantage of their market value or to make further investments. Our analyses have shown that even for this highly motivated and accomplished group the potential for role conflict between career and family is real: family responsibilities disadvantage women by depressing their rates of participation in the labor force or graduate education and by making them less likely than their male peers to pursue S/E careers.

For the period examined in this chapter, our summary statement is that gender differences in career transitions among graduates with an S/E bachelor's degree are small overall. However, our analyses point to two important ways in which women are disadvantaged relative to men, and both are related to gender roles. The first is the gender segregation of majors. The second is the impediment of family responsibility to women's pursuit of S/E careers. Aside from these two important factors, women and men seem to make similar career transitions following the completion of a bachelor's degree in S/E.

CHAPTER SIX

Career Paths after a Science/Engineering Master's Degree

Although the overall conclusion of Chapter 5 is that sex differences in career paths following the completion of a bachelor's degree are rather small, two results from that chapter have significant theoretical implications for women's experiences in the process of becoming a scientist/engineer. The first is that a large portion of the gender disparity in career paths is attributable to the sex segregation of majors. This result points to the real consequences of women's lesser participation in S/E education. The second is that marriage and parenthood seem to impede women's careers in general and their likelihood of working in S/E in particular, suggesting that women face substantial difficulties in combining family responsibilities and career development in S/E. We generalize these results to two broad theoretical explanations of gender differences in S/E careers that are salient at different stages in the life course: (1) gender differences that are rooted in socialization and educational decisions undertaken early in the life course and (2) gender differences that are attributable to gender-specific responses to family and work roles assumed later in the life course. Lacking better terms, we will call the first the "educational-credential" explanation and the second the "role-conflict" explanation.[1]

Both of these explanatory frameworks are potentially powerful explanations of gender differences that develop across the life course, and we are not proposing to test one against the other. Rather, we advocate that one explanation may be relatively more salient than the other at certain points of the life course. In particular, as individuals mature and face career challenges and family obligations more directly, it is reasonable to assume that the relevance of the role-conflict explanation will increase relative to the educational-credential explanation. One way to check this prediction is to examine the determinants of career transitions at different stages in the educational trajectory.

In this chapter, we study gender differences in career transitions following the completion of a master's degree in S/E. Since a master's degree in S/E represents a significant investment in S/E human capital and a sustained commitment to pursuing an S/E professional career, the educational-credential explanation should be of limited importance for explaining gender differences in S/E career paths. In contrast, since receipt of a master's degree occurs later in life than the receipt of a bachelor's degree, the potential is greater for the family-versus-work role conflict to influence subsequent career paths. In addition, scientists and engineers with a master's degree tend to occupy more professionally demanding positions, and these positions often mean a male-dominated work environment (Kanter 1977; Valian 1999). Women scientists with advanced education are therefore more likely to experience an unsupportive work environment and/or patent discrimination than are women with only a bachelor's degree. Thus, we expect that the role-conflict explanation is more relevant for recipients of a master's degree in S/E than for those at the bachelor's level.

Our statistical analyses for this chapter are based on a sample of S/E master's degree recipients from the New Entrants Surveys (NES) and parallel those for NES S/E bachelor's degree recipients in Chapter 5. We first present a descriptive analysis of gender-specific transition rates for different career outcomes and then discuss the results from multivariate sequential logit models of specific transitions made by the recipients of S/E master's degrees.

Career Transitions following a Master's Degree in S/E

As in the earlier analysis of the career transitions of recipients of a bachelor's degree in S/E, we conceptualize the career outcomes of S/E master's degree recipients in terms of five career states: (1) continued graduate education in an S/E field, (2) continued education in a non-S/E field, (3) working in an S/E field, (4) working in a non-S/E field, and (5) neither in graduate school nor working. We again impose a hierarchical structure to the choice set by grouping the two states of graduate education (States 1 and 2) and the two states of work (States 3 and 4). The resulting conceptualization is graphically presented in Figure 6.1.

This conceptualization gives priority to the decision between education and work, rather than to the decision about S/E versus non-S/E career tracks (Figure 5.2b illustrates the alternative conceptualization for S/E baccalaureates). According to this conceptualization, graduates with a master's degree in S/E first make a choice concerning whether to continue graduate education or to work immediately and then decide between S/E versus non-S/E tracks within each level of education. We prioritize the choice between further education and entering the labor force because the decision to continue graduate education is economic, whereas the choice to stay in S/E is a matter of taste. For a typical graduate with a master's degree in S/E, economic constraints are significant and should take priority over taste. As in Chapter 5, the fifth state (neither attending graduate school nor working) is a residual category, representing a cessation of career development.

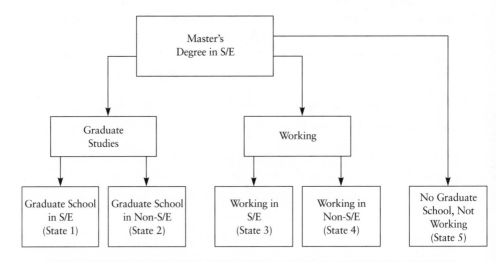

Figure 6.1. Conceptualization of career choices

Measuring Gender Differences in Career Transitions following a Master's Degree

Our statistical analyses are drawn from the NES surveys conducted in 1978, 1979, 1980, 1982, 1984, 1986, and 1988. This dataset was introduced in Chapter 5 and is described in detail in Appendix A. The dataset consists of a series of repeated cross-sectional surveys of recent graduates with a bachelor's or master's degree in S/E. Our analyses in this chapter are restricted to respondents who earned a master's degree in any S/E field two years prior to each survey date. We pool the data from all the available years from 1978 to 1988 and include dummy variables denoting survey year in the regression analyses. Appropriate weights are applied in the statistical analyses to adjust for disproportionate sampling and disproportionate nonresponses. Except for the level of degree attained by the graduates, all the variables are the same as those used for the analysis of the NES data presented in Chapter 5.

Continued graduate education (States 1 and 2) includes both students who are currently enrolled in graduate programs and recipients of a doctoral degree. As explained in the preceding chapter, one serious limitation of the NES series is its failure to identify detailed fields of study for respondents who continued graduate education. We are not able to distinguish between States 1 and 2 and therefore collapse them for our statistical analyses. Although it is reasonable to assume that most of the students who continue graduate education (in States 1 and 2) pursue a doctoral degree, the dataset does not allow us to separate doctoral students from students who are pursuing another master's degree. Thus, the collapsed category of States 1 and 2 is very heterogeneous, including anyone who had either obtained a doctoral degree or remained in graduate school two years after the completion of a master's degree in S/E. To facilitate the interpretation of our statistical results, we assume that most continuing students with a master's degree in S/E who enter States 1 and 2 pursue more advanced education (i.e., a doctoral degree).

Describing Gender Differences in Career Transitions

Table 6.1 presents the transition rates, by gender, field of study or family status, into four distinct destinations: States 1 *or* 2, 3, 4, and 5.

Table 6.1 Outcome distribution of NES respondents by S/E major of master's degree, family status, and gender

| | State following master's degree | | | | | | | | Sample size (n) | |
| | Graduate school (States 1 or 2) | | Working in S/E (State 3) | | Working in non-S/E (State 4) | | Not in graduate school, not working (State 5) | | | |
	Women	Men	Women	Men	Women	Men	Women	Men	Women	Men
Total (%)	25.95	30.95	54.51	59.99	12.76	7.19	6.78	1.87	(2,218)	(9,189)
S/E major (%)										
Biological	34.82	41.90	42.49	42.69	15.20	13.26	7.49	2.15	(649)	(1,320)
Engineering	21.22	26.77	67.86	67.37	5.49	4.61	5.43	1.24	(567)	(4,819)
Mathematical	15.51	22.07	65.97	66.97	13.20	8.44	5.32	2.53	(382)	(993)
Physical	27.87	42.84	48.62	47.68	14.34	6.70	9.17	2.79	(620)	(2,057)
Family status (%)										
Single	31.87	36.06	54.09	55.54	10.71	5.58	3.33	2.82	(1,112)	(4,034)
Married without children	22.74	33.81	58.30	58.60	12.69	6.15	6.26	1.43	(724)	(2,526)
Married with children	16.36	20.89	49.33	67.74	18.00	10.47	16.30	0.90	(382)	(2,629)

Note: Data are from the 1978–1988 New Entrants Surveys. Entries are in percent, except for sample sizes (*n*) given in the last two columns.

The table is of the same format as Table 5.2 and should be interpreted in the same manner.

Comparing Table 6.1 and Table 5.2 lets us contrast transition rates at the master's level and those at the bachelor's level. Overall, we observe similar patterns across the two parallel sets of transition rates, but three noticeable differences emerge. First, the gender gap in the likelihood of making the transition to State 5 (i.e., withdrawal from school and work) persists and is actually greater at the master's level. As the first rows of the two tables indicate, the gender gap increases from 6 percent for women versus 3 percent for men at the bachelor's level to 7 percent for women versus 2 percent for men at the master's level. Second, consistent with the expectation that further investment in S/E capital means a greater likelihood of being retained in S/E, the total rates of entry to State 3 (working in S/E) are higher at the master's level (55 percent for women and 60 percent for men) than at the bachelor's level (41 percent for women and 50 percent for men). Third, the aggregate gender gap in the likelihood of continuing graduate education increased slightly from the bachelor's degree level (34 percent for women versus 36 percent for men) to the master's degree level (26 percent for women versus 31 percent for men).

Despite these differences, the two key results about gender differences in career transitions among degree recipients at the bachelor's level seem to hold true at the master's level as well. The first is that a portion of the observed gender difference in transition rates is due to the sex segregation of majors. For example, we observe from Table 6.1 that women's transition rates to State 3 are similar to men's within each major, although a gender gap of 5 percentage points is present at the aggregate level. The reason for the aggregate gender gap, of course, is the concentration of women in the biological sciences, in which rates of transition to State 3 are low. The second consistent result is that, relative to other women and married men with children, married women with children drop out of the educational trajectory and the labor force at high rates (16 percent). This strong interaction effect between gender and family status suggests that the conflict between work and family roles observed among S/E baccalaureates persists for graduates at the master's level.

Explaining Gender Differences in Career Transitions

Our multivariate analysis here parallels that of the preceding chapter. We run a series of sequential logit models with three nested binary dependent variables. To define these dependent variables, let the destination state be denoted by Y ($Y = 1, 2, 3, 4, 5$) and the probability of making the transition to a particular state be denoted by $P(Y)$. The three outcome odds to be modeled are, respectively,

(6.1) $O_1 = P(Y = 1 \cup 2 \cup 3 \cup 4)/P(Y = 5)$,

(6.2) $O_2 = P(Y = 3 \cup 4 \mid 1 \cup 2 \cup 3 \cup 4)/$
          $P(Y = 1 \cup 2 \mid 1 \cup 2 \cup 3 \cup 4)$,

(6.3) $O_3 = P(Y = 3 \mid 3 \cup 4)/P(Y = 4 \mid 3 \cup 4)$,

where the symbol $\cup$ denotes the union of two or more states. The first quantity, O_1, is the odds of making the transition to either further education or work versus leaving both trajectories. The second, O_2, represents the odds of working versus continuing with education among those who do not drop out altogether. Finally, O_3 represents the odds of working in an S/E versus a non-S/E occupation among those who make the transition to the labor force. The logarithm transformations of these odds are the dependent variables for the logit regression models. As our logit analysis proceeds from O_1 to O_2 to O_3, the size of the analytical sample decreases, as only the cases with positive responses to a particular odds are included for the subsequent analysis. That is to say, the logit analysis of odds O_2 is restricted to the subsample in States 1, 2, 3, and 4, and the logit analysis of odds O_3 is restricted to the subsample in States 3 and 4.

The logit results are presented in Table 6.2. The models in Panel A predict the relative likelihood that a recent recipient of a master's degree in S/E does not exit both the educational trajectory and the labor force, with the logarithm of odds O_1 as the dependent variable. Model A0 is the bivariate baseline model with sex as the only independent variable. It shows that, in the aggregate, female graduates are about one-fourth as likely (in terms of odds) as their male counterparts to enter graduate school or the labor force. By comparison, the estimated gender disparity is much smaller at the bachelor's level, with the sex ratio of odds at 0.41 (see Table 5.4). Adding controls for ma-

Table 6.2 Influence of other covariates on the estimated female-to-male odds ratio in sequential logit models of post–master's degree choices among recent graduates (NES)

Model description	Female-to-male odds ratio
Panel A: Likelihood of either entering graduate school or working (n = 11,407)	
(A0): Sex	0.26***
(A1): (A0) + Master's degree major	0.30***
(A2): (A1) + Year	0.30***
(A3): (A2) + Family status	0.29***
(A4): (A3) + Sex × (Family status)	
Among those single	0.97***
Among those married without children	0.24***
Among those married with children	0.05***
Panel B: Likelihood of working (n = 11,040)	
(B0): Sex	1.19**
(B1): (B0) + Master's degree major	1.39***
(B2): (B1) + Year	1.40***
(B3): (B2) + Family status	1.52***
(B4): (B3) + Sex × (Family status)	
Among those single	1.44***
Among those married without children	1.83***
Among those married with children	1.23
Panel C: Likelihood of working in S/E given working (n = 7,459)	
(C0): Sex	0.51***
(C1): (C0) + Master's degree major	0.71***
(C2): (C1) + Year	0.68***
(C3): (C2) + Family status	0.63***
(C4): (C3) + Sex × (Family status)	
Among those single	0.68*
Among those married without children	0.61*
Among those married with children	0.58**

Source: 1978–1988 New Entrants Surveys.

Note: The logit analysis in Panel B is conditional on the dependent variable in Panel A being 1, and the logit analysis in Panel C is conditional on the dependent variable in Panel B being 1. The interaction between sex and family status is statistically significant at $p = .000$ in Panel A, at $p = .043$ in Panel B, and at $p = .735$ in Panel C.

*$p < .05$, **$p < .01$, ***$p < .001$ (two-tailed test).

jor, year, and family status in subsequent models narrows the sex disparity slightly. In the last model of Panel A, Model A4, we include the interaction between sex and family status and show that almost all of the gender gap lies among married respondents, particularly those with children. For example, married women with children are only 5 percent as likely as married men with children to enter graduate school or the labor force. We note that these large estimated gender gaps for married graduates with an S/E master's degree closely mirror those for married graduates with an S/E bachelor's degree, shown in Table 5.4. The estimated coefficients in exponentiated form and their z-ratios for Model A4, as well as the final models in Panels B and C, are displayed in Appendix Table D6.a.

Among those not exiting both the educational trajectory and the labor force, we model the relative odds of working versus continuing graduate education (odds O_2). The results of the logit models with the logarithm of O_2 as the dependent variable are given in Panel B. Model B0, the bivariate model, shows a gender gap in O_2 that favors women (by 19 percent), meaning that women graduates are more likely than men to work instead of continuing graduate education. The gender gap increases with the addition of controls for major, year, and family status in Models B1 through B3. For Model B3, the relative odds of entering the labor force for women are 52 percent larger than those for men. The finding that women are more likely than men to stop graduate education is consistent between the bachelor's degree level and the master's degree level, although the estimated magnitude of the gender disparity (as measured by female-to-male odds ratios) is greater at the master's level (1.52) than at the bachelor's level (1.34).

The interaction between gender and family status in Model B4 is statistically significant. Results by family status show that women's higher likelihood of working is particularly true for unmarried respondents and married respondents without children. Although the sex ratio of odds among married respondents with children also favors women, the gender gap is not statistically significant. This last result is consistent with the corresponding result for bachelor's degree recipients (see Model B4 in Table 5.4). From parameter estimates reported in Appendix Table D6.a, we observe strong positive effects of marriage and parenthood on the likelihood of working versus continuing graduate education for both men and women. This is similar to the result for bachelor's degree recipients discussed in Chapter 5. As we saw for bachelor's degree recipients, our results show that being married and having children push master's degree recipients to enter the labor force.

Finally, among the S/E master's degree recipients who make the transition to the labor force, we model the relative likelihood that they work in S/E occupations rather than non-S/E occupations (i.e., odds O_3). The logit results are given in Panel C of Table 6.2. Model C0, the bivariate model, reveals a large, observed gender difference in O_3, as women's odds of working in S/E occupations are on average only 51 percent as high as men's. This large gender gap is narrowed by accounting for gender differences in S/E major in Model C1, which increases the estimated female-to-male odds ratio to 0.71. Adding the controls for year and family status in Models C2 and C3 in Table 6.2 increases, rather than reduces, the gender disparity in the odds of working in S/E. According to Model C3, women's conditional odds of making the transition to an S/E job relative to the transition to a non-S/E job is 63 percent as high as men's. Although this estimated disparity appears large, it is important to recall that this estimate is conditional on making the transition to work, the likelihood of which favors women by a 52 percent margin.[2] In Model C4, we allow the estimated gender gap to differ by family status and find the interaction to be insignificant, although, consistent with our expectations, the estimated coefficients suggest that the gender gap is slightly smaller among unmarried respondents than among married respondents.

Conclusion

In this chapter, we have examined career transitions following the completion of a master's degree in S/E. The analyses extend those of the preceding chapter on recipients of a bachelor's degree in S/E, using data from the New Entrants Surveys. Comparing results from this and the earlier chapter, we note that patterns of gender differences in career transitions at the master's level are similar to those at the bachelor's level. For example, married women with a master's degree in S/E are still far more likely than their male peers to withdraw from both the educational trajectory and the labor force, especially when they have children. We find that women recipients of an S/E master's degree, like women recipients of an S/E bachelor's degree, are less likely than men to continue graduate education. Furthermore, we observe that women are clearly less likely than men to make the transition to an S/E occupation at the master's level. As in the case for recipients with an S/E bachelor's degree, the field of the S/E degree plays an important role in sorting graduates with a master's degree into distinct career tracks. Overall, however, the magnitude of the net sex differences in career paths following a master's degree in S/E is similarly small.

Despite the striking similarity of the results from the two chapters, we note a few differences. One major difference is that career transitions at the master's level tend to be more geared toward S/E careers than those at the bachelor's level. The descriptive statistics and the estimates from the logit models reveal that the gender disparity in the likelihood of not exiting from both education and occupation is much larger at the master's level than at the bachelor's level. Upon closer examination with multivariate analysis, we find that most of the difference by level of education is attributable to compositional differences in family status, since the estimated sex differences by family status at the master's level resemble exactly those at the bachelor's level. In other words, the gender disparity in the likelihood of exit is greater at the master's level than at the bachelor's level solely because master's degree recipients are older and thus more likely to be married and have children. Another notable difference between the two levels of educational attainment is that women's greater propensity to make the transition to work instead of graduate education becomes even more pronounced at the master's level than at the bachelor's level.

What theoretical implications should we draw from these findings? We realize that the NES data are not rich enough to support firm conclusions. It seems, however, that the results validate the relevance of the role-conflict explanation. We have shown, for example, that women's pursuit of an S/E career is impeded to a greater extent at the master's level than at the bachelor's level. Since those who attain a master's degree in S/E have made a conscious and costly investment in S/E human capital, it is difficult to explain these sex differences within the educational-credential framework. The family-versus-career role conflict can play out through a number of causal mechanisms. For example, as more individuals get married and have children by the time they complete a master's degree, the disadvantages of marriage and children faced by women accentuate the overall gender differences in career trajectories. Second, as more women attempt to resolve the family and career role conflicts, some give up S/E careers for alternative careers that are perceived to be more compatible with their family roles. Finally, it is also possible that women with a master's degree in S/E (especially those who are married and have children) are more likely to have experienced sex discrimination and thereby to be discouraged in their pursuit of an S/E career than are their counterparts at the bachelor's level, although we have no data to test this speculation directly.

Collectively speaking, results from this chapter and Chapter 5 indicate that sex differences in career transitions upon the receipt of a degree in S/E are real but relatively small, net of the influences of major and family status. Our analyses in these two chapters are, however, too limited to address the larger question of how women's careers in S/E differ from men's after the completion of S/E education. In these two chapters, we are concerned only with transitions made within a short time (one or two years) after the completion of a degree. We have found gender differences in career transitions after the completion of degrees that have the effect of pushing women out of S/E career trajectories, and these gender differences appear to be larger at the master's level than at the bachelor's level. It is possible, and indeed plausible, that these small differences observed earlier in the life course may accumulate and compound with time (Cole and Singer 1991). As more scientists and engineers marry and have children, family responsibilities may play a bigger role in impeding women's aggregate-level progress in S/E careers. In the remainder of the book, we will focus our attention on career outcomes of practicing women scientists in the labor force.

CHAPTER SEVEN

Demographic and Labor Force Profiles of Scientists and Engineers

In the preceding chapters, we have examined gender differences in attaining an S/E education and in career transitions after obtaining a bachelor's or master's degree in S/E. Beginning with this chapter, we shift the focus of our analysis to gender differences among practicing scientists and engineers in the labor force. In the remainder of the book, we focus on a few critical aspects of gender inequality in science: geographic mobility (Chapter 8), research productivity of academic scientists (Chapter 9), and labor force outcomes of immigrant scientists (Chapter 10). In this chapter, we draw together statistics from various sources to provide a broad overview of the demographic and labor force profiles of women and men in science/engineering. The information presented here provides the historical and contextual background necessary for a fuller understanding of the specific topics investigated in the chapters that follow.

We begin our description of the demographic and labor force profiles of women and men in S/E with a review of the two alternative designations of scientists/engineers—the supply- and the demand-based definitions. Recall that the supply-based definition of scientist/engineer includes anyone who completes a postsecondary degree in S/E, and the demand-based definition identifies as a scientist/engineer anyone who works in an S/E occupation. As we have shown in the previous two chapters, the supply-based definition is problematic because many individuals with a formal education in S/E pursue non-S/E

careers. In contrast, the demand-based definition often has the opposite problem—it is too narrow, since it does not recognize as scientists those individuals with an S/E education who are not currently
employed in S/E occupations, even though some of them would wish
to work in S/E occupations if given the opportunity. As argued by
Citro and Kalton (1989), there is no ideal compromise between the
two definitions, and researchers sometimes need to use them both. In
Chapters 2 through 4, we relied on the supply-based definition with a
focus on the attainment of an S/E education. In the previous two
chapters, we analyzed the transition between education and work and
thus implicitly used both definitions. In this and subsequent chapters,
we shift to the demand-based definition since our primary aim now is
to study gender differences in career outcomes among *practicing* scientists.

Gender Composition of Scientists and Engineers

The gender composition of the S/E labor force is influenced by both
the supply of men and women with the skills and education required
for S/E employment and the gender-specific rates of participation in
S/E occupations. So before we shift to the demand-based definition of
scientists/engineers, we assess gender differences in the utilization of
S/E education by comparing the gender composition among S/E degree recipients with the gender composition of the S/E labor force. We
know that a large portion of S/E degree recipients do not enter S/E
occupations or do not stay in S/E occupations for very long. If the proportion of women among S/E degree recipients is greater than the proportion of women in the S/E labor force, it follows that proportionately fewer women than men have transferred their human capital
investment in S/E education to S/E employment.

Gender Composition among Recipients of S/E Degrees

A simple measure of gender composition is the percentage of women
in a subpopulation. In Table 7.1, we present the percentage of women
among S/E degree recipients by level and year of degree from 1966
to 1996. We observe a steady and gradual increase in women's representation among recipients of S/E degrees at all educational levels. Among bachelor's degree recipients, women's representation increased from 16 percent in the beginning of the period to 36 percent

at the end of the period. Over the same period, women's representation increased from 10 percent to 28 percent among master's degree recipients and from 6 percent to 25 percent among doctoral degree recipients. These statistics represent very large and dramatic changes. Although the numbers in Table 7.1 mask subtle but important variation across specific fields of science and engineering, it is clear that the overall gender gap in the attainment of S/E degrees has narrowed substantially since the 1960s. This trend reflects the increasing levels of women's educational attainment and labor force participation and the consequent decline of their economic dependence on men during the same period (Blau 1998; Goldin 1990; Spain and Bianchi 1996). We note that gender disparities are more pronounced at higher levels of education: in any given year, the percentage of women is significantly lower among degree recipients at the master's level than at the bachelor's level, and it is lowest at the doctoral level.

Gender Composition among Incumbents of S/E Occupations

To assess whether the dramatic increase in women's representation among S/E degree recipients has changed the gender composition of practicing scientists and engineers, we calculate the percentage of women in the S/E labor force using the 1 percent Public Use Microsample (PUMS) data from the 1960–1990 U.S. decennial censuses. The statistics presented in Table 7.2 are restricted to individuals who have earned at least an undergraduate degree and are working in an S/E occupation. The data source is explained in more detail in Appendix A, and the occupations comprised in our definition of S/E for the different census years are given in Appendix C.[1] Table 7.2 presents the percent of women among incumbents of S/E occupations by level of degree for two age groups. Trends are revealed by reading down the columns within each panel of the table.

The percentages presented in Panel A are for the entire adult population, ages 25 to 64. These results illustrate trends similar to those evident in Table 7.1: there has been a rapid increase in women's representation in S/E occupations at all three levels of education. For example, women constituted less than 4 percent of all scientists with a bachelor's degree in 1960, but their representation increased to over 20 percent in 1990. Although the 1960 and 1970 data for scientists with advanced degrees are limited by the lack of distinction between those who hold a master's degree from those with a doctoral degree

Table 7.1 Percentage of women among S/E degree recipients by level of degree and year, 1966–1996

Year	Bachelor's degrees	Master's degrees	Doctoral degrees
1966	16.2	9.6	5.8
1967	16.5	10.4	6.3
1968	17.6	10.9	6.6
1969	17.9	11.5	6.7
1970	17.5	13.2	6.6
1971	17.3	12.9	7.4
1972	17.7	13.3	7.9
1973	18.3	12.9	9.2
1974	20.1	14.1	9.6
1975	21.8	14.4	10.6
1976	23.0	14.9	11.3
1977	24.0	16.3	11.9
1978	25.0	17.1	13.2
1979	25.8	18.4	14.1
1980	26.5	18.8	15.4
1981	27.2	19.4	15.9
1982	28.2	20.8	16.9
1983	29.1	21.3	17.6
1984	29.6	22.1	17.6
1985	30.2	22.2	18.4
1986	30.3	23.1	18.9
1987	30.6	23.9	19.2
1988	30.9	23.2	19.5
1989	30.5	23.9	20.9
1990	31.0	24.5	20.6
1991	31.7	25.2	21.0
1992	32.4	25.0	21.6
1993	32.8	24.8	22.7
1994	33.5	25.2	23.1
1995	34.7	26.0	24.1
1996	35.5	27.5	24.6

Source: NSF (2000, Tables 2–4, 2–5, 4.1, 4.2, 4.9, 4.10).

Table 7.2 Percentage of women among incumbents of S/E occupations by
level of degree and year, 1960–1990

Year	Bachelor's degrees	Master's degrees	Doctoral degrees
Panel A: Ages 25–64			
1960	3.6	6.3	
1970	6.4	6.3	
1980	10.9	10.9	10.0
1990	20.5	19.0	14.4
Panel B: Ages 25–34			
1960	4.4	6.2	
1970	9.8	6.6	
1980	16.8	16.3	13.8
1990	27.1	26.9	24.2

Source: Entries for 1960–1990 were computed from the 1 percent PUMS from the
1960, 1970, 1980, and 1990 U.S. censuses.

Note: Degree level was imputed from attained years of schooling before 1990. For the
1960 and 1970 censuses, 16 or 17 years of schooling = bachelor's degree; and 18+ years
of schooling = master's or doctoral degree. For the 1980 census, 16 or 17 years of
schooling = bachelor's degree; 18 years of schooling = master's degree; and 19+ years of
schooling = doctoral degree.

(the two groups are pooled together in this table), the trend toward
increasing representation of women after 1970 is clear and robust.

A comparison of women's representation in the S/E labor force in
Table 7.2 with women's representation in the supply of scientists/engi-
neers in Table 7.1 reveals the severe underparticipation in the S/E labor force of women with an S/E education. For all education levels,
the percentage of women in the S/E labor force is smaller than the
corresponding percentage of women among the S/E degree recipients. For example, women constituted only 21 percent of practicing
scientists and engineers with a bachelor's degree in 1990, whereas
they earned 31 percent of all S/E bachelor's degrees. This comparison
seems to suggest that proportionately more women than men fail to
utilize their S/E education in S/E employment.[2] However, practicing
scientists and engineers at any given time completed their education at
a prior point in time, when women's representation among S/E degree
recipients would have been lower. In other words, the percentages
presented in Panel A are likely to be depressed by very low levels of female representation among workers of older ages. To control for the
lag effect of the increasing trend in women's participation in S/E and

to provide a measure that can be used to assess more accurately gender differences in the actualization of S/E educational investments, in Panel B we present the percent of women among incumbents of S/E occupations aged 25–34 years. Except for scientists with advanced degrees in 1960 and 1970 (whose level of degree attainment, as we have noted, is not precisely measured; see footnote 1), the percentage of women is markedly higher in Panel B than in Panel A. That women's representation is highest among the youngest workers in the S/E labor force reflects women's steadily increasing rates of participation in the S/E labor force.

Comparing corresponding entries in Panel B of Table 7.2 with those in Table 7.1, we observe an interesting pattern: while in the earlier years the percentage of women in the S/E labor force was consistently lower than the percentage of women among S/E degree recipients, around the 1990s the gap narrowed at the bachelor's level and it reversed at the master's and the doctoral levels. In 1990, for example, 31 percent of S/E bachelor's degrees were earned by women, but only 27 percent of young practicing scientists and engineers with a bachelor's degree in the labor force were women. The difference was greater in earlier years, with women constituting 27 percent of bachelor's degree recipients and 17 percent of young S/E workers with a bachelor's degree in 1980. However, 27 percent of young S/E workers with a master's degree in 1990 were women, slightly surpassing the percent of women among recipients of S/E master's degrees in the same year (25 percent). Similarly, the representation of women among young S/E workers with doctoral degrees was higher than that among S/E doctoral degree recipients (24 percent versus 21 percent) in 1990. Although we noted earlier that the percentage of women among degree recipients declines markedly with degree levels, the pattern is much weaker (and indeed absent in 1960) for S/E labor force participation, suggesting that women who have earned an advanced S/E degree are proportionately more likely to utilize their S/E human capital than are those at the bachelor's level. A self-selection process seems to be operating in such a way that those women who continue to pursue S/E education after attaining an S/E baccalaureate are as committed as their male counterparts to S/E careers and thus are as likely as men to work in S/E occupations. However, this observation pertains only to the aggregate level, as we do not observe actual transitions from the attainment of S/E education to S/E occupations.

The percentages presented in Table 7.2 succinctly summarize the gender composition of the S/E labor force, but they are not comparable to the odds ratio scale used throughout this book. To mimic the odds ratio measure, we take the ratio between percentage women and percentage men and call it the "female-to-male representation ratio." For example, the female-to-male representation ratio in the S/E labor force at the bachelor's level increased from 0.04 (3.6 divided by 96.4) in 1960 to 0.26 (20.5 divided by 79.5) in 1990. It is important, however, to recognize that a representation ratio is different from an odds ratio, although the two are comparable under certain assumptions that are not unreasonable in this situation.[3]

The female-to-male representation ratio in the 1990 S/E labor force at the bachelor's level is 0.26 among 25–64-year-olds and 0.37 among 25–34-year-olds. These representation ratios are comparable to the female-to-male odds ratio of 0.37 for aspiring to an S/E degree (Table 3.1) and 0.35 for completing an S/E bachelor's degree among all degree recipients (Table 4.4).

Gender Composition by S/E Field

Since the statistics presented in Tables 7.1 and 7.2 are aggregated across all S/E fields, they obscure any differences by field that may exist. In Figure 7.1, we present the percentage of women among S/E baccalaureates by major field of study from 1967 to 1995. Two patterns emerge from Figure 7.1. First, there has been a steady increase in women's representation across all the fields of science and engineering, with the exception of mathematical science. By 1995, biological science had the highest proportion of female bachelor's degree recipients, at 50 percent. In contrast, women constituted 35 percent of bachelor's degree recipients in both physical science and mathematical science. The lowest percentage of women, 17 percent, was found among recipients of engineering degrees. The second characteristic of the trends presented in Figure 7.1 is that most of the gain in female representation among S/E baccalaureates occurred between 1975 and 1985 (again with the exception of mathematical science). For example, the percentage of women among recipients of bachelor's degrees in physical science increased by a full 10 percentage points from 18 percent in 1975 to 28 percent in 1985. The apparent leveling of the lines in Figure 7.1 after 1985 is consistent with the observation by

Jacobs (1995) that there has been little gender desegregation of S/E fields since 1985.

Compared with the trends in women's representation in other S/E fields, mathematical science appears to be an anomaly. According to the data, from 1967 to 1995 there was virtually no change in women's representation among recipients of bachelor's degrees in mathematical science. As early as 1967, women made up almost 34 percent of all recipients of bachelor's degrees in mathematical science. This number increased slightly to 39 percent around 1985 and then went back to 35 percent toward the end of the period. This leads us to ponder two questions. First, why was the percentage of women in mathematical science relatively high in the 1960s? Second, why did mathematical science not experience an increase in the representation of women as did the other fields during the period? We do not have good answers

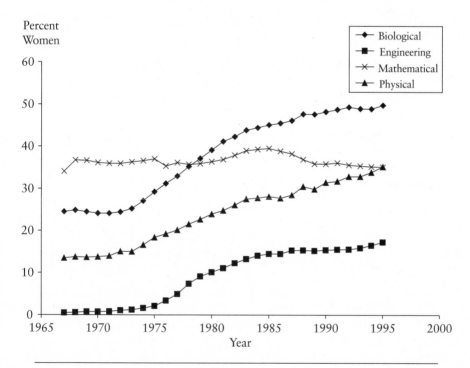

Figure 7.1. Percent women among recipients of S/E bachelor's degrees by field, 1967–1995. *Source:* NSF (1999, Appendix table 4-29).

to these questions. We would, however, like to point out that in this classification of S/E fields, mathematical science is heterogeneous, including mathematics and statistics majors, as well as computer science majors. It is possible that the trend data are misleading for mathematical science because the composition of the field has changed radically since the 1960s.

The increases in women's representation among recipients of S/E bachelor's degrees were paralleled by similar increases in women's representation among incumbents of S/E occupations in the labor force. In Figure 7.2, we present the percentage of women by field of occupation calculated from the 1960–1990 census PUMS. In calculating the statistics for Figure 7.2, we included all incumbents of S/E oc-

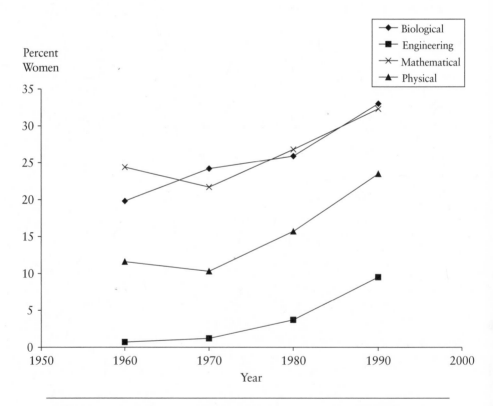

Figure 7.2. Percent women in S/E occupations by field, 1960–1990. *Source:* Entries for 1960–1990 were computed from 1 percent PUMS from 1960, 1970, 1980, and 1990 U.S. censuses.

cupations aged 25–64 with *at least* a bachelor's degree (or 16 years of education for the 1960, the 1970, and the 1980 data). We note that for two reasons the representation of women among degree recipients (Figure 7.1) is not, and should not be, directly reflected in the contemporaneous labor force (Figure 7.2). First, a large fraction of recipients of S/E degrees usually do not end up practicing science. Second, and more importantly, the S/E labor force at any given time is composed of individuals who obtained degrees in many different years. With this caveat, we observe in Figure 7.2 a steady increase in women's representation in the S/E labor force between 1970 and 1990, in all four S/E fields. The trend for women's representation among biological scientists during the period was similar to that among mathematical scientists; in both fields, women's representation increased from around 25 percent in 1960–1970 to about 33 percent in 1990. Finally, given the low rate of female representation among baccalaureates in the physical sciences and engineering, as shown in Figure 7.1, it is not surprising that women's representation was the lowest among engineers, followed by physical scientists, although the post-1970 trend was upward for both of these fields.

In summary, Figure 7.2 illustrates the varying degree to which women have been integrated successfully into different fields of science and engineering and confirms the significant cross-field variation in gender composition. The trend in women's participation in the S/E labor force is clearly one of improvement. According to Figure 7.1, the largest increase in women's representation among S/E bachelor's degrees occurred between 1975 and 1985 (with the exception of degree recipients in mathematical science). However, it is apparent in Figure 7.2 that the largest increase in women's representation among practicing scientists took place between 1980 and 1990. This lag is due largely to the demographic inertia of cohort succession: a cohort of S/E graduates stays in the labor force for a long time before being replaced. Given the dynamics of the demographic change, it is our expectation that women's representation in the S/E labor force should continue to increase into the near future.

Family Status of Scientists/Engineers

In Table 7.3, we present statistics characterizing the family status of scientists and engineers by gender. These statistics are based on all 25–

Table 7.3 Percentage distribution of family status among incumbents of S/E occupations by gender, 1990

Family status	Women	Men
Single	25.0	15.7
Married without children	29.4	33.5
Married with children	34.1	43.7
Divorced	9.5	5.4
Separated	1.3	1.2
Widowed	0.8	0.5
(N)	(6,631)	(30,403)

Source: 5 percent PUMS from the 1990 U.S. census.

Note: The entries are column percentages. The data pertain to incumbents of S/E occupations who have attained a master's degree or higher level of education.

64-year-olds in the 5 percent PUMS of the 1990 U.S. census who are incumbents of S/E occupations and who have at least a master's degree. Our sample includes 30,403 men and 6,631 women. Limiting the analysis to scientists and engineers with a master's degree yields a conservative definition of the population of employed scientists/engineers.[4] Our measure of family status combines the variables measuring marital status and the presence of children in the household.

Gender differences in family status are obvious in Table 7.3. Female scientists are much more likely to be single (25 percent) than male scientists (16 percent), and women are much more likely to be divorced (10 percent) than men (5 percent).[5] As a result, a smaller percentage of women than men are married, regardless of whether or not they have children. Furthermore, a lower percentage of women than men are married and have children in their home (34 percent of women versus 44 percent of men).[6] Although these statistics provide only indirect evidence, they are consistent with the proposition that more women than men may face a conflict between an S/E career and family life (Blau 1998; Goldin 1997). The division of labor within the family that places the responsibility for household labor on women may cause some women who have started a family to forgo an S/E career and others who have started an S/E career to forgo having a family. A less extreme resolution of this conflict occurs when married women scientists leave the S/E labor force temporarily, rather than permanently, to care for children and/or support their husbands. It may also be that the motivation for marriage is low for well-educated women with good jobs such as women scientists, if, as has been theorized (Becker, G. S. 1981), attaining economic security through a husband's income is a major motivation for marriage among women. Regardless of the underlying causes, the available empirical evidence shows that fewer women than men combine a family life with an active S/E career.

Labor Force Outcomes

We now focus on gender differences in labor force outcomes among practicing scientists and engineers. We first use the 5 percent PUMS data from the 1990 census to examine gender differences in labor force participation, employment, full-time employment status, and earnings. These outcomes are relevant measures for all workers, and a large and comprehensive literature on gender differences in these measures for the general population already exists (e.g., Blau 1998; Goldin 1990; Spain and Bianchi 1996). We restrict our analysis of the PUMS data to incumbents of S/E occupations who have attained at least a master's degree.

As argued by Tang (2000), promotion to management is an important marker of career success among engineers. In this chapter, we examine gender differences in the rate of promotion to management among scientists and engineers. We realize that promotion to management is a crude measure of career success, and for some scientists and engineers, management in fact can be seen as an indicator of a sidetracked career. For example, in academia, it is research productivity rather than administrative experience that bestows prestige to scientists (Cole and Cole 1973). Research productivity, however, is a measure of success suitable only for academic scientists. (See Chapter 9 for an analysis of gender differences in publication productivity among academic scientists/engineers.) The drawback of using promotion as a measure of career success is balanced by at least two advantages. First, it is a career outcome applicable to all scientific and engineering personnel. Second, a measure of promotion to management was collected in the longitudinal data from the 1982–1989 Survey of Natural and Social Scientists and Engineers (SSE) that we use for this analysis.

Our statistical analysis consists of two steps. First, we present de-

Table 7.4 Labor force characteristics and promotion rates of scientists and engineers by sex and family status

	Unmarried		Married without children		Married with children	
	Female	Male	Female	Male	Female	Male
Panel A: Employment characteristics from the 1990 census PUMS						
In labor force (%)	96.0	95.1	93.7	93.6	87.3	99.0
Employed (%)[a]	98.6	97.1	97.9	98.4	97.4	98.9
Full-time employed (%)[b]	94.8	95.2	93.7	95.3	82.0	97.9
Earnings[c] (1989)	$38,765	$45,000	$39,198	$54,769	$40,319	$54,101
Log earnings[c]	10.49	10.62	10.49	10.81	10.53	10.82
(n)	(1,982)	(5,492)	(1,508)	(8,436)	(1,345)	(12,291)
Panel B: Rates for promotion to management from the SSE, 1982–1989						
Promotion rate	0.113	0.095	0.051	0.055	0.031	0.112
(n)	(535)	(1,007)	(434)	(873)	(507)	(2,827)

Sources: 5 percent 1990 PUMS for employment status and earnings, and 1982–1989 SSE for promotion to management. The data pertain to incumbents of S/E occupations who have a master's degree or higher education.

a. Percent employed is conditional on labor force participation.

b. Percent full-time employed is conditional on employment.

c. Earnings and log earnings are based on workers employed full-time, year-round with positive earnings in 1989.

scriptive statistics on employment characteristics and earnings from PUMS and on promotion rates from SSE, separately by gender and family status. Second, we use multivariate models to study gender differences in these labor force outcomes net of the influence of demographic and human capital characteristics, field of occupation, sector of employment, and, in the case of earnings, labor supply. For both steps of our analysis, we pay particular attention to the interaction between gender and family status, as this allows us to test if family status affects labor force outcomes differently for men and women.

Describing Labor Force Outcomes by Gender and Family Status

Table 7.4 presents descriptive statistics on labor force outcomes by gender and family status. Panel A presents four nested measures calculated from the 5 percent 1990 census PUMS: the proportion of scientists/engineers participating in the labor force, the proportion employed (versus unemployed) conditional on labor force participation, the proportion employed full-time (versus part-time) conditional on being employed, and the earnings of employed full-time, year-round workers with positive earnings. An individual is considered an active labor force participant if he/she is either currently employed or unemployed (i.e., not working but actively seeking employment). Hence, a person who is not currently participating in the labor force is not only out of a job, he/she is also out of the job market. The census collects information on the current or last occupation only for those who had been actively employed during the past five years. Scientists and engineers who did not work between 1985 and 1990 are thus excluded from the census data. That is, the PUMS data censors, or excludes, scientists and engineers who had moved to nonscientific jobs or had been unemployed or out of the labor force for more than five years. For this reason, our results should be seen as "biased" in the sense that they overrepresent scientists and engineers with continuous S/E work histories.

The first line of Table 7.4, in Panel A, shows the proportion of scientists and engineers in the labor force by gender and family status. According to this measure, labor force participation rates are high, varying between 87 percent and 99 percent. By comparison, the labor force participation rate for the general population with 16 or more years of schooling was 81 percent for women and 95 percent for men in 1990 (Blau 1998, Table 1). Our relatively higher estimates reflect the censoring problem mentioned above and for this reason may not be the best gauge of the level of labor force participation among all scientists/engineers. We use this biased measure mainly to compare differences by gender and family status and to lay the groundwork for our study of other labor force outcomes. The measured rate of labor force participation does not vary much by family status among men, but it varies considerably among women: 96 percent of single women but only 87 percent of married women with children participate in the labor force. It is notable that there is little gender difference in the participation rates for unmarried and childless married scientists/engineers. Only among those who are married and have children do the rates of labor force participation for men and women diverge significantly (88 percent for women and 99 percent for men). The next line of Table 7.4 presents the employment rate among workers who participate in the S/E labor force. We observe little variation in the employment rate by gender and family status: it ranges between 97 and 99 percent.

We define full-time employment as working for 35 or more hours in a typical week. Among employed scientists and engineers, women are less likely than men to work full time. This is shown in the third row of Panel A: for every category of family status, the proportion of full-time workers is lower among women than among men. It is interesting to note that being married with children is again negatively associated with working full-time for women, but the opposite is true for men. The net result is a much wider gender gap for married scientists and engineers with children: 82 percent for women and 98 percent for men. The gender gap for the other two categories of family status is very small.

In the last two lines of Panel A, we present the average annual earnings and logged earnings by gender and family status. To ensure the comparability of this measure for men and women, we restrict the calculation to full-time, year-round employed workers with positive earnings. These statistics therefore represent conservative estimates of gender differences in earnings. Year-round employment is defined as having worked for more than 39 weeks in 1989. Average earnings of full-time, year-round workers is given in the fourth row of the table. We also present the average of logged earnings in the fifth row of Panel A to facilitate the comparison of these descriptive statistics with the multivariate results we present below. Despite the restriction of the analysis to full-time employed workers, the earnings of women are substantially lower than those of men. Women's earnings vary little by family status and average about $39,000–40,000, but men's earnings average about $45,000 if single and $54,000–55,000 if married. These statistics show a relatively small gender gap in earnings among unmarried scientists and engineers ($6,235 in favor of men) but a much larger gender gap among married S/E workers ($15,571 without children and $13,782 with children in favor of men).

Finally, Panel B of Table 7.4 presents the promotion rates for scientists in the SSE data by gender and family status.[7] We use here the same definition of a scientist/engineer as we used for the census data analysis and include in our sample respondents who, at the time of the first wave of the survey, reported being employed in a scientific or engineering occupation and who had attained a master's or doctoral degree. The SSE data allow us to examine longitudinal patterns of promotion to management by gender and family status. The SSE survey is based on a sample of individuals drawn from the 1980 U.S. census and contains four waves of longitudinal data collected in 1982, 1984, 1986, and 1989. See Appendix A for a detailed discussion of the data source. We weighed the statistics to account for stratified, disproportionate sampling and disproportionate nonresponses.

Our analytic strategy for the SSE data is to follow a *new* cohort of scientists and engineers over time in an attempt to avoid confounding the influence of experience with the influence of cohort (Morgan 1998). For this purpose, we restrict the sample to a cohort of scientists and engineers who had ten or fewer years of professional experience in 1982 and focus on their success in attaining promotion to management over time until 1989. Once a scientist/engineer was promoted to management, he or she is excluded from further analyses. Those working in management jobs in 1982 (the first year of the survey) are not included in this analysis. After these restrictions, the sample used for this event-history analysis contains a total of 2,560 individuals yielding information for 6,183 person-periods.

The bottom panel of Table 7.4 presents the rates of promotion to managerial positions by gender and family status, using pooled data for the cohort from the 1982, 1984, 1986, and 1989 waves of the SSE. The promotion rates were calculated for the intervals 1982–1984, 1984–1986, and 1986–1989, with respondents in nonmanagerial positions being at risk of promotion at the beginning of each interval. The promotion rates given in Table 7.4 are aggregated over the three intervals. Panel B shows a small gender difference in favor of women among unmarried scientists/engineers and no gender difference among married scientists without children (around 0.05 per interval). In contrast, a large gender disparity emerges for married scientists/engineers with children (0.11 for men and 0.03 for women).[8]

Explaining Gender Differences in Labor Force Outcomes

We now turn to our multivariate analysis of three labor force outcomes: employment, earnings, and promotion. Analyzing these outcomes with multivariate models allows us to test whether the gender differences observed in the preceding descriptive analysis are statistically significant and to examine whether these gender differences can be explained. For this multivariate analysis, we consider the explanatory influence of six groups of variables.

1. *Demographic characteristics.* Women's observed disadvantage in the labor force could be due, in part, to demographic characteristics such as race and age. We therefore control for these influences in our multivariate analysis. We measure respondent's age continuously and include a squared term to account for the nonlinear effects of age. In all models, we include race as a baseline control. Race is a categorical variable distinguishing the broad categories of white (the reference category), Asian, and other.[9]

2. *Human capital.* Gender differences in labor force outcomes may result from the relatively lesser human capital of women scientists. Our key measure of human capital is education. We differentiate scientists/engineers with only a master's or professional degree from those with a doctoral degree. Another potential measure of human capital is work experience. For the PUMS data, a direct measure of experience is unavailable, and we capture its effect with age. Given the cohort-based design of our SSE data, work experience is approximated by the length of the longitudinal study.

3. *Field.* As shown in earlier chapters, the segregation of men and women in different S/E fields may confound aggregate-level gender comparisons. We control for field-specific differences in gender composition by grouping scientists into four major fields on the basis of their reported occupation: biological science, engineering, physical science, and mathematical science. For the SSE data, we also have information about the field of a scientist's highest degree, which is in-

cluded as an additional control variable. The classification of detailed S/E field codes is presented in Codebook G (posted on www.yuxie .com) for the SSE data and Appendix C for the census data.

4. *Business sector.* We account for variation in career patterns across different sectors of employment by controlling for the sector of the S/E labor market in which a scientist/engineer is employed. Our employment sector variable distinguishes four sectors: industry, academic, government, and other.

5. *Family status.* The descriptive results presented in Table 7.3 show that women scientists are less likely than male scientists to be married in general and married with children in particular. In our multivariate analysis, we consider the influence of family status by including a three-category measure that captures both marital and parental status.

6. *Labor supply.* Finally, for the earnings analysis using the PUMS data, labor supply is controlled using two variables: the number of weeks worked in 1989 (categorized as less than 45, 45 to 49, and 50 and above) and the hours per week typically worked in 1989 (categorized as less than 40, 40 to 44, and 45 and above).

In addition, we include the interaction between gender and family status to identify the unique effects of family status on labor force outcomes for men and women scientists. The multivariate analyses of employment and earnings are based on the 1990 PUMS data, and the analysis for promotion is based on the SSE data. The analysis of employment is limited to labor force participants aged 25–64, and the analysis of earnings is further limited to full-time year-round workers in 1989 who had positive earnings. Logit regressions are used to model the odds of employment and promotion, and linear regressions are used to model the logarithm of annual earnings. The results of the multivariate models for the three labor force outcomes—employment, earnings, and promotion—are summarized in Table 7.5.

The female-to-male ratios presented in Table 7.5 highlight gender differences in the odds of employment, the earnings rate, and the odds of promotion. The upper panel of this table presents the "observed" female-to-male ratios for the three labor force outcomes. Although we calculated these ratios from the sex coefficients from the bivariate statistical models, they can also be derived from the descriptive statistics in Table 7.4 (with small discrepancies due to rounding). The lower panel presents the "adjusted" female-to-male ratios, which

Table 7.5 Observed and adjusted female-to-male ratios measuring gender gaps in employment, earnings, and promotion to management by family status

	Odds of employment	Earnings rate	Odds of promotion
Observed			
Unmarried	2.059***	0.881***	1.205
Married without children	0.726	0.729***	0.937
Married with children	0.434***	0.748***	0.256***
Adjusted			
Unmarried	2.093***	0.929***	1.118
Married without children	0.560***	0.864***	0.985
Married with children	0.406***	0.857***	0.241***

Sources: 5 percent 1990 PUMS for employment status and earnings, and 1982–1989 SSE for promotion to management.

Note: Analysis is restricted to scientists and engineers with a master's degree or higher. "Adjusted" sex ratios control for age, race, education, field of study, employment sector, and, in the case of earnings, weeks and hours worked. See Appendix Tables D7.a and D7.b for details.

*$p < .05$, **$p < .01$, ***$p < .001$ (two-tailed test of the null hypothesis of no gender difference).

were calculated from the sex coefficients in the multivariate models that include the explanatory covariates discussed above. The complete sets of coefficients for the multivariate models are reported in Appendix Tables D7.a and Tables D7.b.

Employment

The first column of Table 7.5 displays the female-to-male ratios for the odds of employment by family status. Unmarried women scientists/engineers are found to be more likely than men to be employed, and the difference is statistically significant for both the observed and the adjusted ratios. The observed ratio of 2 suggests that the odds of employment for unmarried women is twice that for unmarried men. Adjusting for the explanatory covariates in the multivariate analysis does not change this result. Among married scientists who have children, we find a large and statistically significant gender gap in favor of men: women's odds of employment is less than half that of men, and the magnitude of this difference is unaffected by the inclusion of the control variables in the multivariate model. Among scientists and engineers who are married but do not have children, the result lies in between: while the observed gender difference is statistically insignificant, we find a disadvantage faced by women after controlling for the covariates.

Although gender differences in the odds of employment are statistically significant for most of the comparisons, we need to emphasize that these estimated gender differences in terms of probabilities (or rates) lack any practical significance. As shown in Table 7.4, unmarried women are only 1.5 percent more likely than unmarried men to be employed (98.6 percent versus 97.1 percent), and married women with children are only 1.5 percent less likely than married men with children to be employed (97.4 percent versus 98.9 percent).[10] Hence, from a substantive point of view, gender differences in the likelihood of employment among scientists and engineers are rather small (see also NSF 1999, p. 101).

Earnings

The second column of Table 7.5 presents female-to-male ratios in earnings. Let us focus first on the observed ratios in the upper panel of the table. The gender gap in earnings is the smallest for unmarried scientists, with women earning at a rate that is 12 percent below that of men. The gender gap widens for married scientists, regardless of their parental status, with women earning at a rate about 25–27 percent lower than men. Returning to Table 7.4, these gender differences translate into sizable disparities in earnings. For example, unmarried women earn about $39,000 a year, compared to $45,000 for unmarried men, and married women with children earn $40,000 a year, compared to $54,000 for married men with children. The inclusion of the explanatory variables in the multivariate analysis results in a large reduction of the estimated gender gap in earnings, as presented in the lower panel of Table 7.5. The adjusted female-to-male ratio in earnings is estimated to be 0.93, 0.86, and 0.86, respectively, among unmarried scientists, married scientists without children, and married scientists with children.

In our earlier discussion of the descriptive results reported in Table 7.4, we suggested that the large gender gap among married scientists/engineers is not due to a marriage penalty for women; rather, it is due to a significant gain from marriage enjoyed by men. This pattern is confirmed by the multivariate analysis. As shown in Appendix Table D7.a, the exponentiated coefficients for being married are significantly (both statistically and substantively) greater than unity, meaning that marriage increases earnings rates by 7 to 11 percent. However, given the dummy variable coding for sex (1 = female), these coefficients actually represent a large marriage advantage for men. Note that the coefficients for the interactions between sex and family status are statistically significant and in the negative direction, indicating that the earnings of married women are consistently lower than the earnings of married men (by 9 percent). The similar magnitudes of the estimated coefficients for the interaction terms and the coefficients for family status mean that there are no earnings differentials by family status among women.

The gender gaps in earnings reported here may appear small at the first glance. Without any controls, the female-to-male ratio in earnings is estimated to be 0.88 for unmarried scientists/engineers and 0.73–0.75 for married scientists/engineers. With the controls, the estimated sex ratios are 0.93 for unmarried scientists/engineers and 0.86 for married scientists/engineers. By comparison, the observed female-to-male ratio in earnings for the 1989 total labor force was 0.59–0.68, using either median annual earnings (Spain and Bianchi 1996, Table 5.1) or average weekly wages (Blau 1998, Table 4). The main explanation for the relatively small size of our estimated pay gap is that our analysis is restricted to a relatively homogeneous labor force, scientists and engineers with at least a master's degree. By restricting the sample this way, our analysis is not confounded by occupational segregation and differences in the attainment of postsecondary education. Past research has shown that about one-third of the gender gap in earnings can be attributed to occupational segregation (Treiman and Hartmann 1981) and that the gender gap in wages appears to narrow with educational attainment (Blau 1998, Table 4). Thus, it should not be surprising that the earnings gap between men and women with advanced education who work full time in S/E occupations is relatively small.[11] Indeed, Morgan (1998) reports that accounting for variables such as professional experience closes the gender pay gap altogether for recent cohorts of engineers.

Promotion

We now turn to the multivariate results for the likelihood of promotion, displayed in the last column of Table 7.5. For our event-history analysis of the likelihood of promotion to management, we utilize the SSE longitudinal data for the cohort of scientists/engineers who in 1982 had less than 11 years of experience. The dependent variable for the analysis is the odds of promotion within each observed interval. The multivariate results reported in the lower panel of Table 7.5 control for the effects of year, age, race, education, field of degree, occupation, and employment sector. Using female-to-male ratios, we focus on gender differences in the odds of promotion by family status.

Two important findings emerge from these results. First, there is a statistically significant gender gap disadvantaging women in the odds of promotion among married scientists/engineers with children. For unmarried scientists and married scientists who do not have children, however, there is no discernible gender difference in the likelihood of promotion. Second, the inclusion of explanatory variables in the multivariate analysis has little impact on the gender gap in promotion rates, as the observed ratios in the upper panel are similar to the adjusted ratios in the lower panel for all three categories of family status. This means that the disadvantage experienced by married women with children cannot be explained by gender differences in the demographic, educational, or employment characteristics for which we control.

On the basis of these multivariate results, as well as the descriptive results of Table 7.4, we conclude that for married scientists/engineers with children, the odds at which a woman attains a promotion is only a quarter as high as the odds for men. In the original scale of rates (instead of odds), we observe from Table 7.4 that married women with children are promoted at the rate of 0.03 per interval, compared with 0.11 for married men with children. This result indicates that being married with children is a significant career advantage for men but a career disadvantage for women, and it is consistent with past research that shows the potential conflict between family and career for women (Blau 1998; Goldin 1997; Waldfogel 1997). Before we interpret the results as causal, however, we caution the reader that they could be explained by a selection bias: promotion and family status may be jointly determined by unmeasured characteristics such as career ambition. For example, it is possible that more ambitious scientists/engineers may choose not to marry. Further, this selection bias could vary with gender: career ambition may be positively correlated with marriage for men, but negatively correlated for women.[12]

Conclusion

In this chapter, we have characterized the demographic and labor force profiles of men and women scientists/engineers using data from a variety of sources. Beginning in this chapter, and continuing in the chapters that follow, scientists/engineers are defined as incumbents of scientific/engineering occupations. To assess the implications of the two alternative definitions of scientists/engineers—supply-based versus demand-based—we compared the gender composition among recipients of science/engineering degrees with the gender composition among practicing scientists/engineers in the labor force and tracked their trends from the 1960s to the 1990s. We found that women's representation both among recipients of S/E degrees and among incumbents of S/E occupations increased dramatically during these years. The increase occurred in all major S/E fields, with the exception of mathematical science. By 1990, women constituted about a third of practicing biological and mathematical scientists, a quarter of physical scientists, and a tenth of engineers.

Examining the demographic characteristics of scientists and engineers, we found considerable gender differences in family status. Female scientists and engineers are much more likely to be single or divorced than are their male counterparts. Further, even among married scientists and engineers, women are much less likely to have children. These descriptive results suggest the potential influence of a conflict between an S/E career and family life for women. Further analyses in the chapter are concerned with differences in labor force outcomes by gender and family status. Utilizing data from the 1990 5 percent PUMS and 1982–1989 longitudinal SSE, we examine three labor force outcomes: employment, earnings, and promotion. For all three outcomes, we find a clear and persistent pattern in which marriage and parenthood exacerbate gender differences, even after controlling for a variety of demographic and human capital explanatory factors. Gender differences among unmarried scientists are either small or nonexistent, but married women experience large disadvantages relative to men, especially if they have children. This interactive pattern results from two processes: the careers of men benefit from marriage and parenthood, while the careers of women are impeded by family responsibilities. We show that while men benefit from marriage and parenthood in their labor force outcomes, women instead experience a penalty or at best derive no benefit. Altogether, these results suggest that, despite tremendous improvements of women's status in education and the labor force in the past four decades, it is still very difficult for women to "have it all": career and family (Blau 1998; Goldin 1997; Waldfogel 1997).

CHAPTER EIGHT

Geographic Mobility of Scientists/Engineers

In previous chapters, we examined various factors that may produce gender inequalities either in the likelihood of beginning an S/E career or in the labor force outcomes among practicing scientists and engineers. An important finding that has emerged is that family responsibilities, especially those associated with parenthood, seem to impede women's, but not men's, careers in S/E. In this chapter we further explore the relationship among gender, family, and career processes by examining a specific mechanism through which family dynamics may produce gender differences in S/E careers. In particular, we propose that family migration is one means by which family may affect the career development of women and men scientists differently. We examine gender differences in the rate of migration among active scientists and engineers, paying particular attention to the influence of family structure and its interaction with gender.

Much research has shown that the employment positions of women scientists are inferior to those of men (Ahern and Scott 1981; Cole 1979, Table 6–5; Fox 1995; Long 2001; Long, Allison, and McGinnis 1993; Long and Fox 1995; Peek 1995; Xie and Shauman 1998; also see Chapter 7). The persistence of the situation strongly suggests that men and women are sorted, through formal or informal mechanisms, into different positions with access to different career opportunities within the S/E labor force. Since geographic mobility is a primary labor market sorting mechanism, it is theoretically reasonable to suspect that it may play a part in the differential placement of women and men in the S/E labor market. Migration is often a reaction either to employment opportunities in distant locations (pull factors) or to a lack of employment opportunities in one's current location (push factors). Household migration, however, is an event enacted at the family level and as such is influenced by family structure. An individual's ability to react to either push or pull factors is greatly complicated when he or she is involved in a dual-career couple, as women scientists disproportionately are. Although women in the S/E labor force are less likely than men to be married (as we show in Chapter 7), those who are married are much more likely than married men to be part of a dual-career couple.

Our analytical approach for this chapter is informed by two streams of research: the sociological and social psychological literature on dual-career constraints on academic careers (e.g., Marwell, Rosenfeld, and Spilerman 1979) and the economic and demographic literature on family migration decisions and patterns (e.g., Mincer 1978). Researchers in these areas have suggested that married women's inability to initiate a family move may inhibit their career advancement because it may preclude their taking advantage of career opportunities. More specifically, Marwell, Rosenfeld, and Spilerman (1979, p. 1225) propose the following explanation of how gender stratification is produced in the academic labor force:

> [A] considerable part of the disparity between men and women in academic status and earnings derives . . . from the disadvantages that marriages impose on the women. In a two-career family many crucial decisions (for example, whether or not to have children and where to reside) can have an adverse effect on one or both careers. In this situation, two-career couples will be at a handicap, in comparison with one-career couples, with respect to maximizing job prospects. We will argue that, in the aggregate, in academia women's careers suffer more as a result than men's.

Similarly, Mincer (1978, p. 771) suggests a causal link between the migration of dual-career families and the progress of women's careers:

> By interrupting the continuity of women's work, tied migration leads to slower growth of wages over the life cycle. The adverse effect on wage growth can occur even without discontinuity of employment . . . Tied

migration ranks next to child rearing as an important dampening influence in the life-cycle wage evolution of women.

Drawing on these two lines of research, we hypothesize that women
scientists are disadvantaged relative to men because women scientists
are less geographically mobile. We call this the "differential mobility"
hypothesis.

The differential mobility hypothesis rests on two assumptions: first,
that geographic mobility has a positive effect on career advancement;
second, that two-career couples are less able than one-career couples
to make long-distance moves. On the basis of these two assumptions
and the observation that married women scientists are more likely
than their male counterparts to belong to two-career couples, we hypothesize that women scientists are less likely to migrate across labor
market boundaries. We use 1990 U.S. census data to examine this hypothesis among all men and women holding a doctoral degree and
working in the S/E labor force in the United States.

Implications of Geographic Mobility for Women Scientists' Careers

The S/E Labor Market, Geographic Mobility, and Career Advancement

The labor market for doctoral scientists and engineers has several
structural characteristics that are associated with high levels of geographic mobility (Landinsky 1967). S/E doctorates typically occupy
salaried positions in decentralized work settings, where the ratio of
managers to managed workers is low. Scientists and engineers are
generally not subject to standardized work conditions, pay rates, or
state licensing regulations. In addition, they tend to have strong occupational communication networks fostered by nationally circulated
scholarly journals and other periodicals, national funding institutions, and professional organizations. All of these characteristics contribute to the national scope of the scientific labor market and hence
to high long-distance migration rates among doctoral scientists.

The national scope of the labor market for S/E doctorates has implications for individual scientists' career development. For individuals in national labor markets, mobility can be used to compete for
better positions, to accumulate experience rapidly, and to skip rungs

on a promotion ladder (Markham and Pleck 1986). In such markets, the converse is also true: career advancement can suffer from an unwillingness or inability to move. Immobile workers may face more competition for positions and, hence, fewer employment opportunities and lower lifetime earnings. Thus the differential mobility thesis is highly relevant to doctoral scientists because they participate in national labor markets.

Dual-Career Couples and Geographic Mobility

Overall, women scientists are less likely to be married than men scientists. Since women tend to marry men at or above their own educational or professional level, however, women scientists are much more likely than men to be married to other scientists or other highly educated professionals. Furthermore, because proportionately fewer women than men in the U.S. population have S/E doctoral degrees, the supply of career-oriented women does not match that of similarly career-oriented men. Consequently, women scientists and engineers are more often situated in dual-career families in which both partners are highly committed to their careers. Men scientists and engineers are less likely to be part of dual-career couples, and among those who are, their wives' careers are likely to be less advanced than their own (Rosenfeld and Jones 1987, p. 494). If two-career marriages impede scientists' geographic mobility, the gender difference in marriage patterns implies that married women scientists are constrained more often than their male counterparts.

It is at least assumed in the literature, if not empirically shown, that the range of suitable migration destinations and the timing and frequency of family migration may be restricted for dual-career families. With respect to the choice of destination, researchers have suggested that living in large, urban areas with diversified labor markets reduces the degree to which both partners in a dual-career marriage must compromise their individual gains from migration (Marwell, Rosenfeld, and Spilerman 1979; Mincer 1978).[1] The assertion that large urban markets are more likely to satisfy the career needs of both partners in a dual-career marriage is supported by studies of the geographic constraints experienced by dual-career families. Frank (1978), for example, finds that the probability of living in large urban areas is higher among female professionals than among male professionals. In addition, Marwell, Rosenfeld, and Spilerman (1979) show that married academic women are much more likely than married academic men to be located in large metropolitan areas.

The timing and frequency of family migration may also be restricted in dual-career marriages because individuals are not able to react independently to migration push or pull factors. If this is true, women professionals will be less geographically mobile than men professionals because proportionately more women than men are involved in dual-career marriages. In such a marriage, an individual partner may not be able to act on an opportunity that demands geographic relocation because it would disrupt the spouse's career. Implicit in the argument that women's career mobility is hampered by geographic immobility is the assumption that the partnership of two career-oriented individuals necessarily reduces the geographic mobility of such families. It otherwise would be illogical to infer that women professionals are less mobile solely because they are more likely to be in dual-career marriages. This assumption seems to be supported by studies of the influence of women's labor force participation on family migration patterns, which find that women's participation generally depresses the rate of family migration (Bird and Bird 1985; Duncan and Perrucci 1976; Lichter 1980, 1982; Long 1974; Mincer 1978).

Earlier studies of the connection between family migration and women's employment do not, however, inform the specific question of the migration of *dual-career* families. Lacking detailed educational and employment information for both married partners, these studies typically consider the presence of a working wife a proximate indicator of a dual-career union and thus do not distinguish marriages in which only one career may benefit from geographic mobility from those in which the career development of both partners may require geographic mobility. To address this problem, we attempt to distinguish dual-career couples by using information about both spouses' degree attainment, employment status, and occupation. Past studies have also erred by overlooking the possibility that the presence of two careers in a family may generate more career-related opportunities for migration: since two careers in a family generate two sets of career-related opportunities that require migration, two careers may produce more *per-family* migration pulls, although dual-career constraints may diminish the *per-career* realizations of such opportunities. Recognizing this possibility, we subject to empirical test the assumption that dual-career couples are less mobile than one-career couples. Our reasoning does not necessarily contradict the conventional wisdom that dual-career marriages constrain mobility, because migration rates for individuals in dual-career marriages would be much higher than rates for those in single-career situations if no dual-career constraints existed. See Shauman and Xie (1996) for a fuller discussion of our reasoning.

We should not naively assume, however, that women with stocks of human capital equal to those of their husbands command a fully competitive role in career-related migration decisions (Duncan and Perrucci 1976). In the context of studying the migration of academics, Marwell, Rosenfeld, and Spilerman (1979, p. 205) argue that gender roles and the implicit hierarchy of careers within marriage also impede women's career development. More specifically, the husband's career usually takes precedence even in dual-career families, and migrations therefore are likely to be governed by opportunities associated with the husband's career. A sizable body of empirical research supports the notion that gender inequality exists within dual-career families. For example, neither the prestige of the wife's occupation nor the proportionate size of her contribution to the total family income has been found to have a significant effect on family migration behavior (Duncan and Perrucci 1976; Lichter 1980, 1982; Long 1974; Shihadeh 1991).

The difficulty of understanding the asymmetry between husband's and wife's career interests is most evident in the contradictory interpretations of the role of careers in the migration literature. Although it is commonly accepted that career interests often prompt men to migrate, it is assumed that women in professional careers resist mobility because they wish to retain their current employment situation (Lichter 1980, 1982; Long 1974; Mincer 1978). We find this differential treatment of male and female behavior unsettling and in need of an explanation. Whether a wife's professional career decreases or increases a family's propensity for migration is a complicated issue involving the tradeoff between the *addition* of opportunities associated with the wife's career and the *reduction* in the husband's mobility due to dual-career constraints. Although results from past research have shown that a wife's employment is associated with lower migration rates (e.g., Duncan and Perrucci 1976; Lichter 1980, 1982; Long 1974), the pattern may be attributable to the patent sex segregation of the labor force. That is, women are concentrated in female-dominated jobs, which tend to have short career ladders and not to require geographic mobility. Among women doctoral scientists, however, the situation can be quite different. For them, the job market is truly national, and career advancement often requires geographic relocation. It is thus unclear whether or not scientists in two-career families are less likely to migrate than scientists in one-career families—this is the first specific hypothesis we test in this chapter.

Given the possible influence of within-family gender inequality, we further relax the assumption that being in a two-career marriage has the same effect on men and women scientists. For example, being part of a two-career marriage may affect women's geographic mobility but not men's. We examine the interaction between marriage types and gender in order to test the second hypothesis that the effect of two-career marriages on the propensity of migration differs with gender, with women being affected more negatively than men.

Family Structure and Geographic Mobility: The Effect of Children

Parenthood is widely believed to affect the careers of men and women scientists differently, placing an extra burden on women but having neutral or positive effects on men. In her literature review, Zuckerman (1991, pp. 52–53) concludes that empirical research taken as a whole has not supported the notion that childrearing impairs scientists' job performance (also see Cole 1979; Cole and Zuckerman 1987). One exception is a study by Hargens, McCann, and Reskin (1978), who report that having children has a negative effect on research productivity, but the effect does not vary by gender. However, our own research, reported in the preceding three chapters, yields clear evidence that the impact of parenthood on at least some career outcomes of scientists varies by gender, with women more negatively affected. Thus, our expectation that parenthood has a differential effect by gender constitutes the third hypothesis of this chapter.

We propose that the presence of children, especially young children, may affect men and women scientists' careers differentially through its gender-specific effect on geographic mobility. Our proposal is motivated by the life course explanation of family migration patterns, which suggests that married individuals with children are less likely to move than either single people or those who are married but have no children in the household (DaVanzo 1977; Mincer 1978; Sandefur 1985; Speare 1970). Although we recognize the constraining effects of children on the migration of all scientists' families, we expect such effects to differ between men and women scientists. Even when the partners in a dual-career marriage are equally committed to their careers, the arrival of children may cause a division of family duties that enforces traditional gender roles. Since the socially expected role for a woman is that of primary caregiver, she will most likely assume this role and subordinate her nonfamilial roles (Epstein 1974; Maret and Finlay 1984; Sorensen 1983; Spenner and Rosenfeld 1990).

In interviews with a small number of couples in which both partners were heavily invested in their corporate careers, Hertz (1986) found that gender roles become a conspicuous force in the marriage only when childrearing is undertaken. Although these couples did not rely on traditional roles and divisions of labor to make their dual-career marriages successful, "gender becomes a salient issue once children arrive: someone has to be with them. Women are still viewed by these couples as better equipped to nurture young children even though their lives until this point have paralleled those of their male peers and husbands" (p. 145). After the birth of their first child, the majority of the women interviewed by Hertz reported decreasing their work hours and level of responsibility from those they had maintained at their job before they had children. The effect of children on these dual-career families was to disrupt the career equity the couples had enjoyed, negatively affecting the women's careers but having little influence on the careers of their male partners.

The effect of children on family migration depends on the children's age to a more significant degree than on the number of children present in a family. Long (1972) found that the age composition of the children in a family has a consistently differential effect on family mobility, once the age of the household head is controlled: Families with only preschool-age children (0–6) are the most mobile; families with only school-age children are the least mobile; and families with both preschool- and school-age children fall between these two extremes, but their behavior more closely resembles that of the families with only school-age children. Families with only young children are more free to move because their children are not yet involved in a particular school; thus the parents have fewer social ties to any one place. The opposite is true of families with school-age children. The social and emotional costs of migration increase substantially for parents because children's participation in schools tends to increase parents' community involvement. As Long speculates (1972, p. 374), "Perhaps families with school-age children feel that transferring their children from one school district to another is, as a rule, undesirable." This common conception is supported by empirical research documenting the detrimental effect of residential mobility on school achievement (Astone and McLanahan 1994; Coleman 1988; Haveman, Wolfe, and Spaulding 1991; McLanahan and Sandefur 1994).

Describing Gender Differences in Characteristics and Mobility Rates of Scientists/Engineers

The analysis for this chapter is based on a dataset of scientists drawn from the 5 percent PUMS of 1990. We define scientists as U.S. citizens who have attained a doctoral degree, currently are not in school, and report having an occupation that falls into one of four broad S/E categories: biological science, engineering, mathematics and computer science, and physical science.[2] We constructed these categories by collapsing the three-digit census occupational codes listed in Appendix C. We first selected from the PUMS those individuals who fit our definition; then we linked to each scientist's record information about his/her spouse and children, if these family members were present at the time of the census.[3] In brief, our dataset consists of parallel information about each scientist and his or her spouse and about the presence and ages of the children of each scientist.[4]

Migration information for each scientist and spouse is based on a classification of geographic areas that we use to approximate local labor markets. To construct this classification, we used the Public Use Micro Areas (PUMAs) of residence in 1985 and 1990. PUMA is the most detailed geographic identifier available in the PUMS. The PUMA classification, however, tends to divide locales without regard for their economic and social cohesiveness. For a closer representation of local labor markets, we collapsed adjacent PUMAs within a metropolitan area.[5] We define a migration between 1985 and 1990 as a move across the geographic areas thus defined. To be considered a mover, a scientist could have moved across state boundaries or from one geographic area to another within a single state. Those who reported a change of residence but who moved within the boundaries of a defined geographic area are considered nonmovers.

Marital type is a five-category classification referring to the scientist's marital status and the spouse's educational and occupational characteristics. The categories are unmarried scientists, scientists who are married to other scientists, scientists who are married to non-S/E doctorates, scientists who are married to other professionals, and scientists who are married to others. Unmarried scientists include never-married, separated, divorced, and widowed scientists.[6] The "other professionals" category includes spouses with master's and advanced professional degrees. The last category, "others," refers to all remaining spouses, including those out of the labor force in 1990. With this classification, we consider as dual-career families all married scientists except those who fall into the "married to other" category.

The presence of children of specific ages is represented by a set of binary variables. The age categories we use are 0–6 (preschool), 7–12 (elementary school), and 13–18 (teens). Additional control variables are the scientist's field of specialization, the scientist's age, and a dichotomous classification of sector of employment. As a further control, we include in this analysis a continuous variable coded as the age of the scientist's spouse less the scientist's age, with unmarried scientists assigned a value of 0; positive values of this variable indicate that the scientist is younger than his or her spouse.[7]

Descriptive statistics in Table 8.1 document the differences between male and female S/E doctorates by employment field and marital type. As we noted in Chapter 7, women scientists are well represented in the biological sciences but severely underrepresented in engineering and the physical sciences. The breakdown of marital type presented here, more detailed than that used in Chapter 7, reveals interesting gender differences in marriage patterns. In these data, 37.5 percent of women scientists are currently unmarried, compared with 19.4 percent of men. Women are much more likely to be married to fellow scientists and engineers (14.7 percent) and to non-S/E doctorates (16.9 percent) than are their male counterparts (2.7 percent and 4.7 percent, respectively). In addition, women scientists are less likely than men scientists to be married to other professionals, the category that includes spouses who hold a master's or professional degree. These statistics reflect a pattern of educational assortative mating among the women scientists: they tend to marry men with similar educational at-

Table 8.1 Percentage distribution of scientists by marital type, field of science, and sex

Scientists	Unmarried	Married to scientist	Married to non-S/E doctorate	Married to other professional	Married to other	(n)
Females	37.47	14.69	16.85	17.79	13.21	(742)
Biological scientists	42.71	12.20	12.88	20.68	11.53	(295)
Engineers	33.00	20.20	15.27	14.78	16.75	(74)
Mathematical scientists	34.71	12.35	22.35	15.88	14.71	(170)
Physical scientists	35.14	14.86	24.32	18.92	6.76	(203)
Males	19.41	2.74	4.72	25.62	47.51	(4,637)
Biological scientists	20.37	2.82	6.63	23.80	46.38	(815)
Engineers	18.35	3.47	4.60	25.98	47.60	(1,336)
Mathematical scientists	24.22	3.33	5.22	26.56	40.67	(900)
Physical scientists	16.84	1.42	3.37	25.67	52.69	(1,586)

Source: 5 percent PUMS from 1990 U.S. census.

tainment. If we consider as two-career marriages the three types of marriages in which both partners have attained advanced degrees, women clearly are much more likely than men to be in dual-career couples (49.3 percent versus 33.1 percent). Conversely, men are much more likely than women to be married to nonprofessionals (47.5 percent versus 13.2 percent). Female scientists are clearly more likely than male scientists to live in two-career families.

In Table 8.2, the marginal distributions of explanatory variables and the migration rate for each category of the discrete explanatory variables are presented separately for male and female scientists. Female scientists are on average younger than male scientists and are more likely to be childless. Men scientists are more likely than women to have children over age 6. The observed gender differences in family composition, however, are partly an artifact of the relative "youth" of the population of women scientists; that is, on average women scientists belong to more recent cohorts than men. The normative pattern of spousal age gap is evident among scientists as well: male scientists are married to women who are, on average, 1.81 years their junior, while women scientists' husbands are, on average, 1.23 years their senior. Male scientists are more likely than females to be employed in the academic sector.

The migration rate is the proportion of scientists who reported having moved between 1985 and 1990. Contrary to the results of other studies of academics (Marwell, Rosenfeld, and Spilerman 1979), we find that women scientists are significantly more likely than men to have moved during the five years preceding the 1990 census: 38 percent of the women and 28 percent of the men reported undertaking a move during that period.

The descriptive results in Table 8.2 cast some doubt on our first hypothesis that scientists in dual-career marriages are geographically more constrained than scientists in one-career marriages. Doctoral S/E workers married to other professionals with doctoral degrees are more, not less, mobile than those married to less professionally oriented spouses. We also fail to find any evidence for the second hypothesis that the influence of marriage type varies by sex. The descriptive results, however, are consistent with the third hypothesis that women's migration rates are more negatively constrained than men's by the presence of children. Yet the findings from Table 8.2 are preliminary in the sense that they may be contaminated by various confounding

Table 8.2 Percentage distribution and migration rates of scientists by sex and other explanatory variables

	Percentage distribution		Migration rates	
	Females	Males	Females	Males
Total sample			0.38	0.28***
Scientist's age				
25–29	6.74	3.02	0.68	0.83*
30–34	21.83	10.93	0.67	0.66
35–39	24.66	17.45	0.42	0.40
40–44	21.43	20.40	0.21	0.26
45–49	13.88	22.51	0.18	0.15
50–54	7.68	14.92	0.18	0.12
55–59	3.77	10.76	0.04	0.11
Field				
Biological sciences	39.76	17.58	0.38	0.34
Engineering	9.97	28.81	0.38	0.25*
Mathematical sciences	22.91	19.41	0.30	0.24
Physical sciences	27.36	34.20	0.44	0.31*
Marital type				
Unmarried	37.47	19.41	0.42	0.37
Married to scientist	14.69	2.74	0.40	0.37
Married to non-S/E doctorate	16.85	4.72	0.31	0.26
Married to other professional	17.79	25.62	0.34	0.25*
Married to other	13.21	47.51	0.38	0.26*
Children present in home				
None	61.99	49.39	0.43	0.30***
Age 0–6	24.93	23.94	0.36	0.38
Age 7–12	12.94	23.31	0.15	0.25*
Age 13–18	7.95	21.72	0.15	0.14
Employment sector				
Nonacademic	71.29	80.70	0.37	0.29***
Academic	28.71	19.30	0.39	0.28***
Age difference between spouses (married scientists only)	−1.23	1.81		
(n)	(742)	(4,637)		

Source: 5 percent PUMS from 1990 U.S. census.

*$p < .05$, **$p < .01$, ***$p < .001$ (significance levels refer to the Pearson chi-square testing for the hypothesis that the migration rate is the same across the sexes within a category).

factors. For example, the women are younger and more likely to belong to dual-career couples than the men. A more precise test of these hypotheses must control for other factors that are relevant to the relationship between scientists' gender and their geographic mobility. Accordingly we turn to the results from a multivariate analysis.

Explaining Variation in Migration Rates of Scientists/Engineers

We use binary logit models to estimate the effect of each of the independent variables on the likelihood that a member of the S/E labor force undertook a long-distance migration between 1985 and 1990. The estimated coefficients and goodness-of-fit statistics for an additive model and an interactive model are presented in Table 8.3. For the additive model, the exponentiated coefficient for sex is not significantly different from one; this finding indicates that, when we control for gender differences in the characteristics of doctoral scientists and engineers, women are no more or less likely than their male colleagues to have migrated during the period 1985–1990.

The other estimated coefficients for this additive model show that migration rates are affected by the scientist's age and the age difference between spouses. Younger scientists are significantly more likely than older scientists to be geographically mobile. The coefficient of the age difference between spouses is estimated to be significantly less than 1, an indication that net of scientists' own age, the probability of moving is lower for scientists with older spouses. Because married women scientists are more likely to be younger than their husbands, whereas the reverse is true for men, this effect reduces women's mobility but enhances men's mobility.

Migration rates also vary across the S/E fields. Biological scientists and physical scientists are the most likely to have migrated, and mathematical scientists and engineers are the least likely to have migrated. The effect of children on the propensity to migrate deviates slightly from the pattern predicted by the life course model of family migration (Long 1972): migration rates are similarly high among scientists in families without children, families with preschool-aged children, and families with primary-school-aged children; but mobility rates are significantly lower among families with teenage children.[8]

The coefficients for marital type in the additive model are partic-

Table 8.3 Estimated coefficients from logit models of the odds of long-distance migration

	Additive model		Interactive model	
	$\exp(b)$	z-ratio	$\exp(b)$	z-ratio
Constant	5.07	6.40	5.06	6.68
Sex (Female)	0.93	−0.75	1.10	0.91
Scientist's age				
25–29	(Excluded)		(Excluded)	
30–34	0.54	−3.14	0.54	−3.13
35–39	0.19	−8.59	0.19	−8.51
40–44	0.10	−11.74	0.10	−11.66
45–49	0.05	−14.58	0.05	−14.49
50–54	0.04	−15.16	0.04	−15.02
55–59	0.03	−15.01	0.03	−14.83
Field				
Biological sciences	(Excluded)		(Excluded)	
Engineering	0.75	−2.77	0.75	−2.73
Mathematical sciences	0.74	−2.87	0.74	−2.83
Physical sciences	0.92	−0.92	0.93	−0.81
Age difference between spouses	0.96	−4.02	0.95	−3.81
Employment sector				
Nonacademic	(Excluded)		(Excluded)	
Academic	0.95	−0.57	0.90	−0.57
Marital type				
Unmarried	(Excluded)		(Excluded)	
Married to scientist	0.91	−0.47	0.94	−0.50
Married to non-S/E doctorate	0.84	−1.06	1.00	−1.30
Married to other professional	0.90	−0.67	1.00	−0.95
Married to other	0.99	−0.04	0.97	−0.34
Children present in home				
None	(Excluded)		(Excluded)	
Age 0–6	0.87	−1.52	0.91	−0.96
Age 7–12	0.97	−0.39	1.03	0.35
Age 13–18	0.67	−3.81	0.66	−3.73
Sex (Female) × Children				
Sex × No children			(Excluded)	
Sex × Children age 0–6			0.74	−1.43
Sex × Children age 7–12			0.42	−2.65
Sex × Children age 13–18			1.03	0.08
Model χ^2 (df)	1072.48 (19)		1083.47 (22)	

Source: 5 percent PUMS from 1990 U.S. census.
Note: Sample size is 5,379. Indicator variables for missing data were included in all models.

ularly interesting. We find no significant difference in the probability of long-distance geographic mobility among scientists of any marital type. According to this model, the tendency to migrate among scientists in two-career families is no less than among scientists in one-career families; nor is it lower than the migration rate for unmarried scientists.

To test our hypotheses about the gender-specific effects of marital type and the presence of children, we entered the interaction between sex and each of these variables to the additive model. The inclusion of the sex by marital type interaction directly tests the second hypothesis, that women and men are affected differently by their type of marriage. We do not find this interaction to be significant and therefore conclude that the effects of marriage type are the same for men and for women.

The sex by children interaction tests the third hypothesis, that the presence of children affects men and women differently. This hypothesis is confirmed: the significant interaction indicates that the effects of children on scientists' mobility differ between men and women scientists.[9] Figure 8.1 portrays the estimated effects of children on the mobility rates for male and female scientists/engineers, with the other variables in the interactive model held constant at their sample means.

As shown in Figure 8.1, the effects of family composition on migration rates obviously differ between men and women. The migration rates of men scientists with preschool- or elementary-school-age children resemble those of childless men scientists, showing that the presence of young children does not inhibit the mobility of young men. It is only when men have teenage children that their migration rate is low. In contrast, the presence of children has a significantly negative effect on the mobility of women scientists, regardless of the children's age. Although childless women scientists are estimated to be slightly more mobile than childless men scientists, the effect of preschool- and elementary-school-age children on women's geographic mobility is significantly negative, depressing their mobility rates far below those of men in similar families. The gender gap in geographic mobility is the greatest for scientists with children aged 7–12: women scientists with children in this age group are 43 percent less mobile relative to men with children of this age. Among scientists with preschool children, women are 15 percent less mobile. Among scientists with teenage children, the migration rate for women is slightly higher than the rate for men.

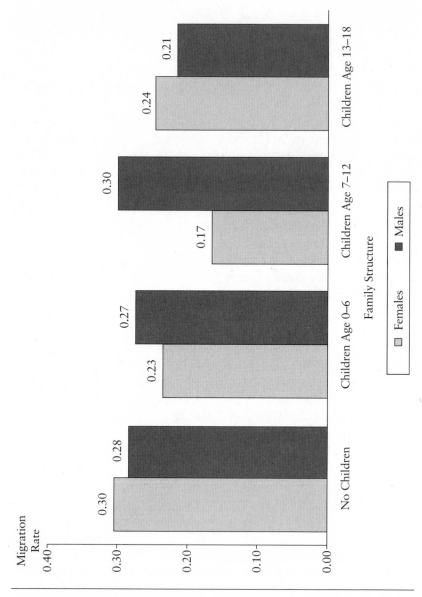

Figure 8.1. Predicted migration rate for scientists by sex and family structure.
Source: 5 percent PUMS from 1990 U.S. census.

Discussion

Census data do not permit us to provide a definitive explanation for the sex differences in the effects of children's presence on scientists' migration. We propose, however, that the pattern of the sex differences can be understood as an outgrowth of gender differences in the responsibilities of parenthood and their consequent effect on labor force behavior. Hertz (1986), for example, suggests that the careers of married women are affected by childbearing negatively because women tend to devote time to childcare that they would otherwise have spent in pursuit of career mobility. To investigate whether this is the case in our sample of scientists, we examined the mean hours and weeks worked by men and women scientists and by their spouses. This information, along with the female-to-male ratios of weeks and hours worked by scientists and their spouses, is presented in Table 8.4.[10]

Average hours worked per week by unmarried women are on a par with those of unmarried men. We also observe near parity in the hours worked by married scientists who do not have children present in the household. For these scientists, the female-to-male ratio of hours worked ranges from 0.93 for scientists who are married to nonscience doctorates to 0.98 for scientists who are married to nonprofessionals. The presence of young children tends to decrease the female-to-male ratio in hours worked regardless of marital type. The largest gender gap in hours worked is observed among scientists who have preschool-aged children. The ratios for scientists with preschool children range from 0.73 (for scientists who are married to non-S/E doctorates) to 0.80 (for scientists who are married to nonprofessionals), indicating that women with very young children work about 25 percent fewer hours than their male counterparts. The disparity is not due to a propensity toward part-time work among women, as the hours reported by women scientists do not fall below full time on average. Rather, it is due to the fact that men scientists are able to work significantly more than 40 hours per week on average, even when they have very young children. The gender gap in working hours narrows as the children's age increases, such that there is near parity in hours worked among scientists with teenage children in all marriage types, except among scientists who are married to non-S/E doctorates.

We interpret this disparity in work hours as a reflection of sex dif-

Table 8.4 Mean hours per week and weeks per year worked by scientists and their spouses, by sex, marital type, and family structure

	Hours worked by scientist			Hours worked by scientist's spouse			Weeks worked by scientist			Weeks worked by scientist's spouse		
	Females	Males	F/M ratio	Females	Males	F/M ratio	Females	Males	F/M ratio	Females	Males	F/M ratio
Unmarried	44.29	43.18	1.03				48.81	48.40	1.01			
Married to scientist												
No children	43.57	45.92	0.95	46.94	42.31	1.11	48.96	51.23	0.96	51.23	48.98	1.05
Children age 0–6	33.57	43.36	0.77	42.60	40.36	1.06	43.02	51.11	0.84	50.50	48.25	1.05
Children age 7–12	43.65	43.35	1.01	49.74	28.31	1.76	42.17	51.31	0.82	49.09	41.65	1.18
Children age 13–18	42.46	44.34	0.96	49.62	31.81	1.56	42.23	50.76	0.83	51.46	44.11	1.17
Married to non-S/E doctorate												
No children	43.60	47.01	0.93	47.38	38.35	1.24	46.57	50.32	0.93	49.81	40.08	1.24
Children age 0–6	34.25	47.22	0.73	47.73	34.77	1.37	43.80	51.48	0.85	51.09	39.25	1.30
Children age 7–12	34.22	46.17	0.74	46.22	35.07	1.32	46.22	51.00	0.91	51.70	42.12	1.23
Children age 13–18	36.28	44.33	0.82	48.17	31.04	1.55	45.00	50.80	0.89	50.56	38.38	1.32

Married to other professional												
No children	43.45	44.93	0.97	36.30	32.72	1.11	47.55	49.72	0.96	43.74	40.17	1.09
	33.60	44.24	0.76	44.75	29.57	1.51	46.00	50.94	0.90	48.68	37.77	1.29
Children age 0–6	37.53	45.23	0.83	46.47	26.85	1.73	45.89	51.04	0.90	51.74	36.31	1.42
Children age 7–12	44.20	45.05	0.98	51.20	22.36	2.29	48.93	50.87	0.96	49.07	32.67	1.50
Children age 13–18												
Married to other												
No children	42.59	43.51	0.98	40.56	22.89	1.77	47.02	49.30	0.95	42.35	32.20	1.32
	35.65	44.54	0.80	46.71	20.06	2.33	43.68	50.72	0.86	48.13	29.54	1.63
Children age 0–6	42.88	45.37	0.95	47.25	16.87	2.80	35.63	50.96	0.70	40.94	27.33	1.50
Children age 7–12	41.33	44.09	0.94	47.67	13.19	3.61	33.33	51.00	0.65	47.17	21.64	2.18
Children age 13–18												

Source: 5 percent PUMS from 1990 U.S. census.

ferences in the spouses' time commitment to childcare tasks. This interpretation is reinforced by the pattern of sex differences in the hours worked by the scientists' spouses. The second set of columns in Table 8.4 shows that, when children are present, male scientists' wives work far fewer hours than do the husbands of female scientists. More specifically, male scientists' wives work substantially fewer hours when a child is present. In contrast, when there are children present in the household female scientists' husbands tend to work more hours than the husbands in childless couples.

The third set of columns of Table 8.4 shows that sex differences in the number of weeks worked per year are affected less drastically by the presence of children than are work hours, although the general pattern of interaction is consistent. We also see no effect of children's age on sex differences in the average weeks worked. In part this is an artifact of our sample selection because the sample includes only scientists in the labor force. Nonetheless, the result is consistent with our argument that the presence of children has differential effects on men and women scientists. We interpret the greater impact of children on the gender differences in hours worked per week as an indicator of women scientists' efforts to balance their commitment to working in science with their commitment to their familial role as primary caregiver.

Conclusion

The migration of dual-career families is interesting because it is a point at which gender dynamics are manifested and become observable through family behavior. Although geographic mobility is not the only route to career mobility, it is an important avenue for developing specific types of careers such as those in S/E. In this chapter, we argue that two careers in a family potentially generate more opportunities for family migration, although realization of such opportunities may be constrained. We find, however, that the mobility rates of dual-career families do not differ significantly from those of unmarried or single-career families. Thus our results do not support the notion that marital type accounts for gender differences in geographic mobility. We also fail to find that being in a dual-career marriage affects women more negatively than men.

We find clear evidence supporting the hypothesis that the presence of children limits women scientists' migration significantly more than that of men scientists. In our sample of doctoral scientists, women with children are less geographically mobile than both women without children and all men scientists. In contrast, men have high rates of mobility when their children are young. We have shown indirectly that the greater mobility among men is probably due to their wives' lesser commitment to career and greater investment in childcare, especially when the children are young. Men scientists' propensity to migrate becomes restricted as their children enter their teens; in this respect, men scientists follow the family migration patterns of the general population (Long 1972). The timing of this restriction for men is likely to coincide with the middle years of career formation— that is, a period of career stability. In contrast, women scientists' geographic mobility is restricted significantly when their children are young. We show that this is probably a result of their assuming the role of primary caregiver. For women, this period of restricted mobility is likely to coincide with the early years of their careers. This is the time of career formation, when a lack of geographic mobility may be most detrimental to a scientist's future career.

CHAPTER NINE

Research Productivity

In this chapter, we study the career achievements of scientists and engineers employed in academic settings. The employment qualifications, work activities, and expected output of academic scientists differ significantly from those of scientists employed in other sectors. First, a doctoral degree in an S/E field is an almost universal requirement for employment as a faculty member in a postsecondary institution. Second, academic scientists are expected to teach in addition to conducting research. Despite the demands of activities that compete with research for time, academic scientists have more freedom than those working in industry and in government to select their research topics and conduct their research projects. Third, for scientists employed in academic settings, research productivity is an important measure of achievement and a primary basis for decisions about career advancement, salary increases, and the distribution of other rewards, such as lab space and access to grant monies.

Numerous studies have found that female scientists publish at lower rates than male scientists, and research efforts to explain this gender gap have been essentially unsuccessful (Long and Fox 1995; Ward and Grant 1995; Zuckerman 1991). In a classic statement of the problem, Cole and Zuckerman (1984, p. 218) characterize sex differences in research productivity as "the productivity puzzle":

> More than 50 studies covering various time periods and fields of science report sex differences in published productivity, more specifically, that

men publish more than women, even when age and other important social attributes are taken into account. Moreover, gender differences in publication rates appear to have persisted for decades. So far, efforts to account for these differences have not been successful; their existence continues to be a puzzle.

From their own research on scientists who received doctorates in 1969–1970, Cole and Zuckerman (1984, p. 217) estimate that "women published slightly more than half (57%) as many papers as men." In a literature review, Zuckerman (1991, p. 43) maintains that "women publish fewer papers than men of the same ages, on average, 50–60 percent as many." Because career advancement is dependent on publication productivity, this large gender gap in publication rates has serious implications for the advancement of women in science and engineering.

So far, Cole and Zuckerman's provocative assertion of a productivity puzzle has not been seriously challenged, and explanations for sex differences in research productivity have remained elusive. This quandary has helped propel the continued acceptance of sex differences in research productivity as a puzzle—a phenomenon we cannot explain. For example, after reviewing many explanations in the literature, Long (1992, p. 160) states, "Unfortunately, none of these explanations has been very successful in accounting for sex differences in productivity. Indeed, Cole and Zuckerman (1984) aptly label these sex differences 'the productivity puzzle.'"

In this chapter, we report empirical findings that challenge the characterization of gender differences in publication productivity as a puzzle. Our findings are from a systematic and detailed analysis of data from four sources: the National Survey of Higher Education conducted by the Carnegie Commission in 1969 (hereafter Carnegie-1969), the Teaching Faculty in Academy study sponsored by the American Council of Education in 1972–1973 (hereafter ACE-1973), the 1987–1988 National Survey of Postsecondary Faculty conducted by the NCES (hereafter NSPF-1988), and the 1992–1993 National Survey of Postsecondary Faculty, also conducted by NCES (hereafter NSPF-1993). These datasets are ideal for our purpose because of their national representation of academic scientists across the complete spectrum of scientific specialties and their coverage of a variety of relevant explanatory factors. In addition, the four datasets are similar in sampling design and survey instrumentation, which allows us to replicate findings and to detect temporal changes over a span of 24 years. See Appendix A for a detailed discussion of the four datasets. We first examine changes in observed sex differences in research productivity over the 24-year period and then apply multivariate negative binomial models in an attempt to uncover explanations for the observed sex differences.

Measuring Sex Differences in Research Productivity

To assess the extent of the gender gap in research productivity, we must first define the scientist population being studied and specify an appropriate measure for quantifying the sex gap in productivity.

The Scientist Population

Both the supply-based and the demand-based approaches to defining the scientist population have advantages and disadvantages for the study of gender differences in publication productivity. The supply-based definition homogenizes the training credentials of scientists and theoretically permits the examination of sex differences in career trajectories (Clemente 1973; Cole and Zuckerman 1984; Long 1992; Reskin 1978). By drawing samples from recipients of doctoral degrees in science, however, supply-based studies could suffer from an "exposure bias" well understood by Cole and Zuckerman (1984, p. 223): "If unequal proportions of men and women have remained in academia, the results . . . could be biased, since academics tend to publish more than government and industrial scientists." In contrast, by restricting the population to academic scientists, the demand-based definition homogenizes the job settings of scientists to those where publication of research results is expected and rewarded (Blackburn, Behymer, and Hall 1978; Fox and Faver 1985). This approach forgoes the potential analysis of sex differences in the processes of entry to and exit from academia.

Hence, the supply-based and demand-based definitions have different implications for our problem: Do sex differences in research productivity result from women's lower likelihood of working in academia or from women's lower productivity within academia? If the former explanation is true, the productivity puzzle should be defined more accurately as a career puzzle (Bernard 1964, p. 154). This proposition is plausible given that women are overrepresented among the ranks of unpublished scientists, many of whom may be "silent" because they are not employed in academic settings (Long 1992; Xie and Akin 1994, Figure 1). Thus, it is useful to restrict the study population to academic scientists, as their publication is generally expected, facilitated, and rewarded. Following Cole (1979), we combine the supply-based and the demand-based criteria and define scientists as individuals with doctoral degrees who occupy faculty positions in science at academic institutions.[1]

To make our results comparable with those from earlier research, we restrict the analysis to doctoral scientists appointed as regular teaching faculty at a postsecondary institution in one of the following major fields: biological science, engineering, mathematical science, and physical science.[2] This definition includes regularly employed lecturers and instructors but excludes graduate student instructors. Using this definition of scientists and restricting our samples to those with valid responses to relevant questions in the four surveys, we extracted information for 12,225 scientists from Carnegie-1969; 6,998 scientists from ACE-1973; 847 scientists from NSPF-1988; and 1,845 scientists from NSPF-1993. The differences in the number of cases across the four datasets reflect the large variation in the sample sizes of the four original studies. We use weights in our analysis so that the samples represent the respective target populations.

Quantifying Sex Differences in Research Productivity

Conceptually, productivity should be measured as the amount of "research output" in a period of "exposure." The concepts of output and exposure both require some discussion. *Research output* is commonly measured by the number of publications, either reported by respondents in surveys or found in bibliographic searches. In general, the publication count is a crude measure of research output, as it does not distinguish between sole-authored and co-authored publications or between significant and insignificant publications. Most survey instruments do not separate peer-reviewed journal articles and books from other forms of publications.[3] In addition, respondents to surveys may misreport their publication counts because of recall error or social desirability pressures. Despite these problems, the count of publications is commonly used because of its simplicity. This practice is supported for the study of gender differences in productivity by the lack of evidence linking sex to the aforementioned factors that would make the measure imprecise. For example, men and women scientists do not differ in their likelihood of collaboration (Cole and Zuckerman 1984; Long 1992; Sonnert 1995a, p. 135). Thus, measurement noise is commonly assumed, as it is in this study, to be innocuous with respect to the main research focus (i.e., sex differences).

Concerning *exposure,* an important distinction must be made between "cumulative" measures and "short-term" measures. Cumulative measures refer to an individual's total research output over the complete span of his/her career; short-term measures refer to research output during a relatively short interval. We contend that the use of short-term measures is preferred for studies of sex differences in research productivity, for three reasons. First, women have only recently increased their participation in science and therefore have fewer years of experience than men on average. Hence, the use of cumulative measures inflates gender differences in any cross-sectional dataset. Second, it is highly plausible that women are more likely to withdraw temporarily from active research owing to spousal/child-rearing constraints. This is particularly true in the earlier decades of the twentieth century (Astin 1969, p. 58). Third, it is difficult to incorporate explanatory variables measuring resource availability into multivariate models when the cumulative count of productivity is the outcome variable, because such explanatory variables are more likely to be endogenous rather than exogenous to one's cumulative productivity. For example, the prestige and type of the employing institution and the scientist's academic rank may in fact result from productivity demonstrated at various points earlier in the career. If this is the case, the causality may run opposite to the direction assumed, or the explanatory and dependent variables may be jointly determined. Although the problem of potential reciprocal causality is not solved by the use of short-term measures, it is at least substantially mitigated.[4]

For a majority of academic scientists, research productivity is a life-long process with a distinct life-cycle profile: it sharply increases to a peak early in life and then gradually declines (Stephan and Levin 1992). For scientists at different points in their life cycles, we expect their short-term rates of productivity to be different. This problem highlights the need to control for experience. Indeed, several major studies (Cole 1979; Cole and Zuckerman 1984; Long 1992; Reskin 1978) were designed to control for experience by following a single cohort of scientists who obtained their doctoral degrees at roughly the same time. With cross-sectional data, it is necessary to control for experience statistically, and the effects of experience can be interpreted as constituting a career profile under the assumption of stationarity (i.e., no substantial changes across successive cohorts).

The dependent variable for our analysis is the count of all publications reported by the respondent scientist for the two years prior to the date of the survey. Included in the publication count are articles published in refereed and nonrefereed journals, chapters in edited volumes, books, and monographs. Unlike the other studies, the NSPF-1988 survey instrument included "creative works" with articles and books in the publication count. This inclusion inflates the average publication count for the NSPF-1988 sample, although it is likely that very few scientists are engaged in the production of creative works. Furthermore, the problem should not bias our study if the relative importance of "creative works" is not related to sex. For both the Carnegie-1969 and ACE-1973 surveys, the publication count was measured in categorical intervals through a closed-ended question. For these datasets, we use the midpoint of response categories as an approximation of publication counts.[5] The NSPF-1988 and NSPF-1993 data provided a detailed count of publications for each scientist.

Assuming that we have a good short-term measure of productivity, how should we quantify sex *differences* in research productivity? Earlier work (Blackburn, Behymer, and Hall 1978; Cole 1979) used the correlation coefficient. As argued in Chapter 1, the correlation measure is not invariant with respect to the sex composition in a sample. Our preference is to use the simple ratio between sex-specific means as a measure of sex differences in research productivity. Easy to compute and interpret, the ratio has been the standard measure used in the labor force literature studying sex differences in earnings (see for example Bianchi and Spain 1986, Chapter 6). It also corresponds well with a key coefficient in the multivariate regression models that are presented below.

Table 9.1 presents summary statistics of two productivity measures, one cumulative and one short-term, by sex and data source. The cumulative measure is the total number of publications in a scientist's entire career (denoted T); the short-term measure is a scientist's total number of publications in the two years prior to the survey date (denoted Y).[6] Both the correlation (r) and the ratio (R) measures for sex differences are presented. As measured by both r and R, sex differences are greater for the cumulative counts of publications than for

Table 9.1 Observed sex differences in self-reported measures of research productivity in four national surveys of postsecondary faculty

Survey and productivity measures	Sex	Mean	Standard deviation	(n)	r	R
Carnegie-1969						
Total publications	Female	9.23	12.70	(459)		
in career (T)	Male	16.30	16.34	(11,706)	−0.091	0.566
Total publications	Female	1.96	2.46	(461)		
in last two years (Y)	Male	3.39	3.32	(11,764)	−0.089	0.580
ACE-1973						
Total publications	Female	13.11	18.20	(239)		
in career (T)	Male	21.47	22.80	(6,720)	−0.074	0.611
Total publications	Female	2.21	2.81	(238)		
in last two years (Y)	Male	3.49	3.42	(6,760)	−0.074	0.632
NSPF-1988						
Total publications	Female	15.96	21.84	(91)		
in career (T)	Male	34.18	50.68	(751)	−0.118	0.467
Total publications	Female	3.38	3.98	(92)		
in last two years (Y)	Male	4.87	6.43	(755)	−0.072	0.695
NSPF-1993						
Total publications	Female	22.90	43.33	(302)		
in career (T)	Male	39.65	52.89	(1,543)	−0.101	0.578
Total publications	Female	4.47	6.50	(302)		
in last two years (Y)	Male	5.47	6.64	(1,543)	−0.072	0.817

the counts of publications in the last two years, which supports our earlier statement that the cumulative count is biased against women scientists.

According to the short-term measure of productivity (Y), the gender gap in productivity rate has appreciably narrowed over the 24-year period covered by these four surveys. In 1969, women's productivity rate was only 58 percent that of men. It increased steadily to 63 percent in 1973, 70 percent in 1988, and 82 percent in 1993. While the Carnegie-1969 data confirm Zuckerman's (1991, p. 43) statement that women publish at "50–60 percent" of men's rate, our results from the more recent surveys point to much smaller gender gaps. Instead of the "50–60 percent" range at earlier times, data from NSPF-1988 and NSPF-1993 suggest that the female-to-male productivity ratio now hovers around 70 to 80 percent.[7] Our result is consistent with the observation of Bentley and Blackburn (1992, p. 702) that "two-year publication differences between men and women have narrowed considerably since 1969." This finding represents a radical departure from the historically persistent pattern observed by Cole (1979, p. 242) and suggests that sex differences in productivity are not immune to social change.

Explaining Sex Differences in Research Productivity

It has long been recognized that sex differences in productivity are confounded by sex differences in other factors that are related to productivity. To explain sex differences in research productivity, we therefore invoke the multivariate approach described in Chapter 1. We attempt to explain the direct effect of sex on publication rate (the observed gender gap in publication productivity) by accounting for the intervening variables through which this effect operates. For each dataset, we build a series of hierarchical negative binomial models with the number of publications during the two years prior to the survey as the dependent variable.[8] We first begin with the bivariate model, with sex as the sole independent variable, and then sequentially introduce other background characteristics, structural locations and resources, and finally family status. We attempt to maintain parallel models across the four datasets, although measurement of the covariates differs slightly because of inconsistencies among the datasets. As variables are added, we are interested in how the net sex difference varies as relevant explanatory factors are controlled. Given the hypothesis that observed raw sex differences may result mainly from confounding factors rather than from sex *per se,* we are interested in whether the magnitude of the sex coefficient shrinks toward zero (or $\exp(b_{sex})$ toward one) as we gradually introduce more intervening covariates.

Previous research on the productivity puzzle has considered many covariates, such as age, time between the bachelor's degree and the Ph.D., prestige of the Ph.D. program, institutional type, and rank (Blackburn, Behymer, and Hall 1978; Clemente 1973; Cole 1979; Fox 1981; Fox and Faver 1985; Reskin 1978; Sonnert 1995a). Despite these efforts, researchers have consistently been concerned with the inadequacy of controls for structural factors that facilitate the production of scientific knowledge but are unequally distributed between men and women scientists. For example, Cole and Zuckerman (1984, pp. 248–49) call for paying closer attention to structural determinants and specifically recommend studying the social organization of scientific laboratories and departments and the allocation of time for teaching versus research. In the report titled *Climbing the Academic Ladder,* the Committee on the Education and Employment of Women in Science and Engineering (1979, p. 87) criticizes the existing literature for lacking adequate controls: "For the specific case of science faculty, factors such as access to appropriate research facilities, division of time between undergraduate and graduate teaching responsibilities, and especially availability of graduate and other research assistants may be of far greater significance to productivity than rank or other variables which have been controlled in [previous studies]." The report suggests, though it does not demonstrate, that sex differences in productivity found in earlier studies may be explained entirely by some important control variables absent from previous analyses.

Since the publication of *Climbing the Academic Ladder,* researchers have responded to these challenges by considering many control factors, particularly the influence of co-authorship and family status. Neither of these factors has been found to account for gender differences in publication productivity. As explained in Chapter 1, two conditions are necessary in order for an explanatory variable to explain gender differences in productivity: (1) the explanatory variable affects productivity in one direction; and (2) the explanatory variable is affected by sex in the opposite direction (with sex coded 1 for females and 0 for males). In the case of co-authorship, condition (2) is not satisfied: Women are just as likely as men to co-author papers (Cole and Zuckerman 1984; Long 1992). In the case of marriage and motherhood, condition (1) is not true: "Women scientists who marry and have families publish as many papers per year, on the average, as single women" (Cole and Zuckerman 1987, p. 125).

To the extent that past efforts have not located explanatory variables that mediate between sex and productivity, our confidence in the search for the mysterious other factors that will account for the gender gap in publication productivity weakens. If we exhaust all plausible explanations, the unexplained differences between the sexes in productivity can legitimately be called a "puzzle." Cole and Zuckerman (1984, p. 219) are skeptical that the control of observed variables measuring resources will explain the observed sex differences in research productivity.[9] We argue that such skepticism is premature, however, and incorporate into this study of sex differences in publication output many of the individual and structural determinants suggested in the literature, including variables that capture the monetary aspect of scientific resources. We, therefore, can clarify the debates, test competing hypotheses, and illuminate the puzzling question of why women scientists publish less than men scientists.

The control variables we include in our analysis are approximately parallel across the datasets. We include a measure of the quality of the employing institution at the time of the survey for all four datasets.[10] We include a measure of the time between the undergraduate and the doctorate degrees, defined as the difference between the year of graduation with a B.S. or B.A. and the year the scientist received his or her Ph.D. We control for years of experience, rank of academic position, and hours devoted to teaching.[11] We also include measures of research resources in the multivariate analysis, as all of the surveys asked questions about access to research assistance and receipt of research funding from five sources (federal, state, private, industrial, and own institution).[12] The final variable added to the hierarchical models measures a scientist's family status. Consistent with the earlier chapters, family status is coded into three categories: unmarried, married without children, and married with children for Carnegie-1969 and ACE-1973. We cannot, however, distinguish the last two categories in NSPF-1988 and NSPF-1993, which did not collect information on parental status. Thus, for NSPF-1988 and NSPF-1993, family status is measured as whether or not a scientist is married. Definitions and descriptive statistics for the complete set of covariate variables used in the multivariate analysis are presented in Appendix Tables D9.a through D9.d.

The descriptive statistics in the appendix tables show that the relative status of women science faculty improved during the study period (Bentley and Blackburn 1992). Consistent with earlier findings (Fox 1995, p. 212; Long and Fox 1995; Rosenfeld 1991), our data indicate that women scientists have been more concentrated in teaching colleges and less likely to be found in research universities than their male counterparts.[13] This was particularly true in early years, although the trend over time is clearly one of convergence toward equity. The average teaching loads of male and female scientists also became more equitable during the period. Similarly, sex differences in research funding appear to have narrowed appreciably. The female-to-male ratio of funding from federal sources, for example, is 0.52 in Carnegie-1969, 0.70 in ACE-1973, 1.08 in NSPF-1988, and 0.99 in NSPF-1993. These statistics illustrating the improvement of women scientists' status and access to resources are consistent with the findings of a recent report commissioned by the National Research Council (Long 2001).

Causality

Cole (1979, p. 68) remarks, "Other variables such as differences in teaching responsibilities, access to research funds, and opportunity to collaborate with other outstanding scientists might account for the differences in published productivity of men and women." Cole's suggestion is tantamount to the statistical control of structural and resource variables in teasing out the net effect of sex on productivity (see Figure 1.2 and associated discussion). However, are structural and resource variables such as institutional affiliation, rank, funding, and teaching hours necessarily causes of productivity?

The answer is no. For example, it is possible that type of current institution, rank, research resources, and so on are consequences as well as causes of productivity. Clearly, the causality between research productivity and resource variables is reciprocal. Without experimental data or at least longitudinal data, we cannot identify the reciprocal causality. We contend that it is still useful to control these variables in our model of publication productivity and to interpret the results descriptively. Our main rationale is that the resource variables are likely to be outcomes of cumulative productivity, whereas our measure of research productivity is short-term. This distinction in timing gives us some leverage for treating the resource variables as exogenous, because for most individuals the resource variables temporarily precede rather than succeed the current level of productivity. Consider the example of research funding. While it is reasonable to expect past productivity to affect the availability of funding, it seems much less likely that current productivity has a large influence on the current availability of funding. Still, causal inference is difficult here because current productivity may merely be a proxy for earlier productivity, where both are caused by some unobserved common factors such as "ability" or "diligence," which can underlie both past productivity and current productivity.

With longitudinal data, it is possible to partial out the unobserved heterogeneity under the assumption that these characteristics are fixed (Allison and Long 1990). With cross-sectional data, unobserved heterogeneity is uncontrolled and may confound the causal relationship between the measured resource variables and productivity. When this is the case, the resource variables are proxies for underlying causes and thus serve as "proximate determinants" of productivity. It is in this sense that we wish to draw descriptive, rather than causal, inferences from our multivariate model.

Some support for tentatively treating the resource variables as exogenous is found in prior research showing the asymmetry of the reciprocal relationship between productivity and resource allocation. Despite the common wisdom that high productivity leads to appointment at prestigious universities, empirical evidence suggests a more complicated picture: although higher productivity does not necessarily mean appointment at prestigious institutions, movement to more prestigious institutions enhances productivity (Allison and Long 1987, 1990; Long 1978; Long, Allison, and McGinnis 1979). Although similar asymmetric relationships may exist between productivity and other resource variables, we are not aware of empirical evidence that supports this conjecture.

Multivariate Results

The main findings from our multivariate analysis are summarized in Table 9.2. Parallel results are presented from each dataset. Four model specifications are presented in hierarchical order for each dataset, with a lower-numbered specification nested within a higher-numbered specification. The simplest specification is Model 0, which includes only the effect of sex. The exponential function of the estimated coefficient for sex ($\exp(b_{sex})$) from this baseline model yields the observed female-to-male ratio of mean productivity (R). Model 1 adds controls for the following individual background variables: field, time lag between bachelor and doctoral degrees, and years of experience beyond the doctoral degree. The introduction of these control variables significantly improves the explanatory power of the model for all of the datasets.[14]

In Model 2, we add the variables measuring type of current institution, academic rank, teaching hours, research funding, and research assistance. While the background variables included in Model 1 are

Table 9.2 Estimated female-to-male ratio of publication count for four negative binomial models of research productivity: Carnegie-1969, ACE-1973, NSPF-1988, and NSPF-1993

Model description	Carnegie-1969	ACE-1973	NSPF-1988	NSPF-1993
(0): Sex	0.580***	0.632***	0.695**	0.817
(1): (0) + Field + Time between BA/BS and Ph.D. + Years of experience	0.630***	0.663***	0.800	0.789*
(2): (1) + Type of current institution + Rank + Teaching hours + Research funding + Research assistance	0.952	0.936	0.775	0.931
(3): (2) + Family/Marital status	0.997	0.971	0.801	0.944

*$p < .05$, **$p < .01$, ***$p < .001$ (two-tailed test for the hypothesis that research productivity is the same between women and men).

clearly exogenous to the dependent variable measuring productivity, the resource variables introduced in Model 2 are potentially contaminated by reciprocal causality with respect to productivity. Again, we observe that the covariates strongly affect the two-year publication count, with a significant improvement in goodness-of-fit over Model 1.[15] Finally, we include the family status variable in Model 3. Except for the Carnegie-1969 data, however, family status does not significantly improve the explanatory power of the statistical model.[16]

For all four datasets, the introduction of the control variables significantly reduces the net sex difference in productivity. Although these control variables are rather crude, their unequal distribution by sex helps explain the estimated gender gap in productivity. For the first two datasets, the estimated female-to-male ratio of publication rates increases dramatically with the inclusion of these controls: for Carnegie-1969, from 0.580 in Model 0 to 0.630 in Model 1 and 0.952 in Model 2; for ACE-1973, from 0.632 in Model 0 to 0.663 in Model 1 and 0.936 in Model 2. For both of these datasets, the female-to-male ratio is no longer significantly different from one in Model 2.

For NSPF-1988, the ratio is statistically insignificant for all the models except the baseline model.[17] For NSPF-1993, the estimated sex ratio is insignificant in Model 0; it becomes marginally significant in Model 1 (at 0.789) but insignificant again in Model 2 (at 0.931).

Between the two earlier surveys and the two later surveys, there is a notable decrease in the power of the resource variables introduced in Model 2 to explain sex differences in productivity. The reason for this trend is *not* a decline in the association between these resource variables and productivity, for there is evidence that the strength of the association has increased over time (Bentley and Blackburn 1992).[18] Rather, this trend is a result of the fact that these resources have become more equally distributed between men and women (Shauman and Xie 1998).

Model 3 includes marital status as an explanatory variable. Although previous research has found childbearing to have a negative effect on productivity for both men and women scientists (Hargens, McCann, and Reskin 1978), there is reason to hypothesize that marriage is a personal asset, especially for men (see Chapter 7). A scientist's work may benefit from marriage because of the additional economic resources and emotional support contributed by a spouse. In addition, a spouse also may provide domestic help that may free up time for the scientist's research. For the Carnegie-1969 data, we found that married scientists, no matter whether they have children or not, have significantly higher (about 10 percent higher) rates of productivity than unmarried scientists, controlling for other factors included in the model. Given that women scientists are less likely than men scientists to be married (Marwell, Rosenfeld, and Spilerman 1979; Shauman and Xie 1996), women scientists, on average, are less likely to benefit from marriage. On the whole, however, family status does not help us further explain sex differences in publication productivity once resources are controlled for in Model 2.

In earlier chapters, we observed that, for at least some labor force outcomes, marriage benefits men scientists more than women scientists. To test whether the effect of marriage on productivity differs by gender, we add an interaction effect between marriage and sex to Model 3. To our surprise, this interaction is not statistically significant.[19]

Parameter estimates for the last model are presented in Appendix Tables D9.a through D9.d. Inspection of the results reveals that the estimated effects for all the remaining covariates included in the multivariate analysis are in the expected direction. Because our main focus is on sex differences in research productivity, we make only two brief observations based on other regression coefficients from the final model. First, the estimated pattern of experience agrees with Levin and Stephan's (1991; Stephan and Levin 1992) finding that scientists' productivity peaks early in their careers and then decreases with experience. Second, time between a bachelor's degree and the Ph.D. has a negative effect on productivity. For example, those who took more than ten years between degrees are 30 to 40 percent less productive than those who completed their Ph.D. within four years. Because women are much more likely (by as much as 50 percent) than men to take 11 or more years between a bachelor's degree and a Ph.D., the negative effect of time to Ph.D. contributes to women scientists' lower rates of productivity relative to men's.

Decomposition of Explanatory Power

To examine the relative explanatory power of each covariate in our analysis, we decompose the total explanatory power to components uniquely attributable to the different explanatory factors, using the method devised by Xie and Shauman (1998) and described in Appendix B. The results presented in Appendix Table D9.e show the extent to which the inclusion or exclusion of an individual factor affects the estimated gender gap in publication productivity ($\exp(b_{sex})$).

Several findings emerge from the decomposition analysis reported in Appendix Table D9.e. First, the range between the "low" and the "high" estimates is fairly large for most of the explanatory factors. This reflects the joint explanatory power among different factors and makes the task of decomposing explanatory power difficult. In other words, the wide range of the estimates indicates that the influence of any single covariate on the estimated gender gap in publication rates depends to a large extent on what other variables are already controlled in the model. Second, the time lag between a bachelor's degree and a Ph.D., institution type, and family status are uniformly positive across all the columns. This finding indicates that gender differences on these characteristics help explain the gender gap in publication independently of other variables. In contrast, the other background and resource variables do not perform consistently.

Selectivity

A clear finding of our analysis is that net sex differences in productivity are small to nil once other personal characteristics, structural settings, and facilitating resources are taken into account. As mentioned earlier, however, interpretation of this result is less clear. The covariates we use may be the effects, rather than the causes, of research productivity, or they may be jointly determined by other unobserved variables, such as motivation and ability. For example, men scientists may score favorably on variables measuring structural locations and resources conducive to research because such structural locations and resources are rewards for high productivity. Consider academic rank, which is highly dependent on productivity (Long, Allison, and McGinnis 1993). As can be calculated from Appendix Tables D9.a through D9.d, full professors are more productive than associate professors, and associate professors are in turn more productive than assistant professors. From the first two columns of the Appendix tables, we observe that women scientists are more likely to be found at lower ranks than men (also see Ahern and Scott 1981, pp. 34–39; Long 2001, pp. 171–180).

Because promotion depends on productivity, promotion is always selective. Unproductive scientists are either kept at the entry (or a relatively low) rank or encouraged to leave academia. With productivity as an important criterion for promotion, women scientists should be promoted more slowly if they indeed publish less than men. Lacking the necessary longitudinal information, we cannot depict the career trajectory of sex differences in productivity as is done by Cole and Zuckerman (1984) and Long (1992). For this reason, the reader should exercise caution in interpreting the results from our statistical models.

Conclusion

Have we solved "the productivity puzzle"? The answer is both yes and no. The answer is yes in the sense that we have successfully identified differences between men and women scientists in personal characteristics, structural positions, and facilitating resources that account for women's lower research productivity. That is, we have found that women scientists publish fewer papers than men because women are less likely than men to have the personal characteristics, structural positions, and facilitating resources that are conducive to publication. There is very little *direct* effect of sex on research productivity. However, we still do not know *why* men and women scientists differ systematically in these important dimensions, and in this sense the puzzle remains unsolved. This research therefore replaces "the old puzzle of productivity differences with a new puzzle involving differences in personal and structural characteristics."[20] In fact, this "new" puzzle is closely related to a long-standing interest in differences in career trajectories between men and women scientists (Bernard 1964; Rossi 1972; Zuckerman 1991). We have simply demonstrated the empirical link between gender differences in career characteristics and the gender gap in publication rates—an important measure of career outcome among academic scientists.

Another important finding of this research is that overall sex differences in research productivity among academic scientists have declined in recent years. With the number of publications in the last two years as the measure of productivity, we find that the female-to-male ratio in productivity increased from around 60 percent in 1969 and 1973 to 70 percent in 1988 and 82 percent and 1993. A major reason for this trend is that the distribution of resources and structural positions, albeit still unfavorable to women, has become more equitable over the observed time period (Long 2001).

The empirical evidence presented in our analysis is significant in its own right, even if theoretical interpretations of it may remain inconclusive for the time being. Some of the debates in the literature are of an empirical nature and can be settled with better data or better data analysis. Our results suggest that the notion of sex differences in research productivity as "the productivity puzzle" may be misleading for three reasons. First, when properly defined and operationalized, the magnitude of raw sex differences in research productivity is smaller than previously claimed.[21] Second, to the extent that sex differences can be explained by personal characteristics, employment positions, and access to resources, sex differences in research productivity have structural causes that can be further investigated. Calling it a puzzle, therefore, mystifies an observed pattern. Finally, as a manifestation of deeper social processes, sex differences in research productivity have declined in response to the improvement of women's representation and status in science, while the notion of a puzzle suggests an inherently static and persistent nature of the phenomenon.

Taken as a whole, the available evidence lends further support to the notion that men and women scientists often pursue or are pushed onto somewhat different career tracks. It has long been recognized that values and career ambitions differ between the sexes (Bernard 1964; Davis 1964, 1965; Turner 1964). Much of the source of this difference is sex-typed socialization (Marini and Brinton 1984). However, a nontrivial part of the difference can also be traced to women's extra family responsibilities associated with childbearing (Shauman and Xie 1996). In this study, we reaffirm the importance of structural sources of gender inequality in science: women and men scientists are located in different academic structures with differential access to valuable resources. Our study confirms the pattern found in other studies (Fox 1995; Long 2001; Zuckerman 1991)—that men generally have positions superior to those of women, although structural differences by gender have appreciably declined over time. Once sex differences in such positions and resources are taken into account, as in this study, net differences between men and women in research productivity are nil or negligible.

CHAPTER TEN

Immigrant Scientists/Engineers

Immigrants are an important part of the scientific workforce in the United States. According to the 1990 census, 11.7 percent of all scientists in the United States are foreign-born (Bouvier and Martin 1995); only 8.5 percent of the general population were born elsewhere (Edmonston and Passel 1994). Based on our estimate from the 5 percent Public Use Microsample (PUMS) of the 1990 U.S. census, we find that immigrants constitute an even higher proportion (24 percent) of scientists with advanced degrees. Despite the potential influence of immigration on the gender composition of the S/E labor force and on gender differences in labor force outcomes of scientists and engineers, past literature on women in science and engineering has paid little attention to immigration. In this chapter we attempt to redress this oversight by presenting empirical information about this important subpopulation—immigrant women scientists/engineers.

The large proportion of immigrants among scientists has led to heated discussions, among policymakers and academics alike, concerning the experiences of immigrant scientists and the impact of immigrant scientists on the S/E labor force. From these discussions, two perspectives have emerged. For the sake of brevity, we name them the "displacement perspective" and the "discrimination perspective." According to the displacement perspective, which is well represented by North (1995), immigrant scientists put downward pressure on the pay structure in science and thereby displace native-born scientists.

One implication of this perspective is that immigrant scientists occupy positions (from fellowships to faculty appointments) that might otherwise be taken by women and native-born minorities, thus slowing their entry into science. In contrast, the discrimination perspective posits that immigrant scientists face unfair treatment in the U.S. labor market. Tang (1993, 2000), for example, argues that Asian-American immigrants are much less likely to be promoted to desirable positions than are their native-born, Caucasian counterparts. By focusing on inequalities in labor market outcomes by nativity, both of these perspectives overlook the intersection between immigration and gender.

There are two important reasons for studying gender differences in the experiences of immigrant scientists. First, immigrant women scientists are numerically a large subpopulation, constituting about a fifth of all immigrant scientists; they potentially influence women's representation in the S/E labor force in the United States. Second, since men and women immigrants may have different labor market outcomes, inattention to gender could result in an inaccurate characterization of the experiences of immigrant scientists. For example, female immigrants' family situations or immigration paths may set them apart from both male immigrants and native-born female scientists.

In this chapter, we invoke the displacement and discrimination perspectives in order to draw attention to immigrant scientists, but we do not directly test hypotheses derived from these two viewpoints. Instead, our main objective is to provide an empirical account of immigrant women scientists' influence on and experience in the S/E labor force. First, we examine whether or not the large influx of immigrant scientists contributes to, or redresses, the underrepresentation of women in science, by documenting the gender composition of immigrant scientists. Next, we explore the ways that the labor force outcomes (i.e., employment, earnings, and promotions) of immigrant women scientists differ from those of immigrant men. We then compare these gender differences among immigrant scientists with differences among native-born scientists.

For the analyses presented in this chapter, we use samples from the 5 percent PUMS from the 1990 U.S. census and longitudinal data from SSE in 1982–1989. These data sources are described in Appendix A, and the analytical samples are described in Chapter 7. As in Chapter 7, we restrict our analysis to scientists and engineers with at least a master's degree. We use the sample of 37,034 individuals from the PUMS data to examine the representation of women immigrants in various scientific fields and differences in employment and earnings by gender and immigration status. Since the cross-sectional PUMS data cannot be used to study dynamic processes of career development, we use the SSE data for a recent cohort of scientists/engineers to examine longitudinal patterns of promotion to management by gender and immigration status. The SSE sample used for this event-history analysis contains a total of 6,183 person-periods during which 2,560 individuals could attain a promotion to management between 1982 and 1989.

Differential attrition by nativity and gender in the SSE sample presents potential problems for our study. However, it is likely that our estimates of differences in promotion rates by nativity are conservatively biased. It is reasonable to postulate that less successful immigrants may return to their native countries if they are not satisfied in the U.S. labor market. Thus, immigrants who had been retained in the SSE follow-up surveys were likely to be more successful than those who had not. If this reasoning holds true, the differences between immigrants and native-born scientists in the observed follow-up surveys are smaller than they would be absent attrition.

The Impact of Immigration on the Gender Composition of the U.S. S/E Labor Force

The displacement perspective asserts that the large influx of immigrant scientists/engineers depresses the representation of women in S/E because immigrants occupy positions that might otherwise be filled by women (e.g., North 1995). This reasoning overlooks the possibility that *female* immigrant scientists/engineers may contribute to a more balanced representation of women in the domestic S/E labor force. In this section, we document the impact of female immigrants on the gender composition of scientists/engineers.

Based on data from the 1990 PUMS, Table 10.1 presents the percentage of women among scientists/engineers with at least a master's degree, by immigration status, field, and education level. Using the sample sizes reported in parentheses, we calculate that about 24 percent of all scientists are immigrants (Panel A). This percentage is higher (at 30 percent in Panel C) for doctoral scientists/engineers than

Table 10.1 The representation of women in science and engineering by immigration status and field

	Total		Native-born		Foreign-born	
	Female %	(*n*)	Female %	(*n*)	Female %	(*n*)
Panel A: Whole sample						
All Fields	17.91	(37,034)	17.76	(28,069)	18.35	(8,965)
Biological	31.38	(3,458)	30.70	(2,743)	33.99	(715)
Engineering	8.20	(16,775)	8.52	(12,423)	7.28	(4,352)
Mathematical	28.07	(11,626)	27.35	(8,874)	30.38	(2,752)
Physical	17.53	(5,175)	16.33	(4,029)	21.73	(1,146)
Panel B: Master's and professional degrees only						
All Fields	18.89	(29,897)	18.59	(23,051)	19.92	(6,846)
Biological	35.26	(1,957)	33.79	(1,598)	41.78	(359)
Engineering	8.56	(14,898)	8.84	(11,295)	7.69	(3,603)
Mathematical	29.77	(10,229)	28.83	(7,839)	32.85	(2,390)
Physical	22.68	(2,813)	20.96	(2,319)	30.77	(494)
Panel C: Ph.D.s only						
All Fields	13.76	(7,137)	13.97	(5,018)	13.26	(2,119)
Biological	26.32	(1,501)	26.38	(1,145)	26.12	(356)
Engineering	5.33	(1,877)	5.32	(1,128)	5.34	(749)
Mathematical	15.60	(1,397)	16.14	(1,035)	14.09	(362)
Physical	11.39	(2,362)	10.06	(1,710)	14.88	(652)

Source: 5 percent PUMS from the 1990 U.S. census.

it is for scientists/engineers with a master's degree (at 23 percent, Panel B). Comparison of the percentage of women by nativity reveals the contribution of immigrants to the gender composition of the S/E labor force. If the percentage of women is lower among foreign-born scientists/engineers than among native-born scientists/engineers, immigration decreases the representation of women in S/E. For each of the three panels, the first row indicates that women constitute a similar proportion among immigrant scientists/engineers as among native-born scientists/engineers. For example, in the whole sample, the proportion of women is about 18 percent both among foreign-born scientists/engineers and among native-born scientists/engineers. Thus, it seems that immigration does not alter the gender composition of scientists/engineers.

The above comparisons are a little misleading, however, because they obscure variation by field of science and engineering. Once the percentages are broken down by field (rows 2 through 5 in Panel A), the percentage of women is higher among immigrant scientists than among native-born scientists for all fields except engineering. For example, 34 percent of immigrant biological scientists are women, compared with 31 percent of native-born biological scientists. Similarly, women make up greater proportions of immigrant scientists in mathematical science (at 30 percent) and physical science (at 22 percent) than do their native-born counterparts (at 27 and 16 percent, respectively). However, the positive contribution of immigration to women's representation in science is limited mostly to scientists with a master's degree, as the above observation does not apply to biological and mathematical scientists with a doctoral degree (shown in Panel C).

The Labor Force Outcomes of Immigrant Women Scientists/Engineers

Research on immigrants' participation in the S/E labor force often finds that immigrants are disadvantaged in comparison with native-born scientists/engineers. Immigrants may experience higher unemployment rates and lower salaries, as well as slower rates of promotion. Consideration of promotion is important, because although immigrants' disadvantage in salaries may be relatively small, given the technical nature of their jobs, their promotion prospects may be significantly less favorable (Takaki 1989; Tang 1993, 2000).

Most research on immigrants has not explicitly considered gender differences in labor market experiences (Koch 1987; North 1995; Tang 1993; Vasegh-Daneshvary, Schlottmann, and Herzog 1987). We therefore have an incomplete picture of immigrants' experience, because immigrant women's labor market characteristics may differ from those of their male peers not only as a result of possible gender discrimination, but also as a result of potential gender differences in human capital characteristics, family experiences, and circumstances of immigration to the United States (Pedraza 1991). Some researchers have studied immigrant women's experiences in the labor market in general (Cobb-Clark 1993; Hughey 1990; Pedraza 1991; Stier 1991), but these studies provide us with few clues as to whether immigrant women encounter distinct disadvantages in the S/E labor force.

Our discussion of the labor force outcomes of immigrant scientists/

engineers proceeds in two stages that parallel the analysis presented in Chapter 7. First, we present descriptive statistics on employment characteristics and earnings from the PUMS and on promotion rates from the SSE, by gender and nativity. Next, we apply multivariate models to the PUMS and SSE data in order to control for factors that could confound the descriptive results. We then compare the observed female-to-male ratios measuring gender differences in employment, earnings, and promotion to adjusted ratios calculated using results from the multivariate models.

Describing Labor Force Outcomes by Immigration Status and Gender

The top panel of Table 10.2 presents a few key statistics measuring aggregate labor force outcomes by gender and nativity. These statistics were calculated from the 1990 PUMS. The first row in Table 10.2 reports the labor force participation rate, which is defined as the ratio of the number of persons in the labor force, including those employed

Table 10.2 Labor force characteristics and promotion rates by sex and immigration status

	Native-born scientists/engineers		Foreign-born scientists/engineers	
	Female	Male	Female	Male
Panel A: Employment characteristics from the 1990 census PUMS				
In labor force (%)	92.4	96.2	92.3	96.6
Employed (%)[a]	98.6	98.6	96.1	97.7
Full-time employed (%)[b]	90.1	96.6	91.4	96.1
Earnings [c] (1989)	$39,617	$52,967	$38,433	$50,565
Log earnings [c]	10.51	10.78	10.48	10.73
(*n*)	(3,673)	(20,129)	(1,162)	(6,090)
Panel B: Rates for promotion to management from the SSE, 1982–1989				
Promotion rate to management	0.070	0.093	0.036	0.117
(*n*)	(1,324)	(3,919)	(152)	(788)

Sources: 1990 PUMS for employment status and earnings, and 1982–1989 SSE for promotion to management.

a. Percent employed is conditional on labor force participation.

b. Percent full-time employed is conditional on employment.

c. Earnings and log earnings are based on earnings of workers employed full-time, year-round with positive earnings in 1989.

as well as those unemployed but seeking jobs, to the total population. Being out of the labor force means that a person is not working and not actively seeking a job. The labor force participation rates calculated from the PUMS data are generally very close to unity for both men and women. For men scientists/engineers, labor force participation is around 96–97 percent; for women scientists/engineers, it is about 92 percent. As discussed in Chapter 7, the large magnitudes of these labor force participation rates are mainly due to the fact that our definition of a scientist/engineer requires current activity or recent experience in the labor force.

In the second row, we report the employment rate, defined as the number of workers employed divided by the number of workers in the labor force. The employment rate does not differ appreciably by nativity status for men, at 98–99 percent. For women, however, the employment rate is slightly higher for native-born scientists/engineers (at 99 percent) than for their immigrant counterparts (at 96 percent). Despite these slight differences in employment rate, the proportion of scientists/engineers reporting full-time employment is comparable between immigrants and their native-born peers. As is shown in the third row of Table 10.2, about 96–97 percent of both native-born and foreign-born employed male scientists/engineers reported working full-time. Among women, about 90–91 percent of both immigrants and their native-born peers were employed full-time in 1989.

We next report summary descriptive results pertaining to earnings among workers who were employed full-time, year-round in 1989. Our calculation is restricted to respondents with positive earnings who worked more than 34 hours in a typical week for more than 39 weeks in 1989. We present, by gender and immigration status, the average annual earnings in the fourth row and the average logged annual earnings in the fifth row.[1] Immigrant men make on average $2,402 less per year (in 1989 dollars) than native-born male scientists/engineers, a 5 percent disadvantage. Among women, this pay penalty for immigrants is smaller: female immigrants earn $1,184 less per year than native-born female scientists/engineers, a 3 percent disadvantage.[2]

The second panel of Table 10.2 presents the rates of promotion to managerial positions, by gender and nativity, among a cohort of scientists/engineers, using pooled data from the 1982, 1984, 1986, and 1989 waves of the SSE. As in Chapter 7, the promotion rates were calculated for three intervals (1982–1984, 1984–1986, and 1986–1989) for respondents in nonmanagerial positions at risk of promotion at the beginning of each interval. Once a respondent is in a managerial position, he/she is removed (or "censored") from risk for promotion in future intervals. The promotion rates given in the second-to-last line of Table 10.2 are aggregated over the three intervals. These descriptive statistics show that while men experience higher promotion rates than women regardless of immigration status, immigration has a slightly positive effect on promotion for men but a negative effect for women. Approximately 9 percent of native-born male scientists/engineers and 12 percent of immigrant male scientists/engineers in this cohort had been promoted to management at the end of the seven years of observation. In contrast, however, about 7 percent of native-born women were promoted during this time while less than 4 percent of immigrant women attained a promotion to management.

Explaining Gender Differences in Labor Force Outcomes by Immigration Status

To tease out the net effects associated with being an immigrant woman scientist/engineer, we must control for other potentially confounding factors and assess the extent to which these factors explain the observed differences by gender and immigration status reported in Table 10.2. Toward this end, we estimate statistical models that parallel the multivariate analysis in Chapter 7. As in Chapter 7, we control for several groups of variables in modeling the odds of employment, the earnings rate, and the odds of promotion: the demographic characteristics, measures of human capital, indicators of field and business sector of employment, and family status (see Chapter 7 for descriptions of the variables). In addition, we include indicators of immigrant status and proficiency with the English language in all the models and measures of labor supply in the model predicting earnings. See Appendix Tables D10.a and D10.b for variable definitions.

Immigration Status. The descriptive statistics show that immigration status affects employment outcomes somewhat differently for men and women. Women scientists/engineers may be more likely than men to be secondary (or tied) migrants; that is, migration may have been motivated by their spouses' career more often for women scientists/engineers than for men (Lichter 1983; Maxwell 1988; Shauman and Xie 1996). If so, labor market prospects for women who are secondary immigrants may not be as good as for those who are primary, employer-sponsored immigrants (Pedraza 1991). Since we do not have a good measure of immigration path, we test this hypothesis by using two proxy indicators: family status and immigration status. Immigration status is measured with two categories: native-born and foreign-born.

English Proficiency. Lack of English skills may also hamper one's success in the labor market (Hughey 1990; Koch 1987; Portes and Rumbaut 1990). Not controlling for English proficiency may lead to an overestimation of the gaps in labor force outcomes between native-born scientists and their immigrant counterparts. In our multivariate analyses of the PUMS data, English proficiency is measured with an indicator variable. Unfortunately, English proficiency was not measured in the SSE survey.

For this analysis we are particularly interested in measuring the effects of family status and immigration status on the career outcomes of scientists/engineers. Given the frequency of secondary migration women immigrants may be more likely to be married and/or to have more young children who need care than native-born women. These family responsibilities may compete with a female scientist's career for her time (Hughey 1990; Koch 1987; Peek 1995; Shauman and Xie 1996; Stier 1991). To test the effects of family status, we include in our analyses the three-category variable contrasting those who are unmarried, married without children, and married with children.

We include an interaction between gender and immigration status to reveal the unique labor force outcomes experienced by immigrant women scientists/engineers. The interaction is intended as an indirect test of the hypothesis that immigrant women scientists/engineers are particularly disadvantaged in the labor market because they are more likely to be secondary immigrants. Note that we do not have direct measures to distinguish secondary immigrants from primary immigrants.

In Table 10.3, we present female-to-male ratios for three outcomes: employment odds, earnings rate, and promotion odds. We first focus on the upper panel of this table, which presents the "observed," or crude, female-to-male ratios. These crude sex ratios can be calculated from the descriptive statistics in Table 10.2 (with small discrepancies due to rounding).

The first column reports the female-to-male ratios for odds of em-

Table 10.3 Observed and adjusted female-to-male ratios measuring gender gaps in employment, earnings, and promotion to management by immigrant status

	Odds of employment	Earnings rate	Odds of promotion
Observed			
Native-born	1.044	0.759***	0.735
Foreign-born	0.595***	0.773***	0.286*
Adjusted			
Native-born	1.084	0.889***	0.750
Foreign-born	0.586***	0.875***	0.321*

Sources: 5 percent 1990 PUMS for employment status and earnings, and 1982–1989 SSE for promotion to management.

Note: Analysis is restricted to scientists and engineers with master's degrees or higher. "Adjusted" sex ratios control for age, race, education, field of study, employment sector, family status, English proficiency, and, in the case of earnings, weeks and hours worked. See Appendix Tables D10.a and D10.b for details.

$*p < .05$, $**p < .01$, $***p < .001$ (two-tailed test of the null hypothesis of no gender difference).

ployment by nativity. We see a substantial difference in the observed sex ratios by immigration status. While native-born women are as likely as their male peers to be employed, immigrant women are only 60 percent as likely (in terms of odds) to be employed as immigrant men. This gender difference is statistically significant. The second column presents the ratio of women's earnings to men's among those who are employed full-time. Here we see similar sex ratios between native-born scientists and foreign-born scientists, with women scientists/engineers making about 76–77 percent as much as men.

In the last column, we present gender differences in the rate of promotion to management positions by nativity.[3] These data come from the cohort of scientists and engineers in SSE with ten or fewer years of professional experience in 1982. We find the gender difference to be large and statistically significant among foreign-born scientists/engineers but statistically insignificant among native-born scientists. The estimates suggest that immigrant women scientists/engineers are promoted at about 29 percent the rate of their male counterparts, and this gender gap among immigrants is statistically significant.

Can other relevant factors explain these observed patterns? To answer this question, in the bottom panel of Table 10.3 we present the adjusted female-to-male ratios from multivariate models that control for demographic characteristics, employment characteristics, human capital, and family responsibilities. Specifically, we calculated female-to-male ratios in the odds of employment, the earnings rate, and the odds of promotion from the coefficients of the sex variable in multivariate models that also include age, race, education, field, employment sector, family status, English proficiency, and, in the case of the earnings rate, labor supply. For the odds of employment and the odds of promotion, a logit model is used. For the earnings rate, linear regression is used with logged earnings as the dependent variable. Appendix Table D10.a and Appendix Table D10.b present the full set of estimated coefficients and the associated z-ratios (or t-ratios) for the multivariate models.

The first column of the bottom panel of Table 10.3 shows the adjusted female-to-male ratios in employment. As is true for the observed ratios in the upper panel, there is virtually no gender difference in the odds of employment among native-born scientists. Immigrant women still face a disadvantage net of other control variables, however, and the magnitude of the estimated difference is hardly changed in the multivariate model. We thus conclude that disadvantages in employment faced by foreign-born women relative to men cannot be explained by such factors as field, human capital, employment sector, and family status.

These same factors explain only a small portion of the entire gap between men and women scientists' earnings. Once employment sector, human capital, labor supply, and family responsibilities are accounted for, women scientists earn about 88–89 percent as much as men. The explanatory power of these factors does not differ much by nativity. For both groups of scientists/engineers, the included covariates account for just over ten percent of women's disadvantage in earnings.

The multivariate analysis of the odds of promotion is conducted using an event-history model. Given that the original 1982 SSE panel was reinterviewed in 1984, 1986, and 1989, our analysis is based on changes over three discrete time intervals: 1982–1984, 1984–1986, and 1986–1989. A scientist/engineer contributes to the sample at risk of promotion until he/she is actually promoted or drops out of the study. The summary results of the event-history model are given in the last column (lower panel). Here, we find that the included explanatory factors do not account for the observed gender differences by immigration status. Among native-born scientists/engineers, there is no significant gender difference. Among immigrant scientists/engineers, the adjusted gender difference remains large, suggesting that for every 100 male immigrants who are promoted, only 32 female immigrant scientists/engineers who share the same characteristics as their male peers are promoted. Part of this large gender gap is due to the slightly higher likelihood of immigrant men being promoted (see Table 10.2). However, most of this gap is due to a unique disadvantage faced by immigrant women. The above results are consistent with the hypothesis that immigrant women may occupy less desirable and less competitive positions in the labor market because they are secondary immigrants.

Conclusion

The preceding results unambiguously highlight the importance of considering immigrant women in studies of women in science. For example, debates about the impact of immigration on women's representation in science and engineering often fail to consider that immigrant women may, in fact, reduce the gender imbalance in some scientific fields. In this study, we find that immigration works to increase women's representation in biological science, mathematical science, and physical science at the master's level.

Our knowledge of disadvantages faced by immigrant scientists/engineers in the labor force (e.g. Tang 1993, 2000) is also improved by explicitly considering gender within the immigrant S/E population. Our analysis of the PUMS data reveals that demographic characteristics, employment characteristics, and family responsibilities account for some of the disadvantages in earnings that immigrant women scientists/engineers face in comparison with immigrant men. However, they do not account for immigrant women's lower rate of employment. Further, in our analysis with the SSE data focusing on a relatively homogeneous group—one cohort of scientists and engineers with little professional experience—over a period of seven years, we find that immigrant women are promoted at a rate that is less than a third as high as the rate for immigrant men. By comparison, native-born women are not similarly disadvantaged.

Our results concerning employment and promotion point to the special disadvantages experienced by immigrant women scientists/engineers. We speculate that this pattern may be caused by a common immigration path taken by many female immigrants—that as the spouses of immigrant men. This speculation is consistent with the migration literature that argues that married women who migrate often do so to benefit husbands' careers rather than their own careers (Lichter 1983; Maxwell 1988). As secondary immigrants, these women scientists/engineers may have more difficulty finding jobs appropriate for their skills that provide opportunities for career mobility.

CHAPTER ELEVEN

Conclusion

In this book, we have presented a systematic study of women in science and engineering. Following a life course approach, our study traces gender differences along the career process of becoming a scientist/engineer as well as in career outcomes among scientists/engineers. The life course approach has led us to recognize that science/engineering careers are multifaceted in nature and are affected by influences at the individual, familial, and social levels. We illustrated the multifaceted nature of S/E careers through our examination of a few important aspects of S/E career processes and outcomes: the attainment of S/E education, career transitions following the completion of undergraduate and graduate S/E education, labor force participation, earnings, promotion, geographic mobility, immigration, and research productivity.

Our research addresses gender differences in the processes and outcomes of S/E careers with detailed statistical analyses of data drawn from seventeen large, nationally representative datasets. Summarizing the findings across these analyses is not an easy task. If we were asked to give a one-word summary, it would be *complexity:* We have found that gender differences in S/E career processes and outcomes are extremely complex, and this complexity necessitates careful and detailed analyses such as those presented in this book. No simplistic explanation should or could substitute for the richness of the empirical results from these analyses. In this concluding chapter, we aim to highlight some of the major findings of the study and discuss their implications.

Major Findings

As discussed in Chapter 1, a sizable literature on women in science already exists. One of the important tasks of our study was to provide an empirical evaluation, with updated data and appropriate analytical methods, of the key hypotheses and claims widely accepted in the literature and commonly believed by the scholarly community and the general public alike. Surprisingly, we found clear evidence rejecting many of these hypotheses and claims.

One of the longstanding hypotheses in the literature is that women are less likely to pursue S/E careers because they are handicapped by deficits in high school mathematics training. For example, discussing career barriers for both minorities and women, Sells (1980, p. 66) claims that "[a] student's level of high-school mathematics achievement acts as a critical filter for undergraduate college admission for blacks and limits choices of an undergraduate major for women in general once they are admitted to college." Although this hypothesis is appealing for its simplicity and the clear remedy it implies, it has not been subjected to a rigorous empirical test. We conducted the analyses in Chapters 2 through 4 in part to test this "critical filter" hypothesis. Two findings emerged: (1) the gender gap in average mathematics achievement is small and has been declining, although boys remain much more likely than girls to attain very high levels of competence; (2) gender differences in neither average nor high achievement in mathematics explain young men's higher likelihood of majoring in S/E fields in college relative to young women. Thus, the empirical results of our study lead us to reject this hypothesis.

A different version of the same hypothesis focuses on math and science coursework. It argues that, since preparation for a science career begins in high school (or before), participation and high performance in high school math and science courses are essential for entry into the S/E career trajectory. This idea is commensurate with and reinforced by the science pipeline perspective that equates membership in the pool of potential scientists with participation in the orderly sequence of high school math and science courses. This "coursework hypothesis," as articulated by Alper (1993, p. 410), states that "[b]y the time

. . . young women graduate high school, they have taken so many fewer math and science courses that it precludes significant numbers of them from pursuing college science and engineering majors." The idea that girls are less likely to pursue S/E majors in college and to become scientists and engineers because they fail to participate in the requisite math and science college preparatory courses during high school is explicitly tested and refuted in Chapters 3 and 4. We found that girls are not only on par with boys in course participation, but they also attain significantly better grades for their science and math coursework. Not surprisingly, we find that coursework participation and performance cannot account for gender differences in students' expectations of and participation in S/E college majors.

In the first chapter, we challenged the prevailing "pipeline" paradigm in the women in science literature as a fruitful conceptualization of the career trajectory. In Chapter 4, we provided concrete evidence demonstrating the drawbacks of the pipeline conceptualization. We showed that, in contrast to the rigid "leaking only" career path dictated by the pipeline metaphor, career processes are fluid and dynamic, with exit, entry, and reentry all being real possibilities at any given point in a career. While this approach was earlier proposed by Xie (1996), the analysis presented in Chapter 4 is far more comprehensive. Contrary to what might be expected according to the pipeline paradigm, we found that most women recipients of S/E bachelor's degrees had actually expected to pursue a non-S/E college major but later shifted to the S/E track during college.

It is widely known, and shown in Chapters 7 and 8, that women scientists are more likely than men to be situated in dual-career marriages. It has been suggested in the literature that the constraints of this marriage pattern contribute to women scientists' low rates of geographic mobility (Marwell, Rosenfeld, and Spilerman 1979; Mincer 1978). As we argued in Chapter 8, however, this view is too simplistic. It overlooks the addition of job-related mobility opportunities associated with two careers in a family. Indeed, our analysis in Chapter 8 shows that women scientists of any marital status are not necessarily less mobile than their male counterparts. We found that gender differences arise only when children are present. More specifically, it is among scientists with young children that men have higher rates of mobility than women.

Another well-known stylized "fact" in the women in science literature is that women academic scientists have lower rates of research productivity than men. In the words of Cole and Zuckerman (1984, p. 217), "women published slightly more than half (57%) as many papers as men." For a long time, this gender gap in research productivity could not be explained and was widely accepted as the "productivity puzzle." In Chapter 9, we conducted a multivariate analysis of four nationally representative datasets on postsecondary faculty that were collected in 1969, 1973, 1988, and 1993. Our analysis yielded two primary findings. First, sex differences in research productivity declined over the time period studied, with the female-to-male ratio increasing from about 60 percent in the late 1960s to 70 percent in the late 1980s and about 80 percent in the early 1990s. Second, most of the observed sex differences in research productivity can be attributed to sex differences in personal characteristics and structural features of employment. These results suggest that sex differences in research productivity are not immutable. Rather, they stem from sex differences in job characteristics and as such respond to the improvement of women's position in science.

A common theme that runs through several chapters in the book is the importance of considering the family in studies of women in science. In particular, we find that it is not marriage per se that hampers women's career development. Rather, married women appear to be disadvantaged only if they have children. Relative to their male counterparts, married women with children are less likely to pursue careers in science and engineering after the completion of S/E education (Chapters 5 and 6), less likely to be in the labor force or employed (Chapter 7), less likely to be promoted (Chapter 7), and less likely to be geographically mobile (Chapter 8). Although some of the gender differences are attributable to the advantages that marriage and parenthood bestow upon men, they clearly suggest that being married and having children create career barriers that are unique to women scientists.

Our research on immigrant scientists is also consistent with the notion that the family plays a distinct role in generating gender differences among immigrant scientists/engineers. In Chapter 10, we found that women immigrant scientists are more severely disadvantaged than native-born women scientists in employment as well as in opportunities for promotion. By comparison, immigrant men scientists fare well relative to their native-born counterparts. Although we do not have the data to verify the explanation, we attribute these differences to the distinct immigration paths taken by women and men scientists. While men scientists are more likely to be primary immigrants, women scientists are more likely to be secondary immigrants, as spouses of primary immigrant husbands. In light of our findings, we echo Pedraza's (1991) call for considering both the "public" and "private" spheres when studying women immigrants. In the future, more research attention should be devoted to the special circumstances experienced by immigrant women scientists—such as their migration paths.

Finally, we have found individual "choice" to be a powerful determinant of gender differences in S/E careers. We put the quotation marks around the word "choice" because we do not believe that choices are necessarily voluntary and/or perfectly rational. On the contrary, career choices always reflect the broad social structure and as such reinforce the current gender segregation of occupations (Marini and Brinton 1984; Xie and Shauman 1997). In Chapter 3, we showed that educational aspirations expressed in high school are gendered, with girls less likely to be interested in pursuing S/E than boys. We further demonstrated in Chapter 4 the consequences of the gender differences in educational aspirations for the actual attainment of S/E education. In Chapters 5 and 6, we showed that a large portion of the aggregate gender differences in career outcomes is attributable to the sex segregation of fields within science and engineering. Clearly, gender equality cannot be achieved as long as women scientists disproportionately "choose" some fields (such as biological science) and avoid others (such as engineering and physical science).

Implications

The results from our study reaffirm our proposition that the career processes and outcomes of women in science are best understood from the perspective of the life course. The benefits of adopting the life course perspective are clear from the analyses we have conducted. For example, while this perspective recognizes that past experiences and "choices" clearly influence the future direction of one's life course, it emphasizes that the interdependence is not a deterministic one. In this sense, the life course perspective directed our attention to the full range of possible life course pathways rather than to those that are most often traveled. The life course perspective also encouraged us to take a broad approach to identifying the factors that influence both individual events and cumulative outcomes. By examining the S/E career trajectory within the broad context of other life course events, we have specified the multiple and interdependent influences of the family as well as institutional structures on the career experiences and outcomes of men and women in science.

The insights gained from the life course perspective highlight the limitations of the dominant pipeline paradigm. For example, according to the pipeline paradigm, entry into the S/E educational trajectory is an insignificant route to S/E careers, and for this reason past research has largely ignored it and instead has focused on the "leaks" from the S/E trajectory. In practice, policies are typically formulated to encourage persistence among those already involved in the S/E educational trajectory rather than to entice students into S/E majors during college. This policy focus is called into question by two findings of our analysis in Chapter 4. First, a significant proportion of students attain S/E bachelor's degrees by shifting from the non-S/E track to the S/E track sometime after high school graduation. Second, gender differences in the prevalence of this "nonconventional" path to S/E account for almost half of the gender differences in S/E degree attainment. Both of these findings suggest that institutional efforts to facilitate the flow of high school students who expected non-S/E college majors into S/E majors during the first year of college may significantly reduce the gender gap in the attainment of S/E bachelor's degrees.

In our effort to contextualize the S/E educational and occupational trajectory, we showed how the career processes and outcomes of women scientists and engineers are intertwined with and influenced by other aspects of their lives. In particular, the results concerning the importance of the family reveal particular challenges that women face in combining an S/E career and a family. In contrast, our results indicate that having a family seems to be a career boost to men scientists and engineers. This conclusion is consistent with the larger literature that addresses the dilemmas faced by professional women pursuing competitive careers in the contemporary United States (Blau 1998; Goldin 1990; Spain and Bianchi 1996). On the surface, it appears that the interaction between gender and family status simply indicates the traditional within-household gender stratification, in which the wife's career is often sacrificed for the benefit of the husband's career. Our empirical results, however, call for a more precise and more qualified interpretation. We have shown that it is not being married per se, but being married *and* having children, that hampers women's careers. Perhaps the past debate on women scientists focused wrongly on the balance between maximizing the husbands' versus wives' careers. Our research suggests instead that, as long as the primary responsibility for childcare continues to fall on the shoulders of women, the real dilemma facing the woman scientist is the choice between maximizing her own career and fulfilling the responsibility for her children's well-being.[1]

The complex and multifaceted nature of women scientists' career processes and outcomes and their close relationship to other life course events make it very difficult to recommend policy interventions intended to increase women's representation in science and engineering. To be sure, such interventions have been proposed and implemented in the past (see, for example, Matyas and Dix 1992). These programs have not been based on findings from empirical research, however, and their effectiveness has not been rigorously evaluated. Although we feel that there are no quick and simple solutions, our results suggest that some policies may effectively increase the representation of women in science and improve the work experiences of women scientists. For example, colleges and universities can institutionalize programs to recruit women from non-S/E majors to the S/E educational trajectory and to address the educational and social needs of the individuals who follow the entry route to S/E education. To mitigate the difficulties of combining an S/E career with family obligations for women (and men), many policies that have been advocated (Hochschild 1989) to help working women in general may be adopted for women scientists in particular. For example, arrangements such as job-sharing and flexible work schedules may enable women scientists to keep their research agenda moving forward while they care for young children. Quality childcare at the site of employment would ease the emotional and temporal burden of childcare responsibilities for working women, enabling them to focus on their work. We believe that structural accommodations of this sort would improve the disciplines of science and engineering by enabling the participation and intellectual contribution of individuals, both women and men, who wish to be active parents as well as active scientists.

These policy suggestions are not new, and we are fully aware that they alone will not bring about gender equality in science. Women's underrepresentation in S/E has deep social, cultural, and economic roots that will not be transformed by a few isolated policy interventions or programs. Rather, we believe that increasing women's representation in S/E requires many social, cultural, and economic changes that are large in scale and interdependent.

In this regard, we note that women *have* indeed made significant and relatively rapid progress in science and engineering. We reported in Chapter 7, for example, that women have increased their representation among S/E degree recipients and in the S/E labor force. In Chapter 9, we also showed that between the late 1960s and the early 1990s women scientists dramatically improved their structural position in the academic S/E labor force, significantly closing the gap with men on such dimensions as institutional affiliation, research resources, teaching responsibilities, and publication productivity. To some observers, these documented improvements in women's representation and status in S/E still may be too slow and too little. To those critics, we offer three responses. First, there is no doubt that there is ample room for further improvement and that the pace of improvement can and should be sped up. This is particularly true when science and engineering are compared with other high-status professions, such as medicine and law. Second, the improvements in women's representation and status in science and engineering in recent decades are real, substantial, and irreversible. We venture to say that they would have been unthinkable only four or five decades ago. Once these trends have started, they are likely to continue into the future. Finally, history has shown that societal changes are often gradual. A successful science career takes a long time to form, through education and training, and may last for decades. Thus, it is a simple demographic impossibility to equalize the representation by gender among those at advanced career stages of S/E careers in a short period of time. When women increase their representation in the S/E labor force, the increase at first occurs among the young (as shown in Chapter 7); it takes time for the impact of the change to be fully realized.

Despite the progress, it remains the case that women are still underrepresented in science and engineering. That individual "choices" result in women's lower likelihood to pursue S/E careers in the aggregate gives credence to social psychological explanations. In the classic Wisconsin status attainment model, educational and occupational aspirations are conceptualized as mediating mechanisms for such background factors as parents' socioeconomic status, an individual's own cognitive ability, and the influences of significant others (Sewell, Haller, and Portes 1969). It has been suggested that gender differences in career aspirations are largely responsible for differences in the career outcomes between men and women (e.g., Turner 1964). Some of the results of our study support this proposition: we found significant gender differences in aspirations for S/E education (in Chapter 3) and in their consequences for achievement of an S/E bachelor's degree (in Chapter 4). To generalize our limited results to the broader life course, we conjecture that social psychological factors may play a prominent role in generating gender differences in career processes and outcomes in S/E. For example, over the life course men and women may react differently to career setbacks, with women more likely than men to forgo their career goals altogether and to replace them with family responsibilities. Carr (2000) vividly describes the gender differences she found from her recent interviews with the original respondents of the Wisconsin Longitudinal Study.[2] Social psychological explanations may be particularly relevant to gender differences in S/E careers, given that S/E training is extensive and S/E work sometimes requires long hours, especially in the early career years when family responsibilities are also the most time-consuming and emotionally demanding. This conjecture is not new, as the "theory of limited differences" (Cole and Singer 1991) also hypothesizes social psychological factors as concrete mechanisms responsible for accumulating and amplifying small gender differences in S/E careers.

In spite of these observations, however, it would be naïve to attribute gender differences in social psychological factors to innate or natural differences between males and females. Indeed, as sociologists, we believe such gender differences are generated and reinforced by the social structures in which individuals are situated and the networks of interaction in which they participate. Causal mechanisms include socialization by parents, teachers, peers, and media, role modeling, and perhaps overt and covert practices of gender discrimination. Thus, we return to our earlier statement that increasing women's representation in science ultimately entails fundamental changes at the societal level. In our earlier work (Xie and Shauman 1997), we showed that an increase in the proportion of women in certain professions that were once male-dominated can induce more girls to aspire to these professions. That is, success breeds future success, in the sense that young cohorts of women see and capitalize on opportunities in occupational areas where preceding cohorts of women have been successful. It is plausible that women's successful inroads to law and certain areas of medicine (such as gynecology and pediatrics) have inspired career-oriented young women to pursue these professions. Although the increase of women in science and engineering may be more gradual by comparison, the long-term trend is sharply upward and considerable and will have a similar inducing effect on the participation of future generations of talented young women in science and engineering.

Directions for Future Research

Our research sheds new light on the structure of the S/E career trajectory and the experiences of women and men who participate in it. In our view, the main contribution of our study lies in the new and rich empirical evidence that has been uncovered from many large and nationally representative datasets. Our empirical results enabled us to dispel some entrenched but flawed ideas about the causes of the underrepresentation of women in science and point to the promise of other explanations. Obviously, there is much more to be learned on the topics we covered in this book. In this sense, our study should be a stimulus for future research in this area.

A significant step for future research will be to take seriously the ample evidence we have presented. We hope that future discourse, theoretical or speculative, on women in science is informed by the empirical facts that have emerged from our study. Taking on the questions that are raised but unanswered by our research will also move research on women in science forward. For example, our analyses showed that the gender gap in the likelihood that a high school student aspires to a science career cannot be explained by differences in achievement, coursework, or familial influences. Given the critical importance of aspirations for later educational decisions and outcomes, the causes of this large gender gap should receive further research attention. Furthermore, we found that most of the observed gender differences in research productivity are attributable to gender differences in structural location and access to research resources. This finding calls for an examination of why women and men scientists are allocated to different structural positions. Filling these and other gaps in our work will significantly advance the collective understanding of the causes of gender inequality in science.

Future research should also aim to overcome the limitations of our research. They are numerous, and we trust that critical readers will identify and exploit them. In our opinion, the most serious limitation, one that actually encompasses others, is that our empirical results are essentially descriptive in nature and hence subject to different interpretations. We encourage future researchers to explore and ascertain the causal mechanisms for the empirical results presented in the book and to test speculative hypotheses suggested in our work and in the literature. We realize that this will be a difficult task and likely will entail the collection of newer and better data. In the following, we discuss three specific limitations of our study and suggest ways to overcome them.

First, our study is based on data from the United States only. Much could be learned from comparative analyses of the career experiences and outcomes of women scientists in the United States and those in European and Asian countries. For example, a comparative analysis involving countries with different childcare arrangements may answer questions about the influence of more readily available childcare on the career mobility of women scientists with children. Second, our study focuses mainly on the influences of individual and familial characteristics, especially in the early chapters, and it largely neglects the influence of social factors such as school influences. While we do examine the influence of some social structural characteristics in the later chapters of the book, much more work needs to be done to specify the social influences on the process of becoming a scientist and the experiences and outcomes of those who are active in the S/E labor force. Third, our research did not explicitly examine the effect of gender discrimination on the participation, experiences, and outcomes of women in S/E education and occupations.[3] A number of high-profile cases of both blatant discrimination (such as neurosurgeon Frances Conley's allegations of sexism and resignation from Stanford University; see Gross 1991; Libman 1991) and structural discrimination (such as the admission of long-term discrimination against female science faculty at MIT; see Goldberg 1999; Wilson 1999) are evidence that both types of discrimination persist and are experienced by individual women scientists and engineers. In addition, although the aggregate representation of women in the S/E labor force has significantly increased, women scientists may still find themselves tokens in their work settings and subject to the negative pressures and interactions that tokenism entails (Kanter 1977). Empirically measuring the occurrence, causes, and consequences of discrimination against women scientists and engineers is therefore integral to a fuller understanding of the career processes and outcomes of women in science.

Although this book is concerned only with women in science and engineering, we hope that the expansive research design of our study contributes both empirically and methodologically to the study of labor force gender stratification, broadly defined. Our research illuminates the life course processes that at times facilitate, and at times inhibit, the career development of women relative to men. Our results speak directly to career development in science, but we suspect that these processes are common to many professional career trajectories. Thus, our approach to the study of women in science may serve as an example for the understanding of gender inequality in other professions.

Appendixes

Notes

References

Index

Descriptions of the Data Sources

This appendix describes the data sources used for the analyses we report in this book. The basic information presented here supplements the summary descriptions of the datasets and the variables used for specific analyses in analytical chapters. We discuss the data sources in the order in which they are introduced in the text.

National Longitudinal Study of the Class of 1972 (NLS-72)

NLS-72 was the first study of the National Education Longitudinal Studies Program at the National Center for Education Statistics (NCES). This program was instituted by the NCES to study the development of students at various points in the life course and the many personal, familial, social, institutional, and cultural influences that affect that development (Ingels et al. 1990). Each of the studies included in the National Education Longitudinal Studies Program collected longitudinal data on a specific cohort, or cohorts, of students. In many instances, the information collected is comparable across the various NCES longitudinal studies, as well as across the multiple waves of each study.

The aim of NLS-72 was to collect information regarding the educational and occupational plans, aspirations, and attitudes of young people in their senior year of high school and the outcomes of their plans at subsequent points in time. The study began in the spring of

1972 and currently consists of the base-year survey and five follow-up surveys conducted in 1973, 1974, 1976, 1979, and 1986. The sample of high school seniors in 1972 was randomly drawn from a probability sample of public and private high schools in all of the 50 states and the District of Columbia. It originally consisted of about 19,000 respondents who completed the base-year student questionnaire in 1972 (Riccobono et al. 1981). We analyzed a sample of 15,485 students from the NLS-72 base-year survey to study the trend in math achievement gender gap in Chapter 2. This sample of respondents had completed the 25-item cognitive test of mathematics achievement that was administered as part of NLS-72. The test consisted of items that were designed to assess basic competence in mathematics (Riccobono et al. 1981). The NLS-72 study did not test the science achievement of the survey respondents.

High School and Beyond Senior and Sophomore Cohorts (HSBSr and HSBSo)

High School and Beyond was designed as a replication of NLS-72 and a continuation of the NCES's Longitudinal Studies program. Base-year data collection was conducted in the spring of 1980 with the survey of two cohorts of students, one in their sophomore year (HSBSo) and the other in their senior year of high school (HSBSr). The samples of students were selected using a two-stage probability sampling design: the first stage was the sampling of public and private schools, and the second stage involved the selection of students enrolled in the sampled schools. Students from schools with a high percentage of Hispanic students, Catholic schools, alternative public high schools, and private schools with high-achieving students were oversampled to ensure that these types of students would be represented in sufficient numbers for separate identification in analyses. After the base-year data collection in 1980, three follow-up surveys of the senior cohort were completed in 1982, 1984, and 1986. Four follow-up studies of the sophomore cohort were conducted in 1982, 1984, 1986, and 1992. Both the HSBSr and HSBSo survey instruments included student, parent, and school administrator questionnaires, a battery of cognitive tests, and a high school transcript study. In addition, a postsecondary transcript study of the HSBSo cohort was conducted in 1987 and supplemented in 1993 (Zahs et al. 1995). Both the HSBSr and HSBSo tested the mathematics achievement of the responding students, but only the sophomore cohort (HSBSo) was tested for science achievement. The HSBSr and HSBSo mathematics tests were designed to be very similar to the NLS-72 test. The HSBSo science test consisted of 20 items designed to assess students' levels of basic science knowledge (Zahs et al. 1995).

For this research we used only the base-year data from the HSBSr. For the descriptive analysis of gender differences in math achievement presented in Chapter 2, we selected from the 28,000 respondents a subsample who had completed the HSBSr math achievement test.

We made more extensive use of data from the HSB sophomore cohort. The base-year and first follow-up samples of the HSBSo included about 30,000 students. Subsequent to the first follow-up survey, NCES conducted a high school transcript study for the HSBSo. The transcript study was based on a probability sample of 18,500 students from the total sample of first follow-up respondents. This sample then became the basis for the selection of a subsample of 15,000 respondents for the second follow-up, conducted in the spring and summer of 1984, and was retained for the third follow-up survey in 1986 and the fourth follow-up in 1992. Postsecondary transcript studies were conducted in 1987 and 1993 as part of the third and fourth follow-ups of the HSBSo. These two studies collected postsecondary transcripts for all HSBSo members who reported attending at least one postsecondary institution since graduating from high school. The resulting integrated transcript file includes information on each institution that a student attended, the dates of attendance, status of enrollment, courses taken, grades attained in each course, and the types of degrees attained.

We used a subsample of about 10,601 students from the base year and 10,421 from the first follow-up of the HSBSo for the descriptive analysis of Chapter 2. For the analyses in Chapters 4, we made extensive use of the high school and college transcript data in conjunction with the student survey data. The analytical sample included individuals for whom the study had complete data on educational expectations in 1982 and educational status for the years 1982, 1984, 1986, and 1988, from either the follow-up surveys or the college transcript file. We also restricted the sample to those who had received their high school diploma by 1984 (before the administration of the second follow-up). These records were merged with data on high school course participation and grades extracted from the 1982 HSBSo high school transcript file and data on college course enrollment and grades extracted from the 1992 college transcript study. Students whose postsecondary educational activities could not be ascertained were excluded from the sample. The sample used in Chapter 4 consisted of 6,728 students. We used appropriate weighting to correct for unequal probability of selection into the sample, nonresponse bias, and unequal rates of high school dropout.

National Education Longitudinal Study of 1988 (NELS)

The National Education Longitudinal Study of 1988 was the third major study of the NCES's Longitudinal Studies program. The NELS began in 1988 with a cross-section of eighth graders selected via a two-stage probability sampling design from public and private schools in the United States. These students were resurveyed in 1990, 1992, and 1994. The base-year sample of NELS consists of about 25,000 eighth-grade students. Over 21,000 of these eighth graders were retained in the samples of the first and second follow-up studies. In addition to the panel of students who were followed from eighth grade through twelfth grade, the samples for the first and second follow-ups were freshened to ensure that they would be nationally representative of the students who were sophomores in 1990 and seniors in 1992 (Ingels et al. 1994). The NELS instruments included questionnaire surveys and tests of students and questionnaire surveys of parents, teachers, and school administrators. Additionally, as part of the second follow-up in 1992, a high school transcript study was conducted that compiled detailed information about the respondents' participation and performance in math and science courses during high school. The cognitive tests that were developed for NELS are comparable to those for NLS-72, HSBSo, and HSBSr. For the base year, the first follow-up, and the second follow-up, a mathematics achievement test with 40 items was given to assess both simple and advanced computational and problem-solving skills (Ingels et al. 1990, 1992, 1994). Similarly, a science achievement test with 25 items was used to assess basic understanding of concepts in the fields of life, earth, and physical sciences (Ingels et al. 1990, 1992, 1994).

We analyzed NELS data from the base-year, the first follow-up, and the second follow-up files in Chapters 2 and 3. These analyses drew on data from the student survey, cognitive tests, and transcript files for the investigation of gender differences in math and science achievement (Chapter 2) and in student expectations for pursuing postsecondary S/E education (Chapter 3). The samples for Chapter 2 included 23,648 eighth-grade students, 17,424 tenth-grade students, and 16,489 high school seniors. We weighted these samples to account for the sampling design effects. For the analysis of educational expectations in Chapter 3, we used a subsample of 12,784 from the NELS second follow-up that, after weighting, is representative of all U.S. high school seniors in the spring of 1992.

Longitudinal Study of American Youth, Cohorts 1 and 2 (LSAY1 and LSAY2)

LSAY was sponsored by the National Science Foundation. It was designed to focus specifically on students' attitudes toward science and mathematics, as well as their participation and performance in math and science during middle and high school. The LSAY sample was smaller than those of the NCES studies discussed above, and it did not include students from private schools (Miller et al. 1992). LSAY was begun in the fall of 1987 with two nationally representative samples of students from public schools: Cohort 1, a cross-section of tenth graders (LSAY1), and Cohort 2, a cross-section of seventh graders (LSAY2). The base-year sample sizes were 2,829 and 3,116 for LSAY1 and LSAY2, respectively. Both the LSAY1 and LSAY2 cohorts were surveyed each year for five years. In addition to student questionnaires and achievement tests, data were collected from the parents and teachers for both the LSAY1 and LSAY2 cohorts.

We utilized the LSAY1 and LSAY2 data only in the descriptive analysis of gender differences in math and science achievement in Chapter 2. The small size of the LSAY1 and LSAY2 samples makes these data less suitable than HSBSo and NELS for multivariate analyses. In addition, the exclusion of students in private schools from the LSAY study limits the generalizability of the results of analyses based on LSAY.

The tests of math and science achievement administered to the LSAY1 and LSAY2 respondents differ from those in the NCES studies. The LSAY tests were significantly longer than those administered in NLS-72, HSBSo, HSBSr, and NELS. The LSAY tests were designed to require 50 minutes to complete, although students were given additional time to complete the tests if needed (Miller et al. 1992). They included many more items than the cognitive tests that were part of the NCES data sources. Hence, the comparability of the scores from the LSAY and the NCES data sources is questionable, as we note in Chapter 2.

Baccalaureate and Beyond Longitudinal Study (B&B)

The Baccalaureate and Beyond Longitudinal Study is also part of the NCES Longitudinal Studies program. The B&B study was designed to collect information about the educational and work experiences of a cohort of individuals after they had completed their bachelor's degrees. The B&B first follow-up sample consisted of more than 11,000 students who completed their undergraduate degree in the 1992–93 academic year. The baseline data for the B&B cohort were collected as part of the 1993 National Postsecondary Student Aid Study (NPSAS). Students were selected for inclusion in NPSAS via a stratified multistage sample design with postsecondary institutions selected in the first stage and students selected in the second stage of the sampling process (Green et al. 1996). The NPSAS respondents eligible for the B&B study were reinterviewed in 1994, one year after they received their bachelor's degrees. Through telephone interviews, the B&B survey collected information about the respondents' job search activities, education, and employment experiences. A transcript study of a sample of the schools from which the B&B respondents had graduated was also conducted as part of the first follow-up. The second follow-up survey, in 1997, collected detailed information on education, employment, family formation, and other experiences since the first follow-up interviews.

We used the B&B first follow-up data for the analysis of gender differences in career paths after attainment of a bachelor's degree in S/E in Chapter 5. For that analysis, we selected a subsample of 2,086 B&B respondents who had attained a bachelor's degree in either biological science, engineering, mathematical science, or physical science, and who had nonmissing information about enrollment, employment, and family status. After weighting, the sample is representative of the population of U.S. students who completed an S/E bachelor's degree in 1992–93.

New Entrants Surveys (NES)

The New Entrants Surveys (NES) were a series of cross-sectional studies conducted by the National Science Foundation to collect data on the personal and employment characteristics of individuals who had completed bachelor's and master's degrees in S/E fields. The study was conducted in 1978 and 1979 and then biannually from 1980 to 1988. Each NES sample was drawn from the population of U.S. citizens or permanent residents who received a bachelor's or master's degree in any field of science or engineering during the two academic years preceding the date of the survey. The study design involved a two-stage probability sampling procedure in which S/E degree-granting postsecondary institutions in the United States were selected, and then individual S/E graduates were selected from the sampled schools. The probability that an institution was selected was proportional to its relative contribution to all S/E degrees. Individual graduates within specific S/E fields were then selected for inclusion in the sample according to the size of the field, with sampling rates being greater for smaller fields. Using a mail survey, NES collected data on major demographic, educational, and employment variables (Citro and Kalton 1989, pp. 69–71; Westat 1979). Some variables were not measured and/or coded consistently across the multiple years. We first recoded all variables to consistent coding schemes before pooling the year-specific data files.

The information about the early career experiences of scientists and engineers makes NES particularly useful for studying the transition from S/E education to S/E employment. We used this information to study the career paths of S/E degree recipients in Chapters 5 and 6. For the 1978–1988 survey years the sample sizes ranged from 7,935 to 11,058 for baccalaureates and from 3,435 to 5,632 for master's degree recipients. The samples were weighted to represent the population of S/E bachelor's and master's degree recipients in a given year. After excluding respondents for whom we had incomplete information on gender, education, employment, or family status, our analytical sample, pooled across all survey years, consisted of 25,170 S/E baccalaureates (Chapter 5) and 11,407 S/E master's degree recipients (Chapter 6).

U.S. Census Public Use Microdata Samples, 1960, 1970, 1980, 1990 (PUMS)

The Public Use Microdata Samples (PUMS) from the U.S. decennial censuses contain individual-level and household-level information from the "long-form" questionnaires distributed to a sample of the population. The PUMS data files include (1) housing information such as the year the structure was built, description of the household facilities, vehicles available, mortgage, rent, and taxes, (2) household information such as the number of persons in the household, household income, and household composition, and (3) for each person in the household, personal information such as demographic characteristics, schooling, occupation, place of work, transportation to work, and earnings. Although much of the information solicited by the census long-form questionnaire is consistent across the four decennial censuses from 1960 to 1990, there are differences. Some items were dropped or added from one census to another, but more often the coding of variables changed. For example, the detailed (three-digit codes) classification of occupations changed for every census, and a major change of occupational coding occurred in 1980. See Appendix C for the specific occupational codes we included in our classification of S/E occupations. Similarly, the coding of educational attainment changed slightly in 1980 and significantly in 1990.

In Chapter 7 we use the 1 percent PUMS data from the 1960, 1970, 1980, and 1990 censuses to sketch the historical profile of men and women in the S/E labor force. We use the 1990 5 percent PUMS for the study of gender differences in labor force outcomes of scientists in Chapter 7, in the geographic mobility of scientists in Chapter 8, and in the influence and experience of immigrant women scientists in Chapter 10.

1982–1989 Survey of Natural and Social Scientists and Engineers (SSE)

The Survey of Natural and Social Scientists and Engineers is a longitudinal study that provides information on workers engaged in natural science, social science, engineering, and related occupations. The aim of the survey was to collect information about employed scientists' education and training both on and off the job, employment status and job characteristics, marital status and presence of children at home, and physical disabilities or limitations. The SSE survey was based on a sampling frame drawn from the 1980 U.S. census that included those who completed four or more years of college and were currently incumbents of science and engineering occupations and those who were not employed or in the labor force but reported a scientific occupation as the last occupation held in the past five years.

The sampling frame was then stratified by 11 occupational fields, race/ethnicity, and gender. Minorities and women were oversampled. The study contains longitudinal data from four waves: 1982, 1984, 1986, and 1989. For the first wave, about 88,000 out of 122,000 mailed questionnaires were returned, yielding a response rate of 72 percent. The response rates from panel to panel are high, ranging around 72–84 percent. For the final wave, however, only 47 percent, or approximately 41,000, of the original 88,000 respondents remained. After weighting of the data to account for stratified, disproportionate sampling, disproportionate nonresponses, and disproportionate attribution, the data are representative of the population of scientists/engineers employed in the U.S. labor force in the 1980s (except for new entrants).

We used the SSE data for the analyses of differential promotion rates in Chapters 7 and 10. In both of these chapters, we selected the survey respondents for whom we had valid information about their educational attainment and their employment, immigration, and family status. Our restricting criteria—including only those respondents with a master's or doctoral degree who reported being employed in a scientific or engineering occupation but with ten or fewer years of professional experience in 1982—resulted in an analytical sample of 2,560 scientists/engineers.

Carnegie Commission National Survey of Higher Education, 1968–69
(Carnegie-1969)

The 1968–69 Carnegie Commission National Survey of Higher Education covered 303 postsecondary institutions that were originally selected in 1966 via a stratified random sample of all two- and four-year colleges and universities in the United States. Information was collected from 60,028 respondents from the 100,290 "regular faculty" sampled, yielding a 60 percent response rate (Trow 1975, p. 307). The study collected information about the educational background, professional activities, and views about a range of social, political, and educational policy issues of faculty members employed in U.S. postsecondary educational institutions.

For the analysis of gender differences in the publication rates of academic scientists and engineers presented in Chapter 9, we used a subsample of the Carnegie-1969 data that included all regular faculty members in the biological sciences, engineering, mathematical sciences, and physical sciences. The sample included 12,225 respondents and is representative of all S/E postsecondary faculty in the United States in the late 1960s.

American Council of Education Teaching Faculty in Academe, 1972–73 (ACE-1973)

The ACE Teaching Faculty in Academe study was undertaken as a partial replication of the Carnegie-1969 survey. As such, it paralleled the Carnegie-1969 in both sampling and data collection. The two studies differed somewhat in the actual items included in the survey instrument. The names of 108,722 faculty on the staffs of 301 colleges and universities were selected for participation in the ACE-1973 mail survey. A total of 53,034 people responded to the questionnaire, for an overall response rate of 49 percent. Of them, 42,345 respondents fit the definition of regular faculty and were included in the dataset. (See Bayer 1973 for a full description of the ACE-1973.)

The sample that we analyzed for the study of gender differences in publication productivity in Chapter 9 included all regular faculty in the four S/E fields. After the exclusion of individuals with missing data on the variables measuring background characteristics, structural locations and resources, and marital status, the subsample in our analysis included 6,998 respondents.

National Survey of Postsecondary Faculty, 1988 and 1993 (NSPF-1988 and NSPF-1993)

The National Survey of Postsecondary Faculty was sponsored by the NCES and conducted in 1988 and 1993 by the National Opinion Research Center (NORC). The sampling framework for NSPF-1988 and NSPF-1993 studies was similar to that of the Carnegie-1969 and ACE-1973 studies: a two-stage sample selection procedure in which individual faculty members were selected from a sample of postsecondary institutions. One design difference between the NSPF surveys and the Carnegie-1969 and ACE-1973 studies is that telephone interviews were used for sampled individuals who failed to return mail surveys in NSPF-1988 and NSPF-1993. This resulted in greatly improved response rates for NSPF-1988, at 76 percent, and NSPF-1993, at 87 percent. In addition, the NSPF-1993 sample is substantially larger (31,354 respondents) than NSPF-1988 (11,000 respondents) (NORC 1993).

The NSPF-1988 and NSPF-1993 data sources provided the most recent information on faculty characteristics and publication productivity for the study of the gender differences in publication rates in Chapter 9. The analytical samples numbered 847 and 1,845, respectively, for NSPF-1988 and NSPF-1993.

Method for Decomposition Analysis

A typical multivariate analysis presented in this book consists of a series of hierarchical, nested models, which means that a later model necessarily includes the variables present in earlier model(s). While this is an effective way to examine the *additional* explanatory power of the variables being added in the later model, this strategy does not allow the decomposition of the explanatory power attributable to individual factors. In fact, it is not possible to establish the "pure" explanatory power of the individual factors. In this appendix, we illustrate a decomposition method introduced by Xie and Shauman (1998), with loglinear (or negative binomial) and logit models as examples. For our study, the focus of such models is on $\exp(b_{sex})$. Since the explanatory factors are correlated with each other, how much $\exp(b_{sex})$ is altered by the inclusion of a particular factor depends on what other variables are included in the model. It is thus informative to know how the inclusion or exclusion of an individual factor affects $\exp(b_{sex})$ under certain conditions. We examine the changes in $\exp(b_{sex})$ under two starkly different conditions and use the changes to measure the potential explanatory power of the individual factor.

The first measure of explanatory power is based on the *change* in $\exp(b_{sex})$ after an explanatory factor is taken out of the full model including all potential covariates considered for an analysis. Define D_1 as:

(B.1) $D_1 = \exp(b^F) - \exp(b^{F-k})$

where b^F denotes the sex coefficient for the full model, and b^{F-k} denotes the sex coefficient for the model in which the kth factor is excluded from the full model (omitting the subscript for sex). If a particular factor contributes additional explanatory power in the presence of all other variables, we expect D_1 to be greater than 0. A zero or negative D_1 means that a particular factor does not appear to explain the sex difference in the presence of other covariates. If the explanatory power of the full model were entirely due to this factor, $\exp(b^{F-k})$ would be the same as $\exp(b^0)$, the sex ratio from the baseline bivariate model, and D_1 would be $[\exp(b^F) - \exp(b^0)]$.

Our second measure, D_2, is based on the *change* in $\exp(b_{sex})$ after an explanatory factor is added to the bivariate baseline model (again omitting the subscript for sex):

(B.2) $D_2 = \exp(b^{0+k}) - \exp(b^0)$

where b^{0+k} denotes the sex coefficient for the model with the kth factor added to the baseline model. For a well-behaved explanatory factor k, D_2 should also vary between 0 and $[\exp(b^F) - \exp(b^0)]$. Zero means no explanatory power, and $[\exp(b^F) - \exp(b^0)]$ means the maximum explanatory power. In general, the D_1 measure tends to be conservative whereas the D_2 measure tends to be liberal. For this reason, we call D_1 the "low" method and D_2 the "high" method. For an actual explanatory factor in our empirical work, a "low" estimate can be higher than a corresponding "high" estimate, and both can take negative values, in which case controlling a factor increases, rather than reduces, the estimated gender gap in the dependent variable.

Detailed Occupation Codes in Science and Engineering

The following codes (from U.S. census PUMS Data 1960, 1970, 1980, 1990) are arranged by field of science.

Science Category	1960	1970	1980	1990
(1) Biological scientists	031 Professors and instructors, agricultural sciences 032 Professors and instructors, biological sciences 130 Agricultural scientists 131 Biological scientists 052 Professors and instructors, natural sciences, n.e.c. 145 Miscellaneous natural scientists	042 Agricultural scientists 044 Biological scientists 052 Marine scientists 102 Agriculture teachers 104 Biology teachers	077 Agricultural and food scientists 078 Biological and life scientists 079 Forestry and conservation scientists 083 Medical scientists 113 Earth, environmental, and marine science teachers 114 Biological science teachers 117 Natural science teachers, n.e.c. 133 Medical science teachers 136 Agriculture and forestry teachers	077 Agricultural and food scientists 078 Biological and life scientists 079 Forestry and conservation scientists 083 Medical scientists 113 Earth, environmental, and marine science teachers 114 Biological science teachers 117 Natural science teachers, n.e.c. 133 Medical science teachers 136 Agriculture and forestry teachers
(2) Engineers	040 Professors and instructors, engineering 075 Editors and reporters 080 Engineers, aeronautical 081 Engineers, chemical 082 Engineers, civil 083 Engineers, electrical 084 Engineers, industrial	006 Aeronautical and astronautical engineers 010 Chemical engineers 011 Civil engineers 012 Electrical and electronic engineers 013 Industrial engineers 014 Mechanical engineers 015 Metallurgical and materials engineers 020 Mining engineers	044 Aerospace engineers 045 Metallurgical and materials engineers 046 Mining engineers 047 Petroleum engineers 048 Chemical engineers 049 Nuclear engineers 053 Civil engineers 054 Agricultural engineers 055 Electrical and electronic engineers	044 Aerospace engineers 045 Metallurgical and materials engineers 046 Mining engineers 047 Petroleum engineers 048 Chemical engineers 049 Nuclear engineers 053 Civil engineers 054 Agricultural engineers 055 Electrical and electronic engineers

085 Engineers, mechanical	021 Petroleum engineers	056 Industrial engineers	056 Industrial engineers
090 Engineers, metallurgical, and metallurgists	022 Sales engineers	057 Mechanical engineers	057 Mechanical engineers
091 Engineers, mining	023 Engineers, n.e.c.	058 Marine engineers and naval architects	058 Marine engineers and naval architects
092 Engineers, sales	111 Engineering teachers	059 Engineers, n.e.c.	059 Engineers, n.e.c.
093 Engineers, n.e.c.		063 Surveyors and mapping scientists	063 Surveyors and mapping scientists
		127 Engineering teachers	127 Engineering teachers
		258 Sales engineers	258 Sales engineers

(3) Mathematical and computer scientists

042 Professors and instructors, mathematics	112 Mathematics teachers	066 Actuaries	066 Actuaries
051 Professors and instructors, statistics	034 Actuaries	067 Statisticians	067 Statisticians
135 Mathematicians	035 Mathematicians	068 Mathematical scientists, n.e.c.	068 Mathematical scientists, n.e.c.
174 Statisticians and actuaries	036 Statisticians	128 Mathematical science teachers	128 Mathematical science teachers
	003 Computer programmers	064 Computer systems analysts and scientists	064 Computer systems analysts and scientists
	004 Computer systems analysts	065 Operations and systems researchers and analysts	065 Operations and systems researchers and analysts
	005 Computer specialists, n.e.c.	129 Computer science teachers	129 Computer science teachers
	055 Operations and systems researchers and analysts	229 Computer programmers	229 Computer programmers

(4) Physical scientists

021 Chemists	043 Atmospheric and space scientists	069 Physicists and astronomers	069 Physicists and astronomers
034 Professors and instructors, chemistry	045 Chemists	073 Chemists, except biochemists	073 Chemists, except biochemists
041 Professors and instructors, geology and geophysics	051 Geologists	074 Atmospheric and space scientists	074 Atmospheric and space scientists
	053 Physicists and astronomers		

Science Category	1960	1970	1980	1990
	045 Professors and instructors, physics	054 Life and physical scientists, n.e.c.	075 Geologists and geodesists	075 Geologists and geodesists
	134 Geologists and geophysicists	103 Atmospheric, earth, marine, and space teachers	076 Physical scientists, n.e.c.	076 Physical scientists, n.e.c.
	140 Physicists	105 Chemistry teachers	115 Chemistry teachers	115 Chemistry teachers
		110 Physics teachers	116 Physics teachers	116 Physics teachers

Note: n.e.c. = not elsewhere classified.

Detailed Statistical Tables

The tables in this appendix are intended for readers who are interested in detailed statistical results. Appendix Table D2.a describes the data sources and sample sizes for the analyses in Chapter 2. All other tables present descriptive statistics, full coefficients of final multivariate regression models, or results of decomposition analyses. Linear (OLS) regression coefficients are denoted b, and logit and negative binomial coefficients are denoted $\exp(b)$. All t-ratio or asymptotic z-ratio statistics refer to the null hypothesis of no difference: $b = 0$ or $\exp(b) = 1$.

Table D2.a Samples used for descriptive analysis of sex differences in math and science achievement by grade, data source, and type of achievement

School cohort	Sample sizes in grade						Data source
	7	8	9	10	11	12	
Panel A: Math achievement							
1960						15,485	NLS-72
1968						9,161	HSBSr
1970				10,601		10,421	HSBSo
1978				2,716	2,198	1,881	LSAY1
1980		23,648		17,424		16,489	NELS
1981	3,063	2,748	2,428	2,255	1,828		LSAY2
Panel B: Science achievement							
1960							NLS-72
1968							HSBSr
1970				10,619		10,506	HSBSo
1978				2,679	2,212	1,902	LSAY1
1980		23,617		16,181		13,291	NELS
1981	3,065	2,739	2,437	2,242	1,530		LSAY2

Table D2.b Female-to-male ratio of the variance of math and science achievement scores by grade and cohort

School cohort	Variance ratio (VR) in grade						Data source
	7	8	9	10	11	12	
Panel A: Math achievement							
1960						0.95*	NLS-72
1968						0.84***	HSBSr
1970				0.83***		0.83***	HSBSo
1978				0.72***	0.65***	0.76***	LSAY1
1980		0.93***		0.93***		0.93***	NELS
1981	0.81***	0.72***	0.73***	0.71***	0.72***		LSAY2
Panel B: Science achievement							
1960							NLS-72
1968							HSBSr
1970				0.89***		0.91***	HSBSo
1978				0.81***	0.72***	0.70***	LSAY1
1980		0.79***		0.80***		0.89***	NELS
1981	0.77***	0.78***	0.74***	0.71***	0.71***		LSAY2

Note: Variance ratio (VR) is defined as the ratio in the variance of achievement scores between males and females.

$*p < .05, **p < .01, ***p < .001$ (two-tailed test) for the hypothesis that there is no variance difference between males and females.

Table D2.c Sex-specific distributions of variables measuring individual and familial influences by grade

	8th grade		10th grade		12th grade	
	Females	Males	Females	Males	Females	Males
Total sample	11,607	11,629	7,733	7,741	5,750	5,933
Background characteristics						
Race/ethnicity (%)						
White	71.19	71.56	72.55	73.34	72.59	74.92
Black	12.94	12.43	12.04	11.67	12.00	10.70
Hispanic	10.12	10.07	9.63	9.40	9.44	9.10
Other	4.80	5.05	4.93	4.99	5.20	4.72
Missing	0.96	0.89	0.85	0.61	0.77	0.56
High school program (%)						
Non–college preparatory	44.56	45.23	55.21	57.56	48.96	50.33
College preparatory	29.06	28.27	36.06	32.23	46.68	43.81
Missing	26.38	26.50	8.73	10.21	4.37	5.87
Educational aspirations (%)						
Less than four years of college	31.33	36.72	35.82	42.33	27.23	29.89
Four years of college or more	68.29	62.55	63.30	56.39	66.67	60.82
Missing	0.39	0.73	0.88	1.28	6.10	9.29
Family of origin influences						
Father's educational attainment (%)						
Less than four years of college	58.93	58.61	58.85	57.77	57.99	57.05
Four years of college or more	23.37	25.82	24.23	27.90	25.98	29.92
Missing	17.70	15.56	16.91	14.33	16.03	13.03
Mother's educational attainment (%)						
Less than four years of college	70.02	65.40	69.68	64.88	68.44	64.03
Four years of college or more	19.01	21.56	19.68	22.53	21.28	23.92
Missing	10.97	13.04	10.64	12.60	10.28	12.05
Parental expectations for student's educational attainment (%)						
Less than four years of college	18.31	21.27	21.61	27.80	18.11	18.37
Four years of college or more	71.69	68.13	70.67	62.56	71.26	66.32
Missing	10.00	10.59	7.72	9.64	10.63	15.30
Family income (%)						
Under $7,500	8.28	6.74				
$7,500–$14,999	11.60	10.84				

Table D2.c (continued)

	8th grade		10th grade		12th grade	
	Females	Males	Females	Males	Females	Males
$15,000–$24,999	16.51	16.53				
$25,000–$34,999	17.03	16.49				
$35,000–$49,999	17.89	19.15				
$50,000–$74,999	12.73	12.93				
$75,000 or more	6.37	6.94				
Missing	9.60	10.37				
Family owns a computer (%)						
Yes	35.98	45.18	37.49	46.85	38.47	47.87
No	60.39	50.26	58.98	49.09	58.14	48.51
Missing	3.63	4.56	3.53	4.06	3.39	3.62

Student's dating attitudes, family expectations, and family vs. work attitudes

	8th grade		10th grade		12th grade	
How important is it to have a steady girl/boyfriend (%)						
Not important			23.05	17.63	30.99	27.14
Somewhat important			54.29	54.06	50.77	51.79
Very important			19.78	22.19	13.81	13.45
Missing			2.87	6.11	4.43	7.62
Expected age at first marriage (mean)					25.88	
Expected age at first birth (mean)					27.61	
Family-work attitude scale (mean)			−0.42		−0.35	

High school math/science course participation and grades

	8th grade		10th grade		12th grade	
Math course taken (% among those taking math courses)						
Algebra 1			62.70	58.95	74.24	74.03
Geometry			44.52	39.58	70.98	67.47
Algebra 2			18.90	17.20	57.27	53.42
Trigonometry			2.19	2.83	26.78	27.12
Precalculus			0.41	0.49	18.68	19.14
Calculus			0.00	0.08	10.38	11.26
Science course taken (% among those taking science courses)						
Earth science			17.07	17.00	21.40	22.55
Biology			80.27	77.74	95.09	93.14
Chemistry			11.97	11.18	60.12	56.91
Physics			0.94	1.50	24.16	31.36
Advanced biology			3.29	3.73	22.51	18.71
Advanced chemistry			0.31	0.49	5.19	5.79
Mean high school course grades						
Math course grades (mean)			79.81	78.12	77.89	75.61
Science course grades (mean)			78.46		77.94	

Table D2.c (continued)

	8th grade		10th grade		12th grade	
	Females	Males	Females	Males	Females	Males
Grade during which student took last math course (%)						
Grade 9					2.07	2.38
Grade 10					10.19	9.56
Grade 11					28.41	25.72
Grade 12					48.63	53.02
Missing					10.70	9.32
Grade during which student took last science course (%)						
Grade 9					1.43	1.82
Grade 10					17.50	17.11
Grade 11					30.77	29.13
Grade 12					39.51	42.42
Missing					10.79	9.52
Student attitudes about math/science						
Math will be useful in my future (%)						
Agree	84.27	83.81				
Disagree	12.74	10.36				
Missing	2.99	5.83				
Afraid to ask questions in math class (%)						
Agree	22.29	17.53				
Disagree	74.85	76.76				
Missing	2.86	5.70				
I look forward to math class (%)						
Agree	52.81	55.33				
Disagree	44.39	39.16				
Missing	2.80	5.51				
Science will be useful in my future (%)						
Agree	62.46	67.50				
Disagree	33.70	25.83				
Missing	3.83	6.66				
Afraid to ask questions in science class (%)						
Agree	14.78	13.34				
Disagree	81.71	80.20				
Missing	3.52	6.47				
I look forward to science class (%)						
Agree	55.39	60.90				
Disagree	41.12	32.89				
Missing	3.50	6.22				
Math is one of my best subjects (%)						
Agree			37.21	44.30		
Ambivalent			32.45	33.00		

Table D2.c (continued)

	8th grade		10th grade		12th grade	
	Females	Males	Females	Males	Females	Males
Disagree			28.04	18.59		
Missing			2.29	4.11		
I have always done well in math class (%)						
Agree			40.41	47.09		
Ambivalent			33.29	33.64		
Disagree			23.39	15.14		
Missing			2.91	4.12		
I have always gotten good grades in math (%)						
Agree			45.05	49.48		
Ambivalent			31.83	30.57		
Disagree			19.59	14.96		
Missing			3.53	4.99		

Source: NELS Base Year (1988), First Follow-up (1990), and Second Follow-up (1992).

Table D2.d Estimated coefficients from OLS regression model of math and science achievement score and binary logit models of the odds of being in the top 5 percent of the achievement distribution, 8th grade

	Math				Science			
	d		AR		d		AR	
	b	t-ratio	exp(b)	z-ratio	b	t-ratio	exp(b)	z-ratio
Constant	2.21	73.42	0.00	-15.75	3.24	110.87	0.01	-15.43
Sex (female)	-0.02	-2.01	0.81	-2.94	-0.14	-11.29	0.55	-7.94
Background characteristics								
Race/ethnicity (excluded = white)								
Black	-0.57	-32.36	0.20	-7.26	-0.62	-34.22	0.20	-6.27
Hispanic	-0.33	-18.30	0.42	-4.90	-0.36	-19.05	0.40	-5.20
Other	-0.05	-1.82	1.36	2.90	-0.22	-7.95	0.89	-0.96
High school program (excluded = non-college preparatory)								
College preparatory	0.41	25.62	2.98	11.98	0.37	22.70	2.67	11.47
Educational aspirations (excluded less than four years of college)								
Four years of college or more	0.32	20.89	3.28	6.29	0.28	16.97	2.66	5.63
Family of origin influences								
Father's educational attainment (excluded = less than four years of college)								
Four years of college or more	0.25	12.85	1.74	5.60	0.20	10.51	1.71	5.89
Mother's educational attainment (excluded = less than four years of college)								
Four years of college or more	0.14	7.01	1.62	5.44	0.12	6.02	1.36	3.60
Parental expectations for student's educational attainment (excluded = less than four years of college)								
four years of college or more	0.19	10.98	1.83	3.04	0.18	9.44	1.27	1.27

Family income (excluded = under $7,500)								
$7,500–$14,999	0.07	2.97	2.84	2.39	0.09	3.51	0.96	−0.12
$15,000–$24,999	0.17	6.98	3.78	3.31	0.17	6.48	1.34	0.98
$25,000–$34,999	0.23	9.31	3.44	3.08	0.24	9.25	1.43	1.23
$35,000–$49,999	0.27	10.89	4.18	3.61	0.26	9.88	1.74	1.93
$50,000–$74,999	0.31	11.23	4.20	3.60	0.27	9.05	1.56	1.53
$75,000 or more	0.49	14.04	5.62	4.29	0.36	9.97	1.85	2.07
Family owns a computer (excluded = no)								
Yes	0.11	8.16	1.45	4.68	0.10	7.10	1.38	4.09
Student attitudes about math/science								
Math will be useful in my future (excluded = disagree)								
Agree	−0.20	−13.15	0.75	−2.75	−0.19	−10.74	0.76	−2.22
I usually look forward to math/science class (excluded = disagree)								
Agree	0.05	3.82	1.40	4.19	0.01	0.69	1.23	2.60
R^2 / Model χ^2 (df)	0.34	1,121.62 (30)			0.29	938.20 (30)		

Source: NELS Base Year, 1988.
Note: Sample size is 23,236 for the linear regression and logit models of the math and science achievement and high performance. All models include missing data indicator variables for each of the covariates.

Table D2.e Estimated coefficients from OLS regression model of math and science achievement score and binary logit models of the odds of being in the top 5 percent of the achievement distribution, 10th grade

	Math				Science			
	d		AR		d		AR	
	b	t-ratio	exp(b)	z-ratio	b	t-ratio	exp(b)	z-ratio
Constant	1.52	20.27	0.00	-8.96	1.87	16.94	0.00	-10.57
Sex (female)	-0.09	-5.10	0.62	-3.97	-0.35	-18.16	0.34	-9.73
Background characteristics								
Race/ethnicity (excluded = white)								
Black	-0.43	-15.64	0.35	-2.65	-0.58	-18.31	0.17	-3.95
Hispanic or Spanish	-0.25	-9.84	0.67	-1.22	-0.36	-12.36	0.27	-4.06
Other	-0.09	-2.26	1.54	2.65	-0.20	-4.72	0.84	-0.95
High school program (excluded = non-college preparatory)								
College preparatory	0.20	9.85	1.36	2.25	0.27	11.60	1.64	4.29
Educational aspirations (excluded = less than four years of college)								
Four years of college or more	0.23	10.63	3.31	4.64	0.22	9.54	1.52	2.19
Family of origin influences								
Father's educational attainment (excluded = less than four years of college)								
Four years of college or more	0.12	4.87	1.41	2.17	0.19	5.82	1.63	3.45
Mother's educational attainment (excluded = less than four years of college)								
Four years of college or more	0.11	4.25	1.49	2.71	0.09	2.98	1.03	0.19
Parental expectations for student's educational attainment (excluded = less than 4 years of college)								
Four years of college or more	0.14	6.59	2.99	4.60	0.17	7.27	1.82	3.18
Family income (excluded = under $7,500)								
$7,500–$14,999	0.11	2.92	0.59	-0.94	0.11	2.54	3.12	1.83
$15,000–$24,999	0.16	4.32	1.26	0.45	0.16	3.62	3.51	2.18
$25,000–$34,999	0.19	5.08	1.53	0.85	0.17	3.92	3.79	2.34
$35,000–$49,999	0.25	6.41	1.64	0.99	0.21	4.70	4.23	2.53

$50,000–$74,999	0.22	5.26	1.65	1.01	0.18	3.60	3.51	2.19
$75,000 or more	0.32	6.72	2.04	1.41	0.28	5.03	4.77	2.64
Family owns a computer (excluded = no)								
Yes	0.08	4.77	1.67	3.97	0.10	5.00	1.69	4.91
Student's dating attitudes, family expectations, and family vs. work attitudes								
How important is it to have a steady girl/boyfriend (excluded = not important)								
Somewhat important	−0.05	−2.65	0.70	−2.54	−0.08	−3.58	0.81	−1.78
Very important	−0.21	−7.66	0.46	−3.82	−0.26	−8.70	0.48	−4.59
Family-work attitude scale	0.03	4.35	1.06	1.17	0.02	2.78	0.98	−0.43
High school math/science course participation and grades								
Math/science courses taken								
Algebra 1/earth science	−0.09	−3.66	0.49	−4.39	0.10	3.91	1.07	0.47
Geometry/biology	0.33	16.44	2.40	4.05	0.02	0.39	0.66	−1.27
Algebra 2/chemistry	0.33	14.40	2.85	6.78	0.37	12.40	2.37	7.00
Trigonometry/physics	0.50	11.88	4.67	5.18	0.20	1.85	1.58	1.48
Precalculus/adv. biology	0.40	4.02	9.50	4.56	0.02	0.33	0.74	−1.03
Calculus/adv. chemistry	0.33	3.25	2.35	0.80	0.44	3.90	3.22	2.75
Avg. math/science grade	0.01	14.53	1.09	4.38	0.02	17.63	1.11	9.02
Student attitudes about math								
Math is one of my best subjects (excluded = disagree)								
Ambivalent	0.12	3.30	1.15	0.43				
Agree	0.16	4.16	1.82	1.79				
I have always done well in math class (excluded = disagree)								
Ambivalent	0.07	2.32	1.53	0.97				
Agree	0.20	5.88	2.94	2.55				
I have always gotten good grades in math (excluded = disagree)								
Ambivalent	−0.02	−0.65	0.97	−0.09				
Agree	0.06	1.93	1.20	0.55				
R^2 / Model χ^2 (df)	0.54	1,155.06 (46)			0.40	834.57 (37)		

Source: NELS First Follow-up, 1990.

Note: Sample size is 15,474 for the linear regression and logit models of the math and science achievement and high performance. All models include missing data indicator variables for each of the covariates.

Table D2.f Estimated coefficients from OLS regression model of math and science achievement score and binary logit models of the odds of being in the top 5 percent of the achievement distribution, 12th grade

	Math				Science			
	d		AR		d		AR	
	b	t-ratio	exp(b)	z-ratio	b	t-ratio	exp(b)	z-ratio
Constant	1.55	14.58	0.00	−9.81	2.18	14.87	0.00	−9.23
Sex (female)	−0.15	−8.90	0.52	−4.69	−0.34	−15.16	0.35	−7.93
Background characteristics								
Race/ethnicity (excluded = white)								
Black	−0.40	−13.46	0.16	−3.42	−0.59	−17.58	0.14	−4.34
Hispanic	−0.24	−8.17	0.87	−0.36	−0.36	−10.86	0.73	−0.97
Other	−0.06	−1.31	1.50	2.04	−0.22	−4.67	1.07	0.37
High school program (excluded = non-college preparatory)								
College preparatory	0.15	7.38	1.56	2.35	0.21	8.34	1.76	3.82
Educational aspirations (excluded = less than four years of college)								
Four years of college or more	0.19	7.84	4.08	3.04	0.15	5.28	2.48	3.49
Family of origin influences								
Father's educational attainment (excluded = less than four years of college)								
Four years of college or more	0.07	2.77	1.75	3.50	0.12	3.27	1.18	1.12
Mother's educational attainment (excluded = less than four years of college)								
Four years of college or more	0.08	3.26	1.41	2.21	0.09	2.35	1.44	2.52
Parental expectations for student's educational attainment (excluded = less than four years of college)								
Four years of college or more	0.10	3.85	1.13	0.29	0.10	3.15	1.71	1.49
Family income (excluded = under $7,500)								
$7,500–$14,999	0.06	1.52	1.39	0.50	0.10	2.25	3.21	1.60
$15,000–$24,999	0.10	2.46	1.90	1.02	0.10	2.38	3.86	1.95
$25,000–$34,999	0.09	2.39	2.43	1.40	0.14	3.06	4.21	2.07
$35,000–$49,999	0.13	3.19	2.04	1.14	0.14	3.31	5.03	2.35

$50,000–$74,999	0.08	1.79	1.51	0.66	0.07	1.21	5.22	2.36
$75,000 or more	0.21	4.14	2.22	1.25	0.15	2.38	4.44	2.12
Family owns a computer (excluded = no)								
Yes	0.07	3.88	1.78	4.14	0.08	3.80	1.49	3.13
Student's dating attitudes, family expectations, and family vs. work attitudes								
How important is it to have a steady girl/boyfriend (excluded = not important)								
Somewhat important	−0.01	−0.75	1.00	0.02	−0.04	−1.33	0.91	−0.74
Very important	−0.11	−3.53	1.22	0.69	−0.16	−4.40	0.69	−1.46
Expected age at first marriage	0.00	−0.75	1.02	0.58	−0.01	−1.76	0.98	−1.10
Expected age at first birth	0.01	2.14	1.00	−0.03	0.01	4.20	1.06	2.46
Family-work attitude scale	0.03	5.07	1.06	1.03	0.04	4.89	1.05	0.97
High school math/science course participation and grades								
Math/Science courses taken								
Algebra 1/earth science	0.16	−7.15	0.54	−3.96	0.07	3.05	1.20	1.35
Geometry/biology	−0.16	5.65	1.02	−2.22	0.07	7.56	1.11	0.60
Algebra 2/chemistry	0.13	8.45	0.70	0.08	0.22	−0.47	0.82	−0.57
Trigonometry/physics	0.28	13.57	1.00	−0.02	−0.02	10.76	2.45	5.21
Precalculus/adv. biology	0.39	17.78	2.15	4.70	0.21	2.56	1.10	0.66
Calculus/adv. chemistry	0.47	18.85	6.02	10.74	0.22	4.76	1.98	4.32
Avg. math/science grade	0.01	15.84	1.16	8.44	0.01	13.25	1.09	7.53
Grade during which student took last math/science course (excluded = grade 9)								
Grade 10	0.22	4.59	0.88	−0.13	0.00	0.02	2.19	0.85
Grade 11	0.25	5.31	1.05	0.06	−0.01	−0.07	1.62	0.54
Grade 12	0.22	4.61	1.82	0.70	0.06	0.78	1.96	0.75
R^2 / Model χ^2 (df)	0.60		1,030.47 (42)		0.43		638.69 (42)	

Source: NELS Second Follow-up, 1992.

Note: Sample size is 11,683 for the linear regression and logit models of the math and science achievement and high performance. All models include missing data indicator variables for each of the covariates.

Table D2.g Change in the estimated female-to-male high achievement ratio attributable to each set of explanatory factors

	8th grade		10th grade		12th grade	
Explanatory variables	"Low" (D_1)	"High" (D_2)	"Low" (D_1)	"High" (D_2)	"Low" (D_1)	"High" (D_2)
Panel A: Math achievement						
Background characteristics	−0.03	−0.05	−0.01	−0.09	0.01	−0.06
Family of origin influences	0.09	0.05	0.07	0.05	0.05	0.05
Student's dating attitudes, family expectations, and family vs. work attitudes	n/a	n/a	−0.04	−0.11	0.00	−0.04
High school math course participation and grades	n/a	n/a	−0.12	−0.15	−0.13	−0.17
Student attitudes about math	0.02	0.01	0.07	0.10	n/a	n/a
All factors	0.05		−0.08		−0.13	
Panel B: Science achievement						
Background characteristics	−0.03	−0.04	0.00	−0.05	0.00	−0.04
Family of origin influences	0.05	0.03	0.04	0.02	0.02	0.01
Student's dating attitudes, family expectations, and family vs. work attitudes	n/a	n/a	−0.01	−0.05	−0.01	−0.03
High school science course participation and grades	n/a	n/a	−0.04	−0.08	−0.03	−0.04
Student attitudes about science	0.02	0.02	n/a	n/a	n/a	n/a
All factors	0.03		−0.07		−0.04	

Note: The entries represent the amount of change in the female-to-male odds ratio of high achievement that is attributable to each set of explanatory factors included in the model. The "Low" estimate (D_1) is the change in the exponentiated coefficient of sex after a set of factors is removed from the full model. The "High" estimate (D_2) is the increase in the exponentiated coefficient of sex after an explanatory factor or set of factors is added to the model that includes only sex as an explanatory variable. All calculations ignore sampling error.

Table D3.a Sex-specific distributions of variables measuring individual and familial influences

	Total sample		Those who expect to attend college	
	Females	Males	Females	Males
Sample size	6,558	6,226	4,759	4,159
Background characteristics				
Race/ethnicity (%)				
White	73.79	75.59	73.58	76.31
Black	11.88	10.53	12.35	9.89
Hispanic	9.01	8.56	7.94	8.05
Other	4.55	4.75	5.21	5.32
Missing	0.77	0.57	0.91	0.44
High school program (%)				
Non–college preparatory	48.98	51.34	37.30	36.09
College preparatory	47.17	44.61	60.24	61.51
Missing	3.84	4.06	2.46	2.40
Math and science achievement				
Math achievement score	0.06	0.15	0.34	0.51
Science achievement score	-0.05	0.27	0.18	0.55
Math achievement high performance	0.05	0.07	0.07	0.11
Science achievement high performance	0.04	0.09	0.05	0.13
Family of origin influences				
Father's educational attainment (%)				
Less than four years of college	57.07	56.28	50.64	47.01
Four years of college or more	26.51	30.66	34.24	41.57
Missing	16.42	13.06	15.12	11.42
Mother's educational attainment (%)				
Less than four years of college	67.90	64.51	62.48	57.88
Four years of college or more	21.91	24.41	27.92	32.59
Missing	10.19	11.08	9.60	9.53
Parental expectations for student's educational attainment (%)				
Less than four years of college	19.00	19.49	2.94	3.40
Four years of college or more	72.66	68.62	91.64	90.43
Missing	8.34	11.89	5.41	6.17
Family income (%)				
Under $7,500	5.78	4.34	3.79	2.65
$7,500–$14,999	9.45	9.06	7.56	6.53
$15,000–$24,999	15.43	15.48	13.96	12.83
$25,000–$34,999	18.31	17.13	16.89	16.72
$35,000–$49,999	20.33	20.23	21.60	21.33
$50,000–$74,999	15.06	17.05	18.05	20.00
$75,000 or more	7.31	8.51	9.80	12.22
Missing	8.34	8.19	8.36	7.73

Table D3.a (continued)

	Total sample		Those who expect to attend college	
	Females	Males	Females	Males
Family owns a computer (%)				
Yes	57.81	48.17	53.71	41.09
No	38.90	48.63	43.22	56.74
Missing	3.29	3.20	3.08	2.16
Student's dating attitudes, family expectations, and family vs. work attitudes				
How important is it to have a steady girl/boyfriend (%)				
Not important	31.63	27.95	34.64	30.54
Somewhat important	51.05	53.24	51.38	54.21
Very important	14.18	14.38	11.47	12.33
Missing	3.14	4.44	2.51	2.92
Expected age at first marriage (mean)	24.31	25.89	24.96	26.22
Expected age at first birth (mean)	26.47	27.69	27.33	28.17
Family-work attitude scale (mean)	0.09	−0.32	0.07	−0.25
Student attitudes about math/science				
Math is one of my best subjects (%)				
Disagree	58.55	49.24	55.09	45.37
Agree	37.38	44.26	41.26	50.18
Missing	4.07	6.50	3.65	4.45
I have always done well in math class (%)				
Disagree	54.20	45.96	49.91	40.79
Agree	41.38	47.64	46.04	54.65
Missing	4.43	6.40	4.05	4.56
I have always gotten good grades in math (%)				
Disagree	48.84	42.63	44.58	37.77
Agree	46.13	50.15	50.85	57.10
Missing	5.04	7.22	4.57	5.14
High school math course participation and grades				
Participation in advanced math courses during high school (%)				
No	51.82	54.00	41.89	40.82
Yes	29.91	30.53	39.36	43.33
Missing	18.26	15.47	18.75	15.84
Average math course grades	79.00	76.72	81.16	79.78
Grade during which student took last math course (%)				
Grade 10	11.35	11.86	5.60	4.19
Grade 11	26.21	23.29	23.30	19.24
Grade 12	44.16	49.35	52.35	60.68
Missing	18.29	15.49	18.75	15.88

Source: NELS Second Follow-up, 1992.

Table D3.b Estimated coefficients from sequential logit models of the expectation of college attendance and pursuing an S/E major among those who expect to attend college

	Attend college		Major in S/E	
	exp(*b*)	*z*-ratio	exp(*b*)	*z*-ratio
Constant	0.00	−11.80	0.05	−4.67
Sex (female)	1.69	6.34	0.34	−12.75
Background characteristics				
Race/ethnicity (excluded = white)				
Black	1.91	3.99	1.55	2.69
Hispanic	1.38	2.45	1.25	1.46
Other	1.25	1.22	1.07	0.51
High school program (excluded = non–college preparatory)				
College preparatory	3.12	12.41	1.28	2.77
Math and science achievement				
Math achievement score	1.74	7.01	1.03	0.34
Science achievement score	1.03	0.43	1.39	4.25
Math achievement high performance	n/a	n/a	1.52	2.92
Science achievement high performance	n/a	n/a	1.04	0.28
Family of origin influences				
Father's educational attainment (excluded = less than four years of college)				
Four years of college or more	1.73	4.62	0.87	−1.34
Mother's educational attainment (excluded = less than four years of college)				
Four years of college or more	1.29	1.99	0.95	−0.54
Parents' expectations for student's educational attainment (excluded = less than four years of college)				
Four years of college or more	29.32	29.44	1.19	0.68
Family income (excluded = under $7,500)				
$7,500–$14,999	1.34	1.49	1.60	1.61
$15,000–$24,999	1.61	2.42	1.03	0.11
$25,000–$34,999	1.40	1.82	1.13	0.46
$35,000–$49,999	1.47	2.05	1.18	0.60
$50,000–$74,999	1.45	1.65	1.20	0.64
$75,000 or more	3.28	4.23	0.75	−0.95
Family owns a computer (excluded = no)				
Yes	1.16	1.73	1.06	0.66
Student's dating attitudes, family expectations, and family vs. work attitudes				
How important is it to have a steady girl/boyfriend (excluded = not important)				
Somewhat important	0.78	−2.73	0.91	−1.06
Very important	0.69	−2.84	0.85	−1.15
Expected age at first marriage	1.05	3.34	0.99	−0.88
Expected age at first birth	1.04	3.18	1.00	0.29
Family-work attitude scale	1.04	1.08	0.91	−2.86

Table D3.b (continued)

	Attend college		Major in S/E	
	exp(b)	z-ratio	exp(b)	z-ratio
Student attitudes about math				
Math is one of my best subjects (excluded = disagree)				
Agree	1.09	0.69	1.49	3.16
I have always done well in math (excluded = disagree)				
Agree	1.14	1.06	1.45	2.93
I get good marks in math (excluded = disagree)				
Agree	0.80	−1.58	0.86	−1.08
High school math course participation and grades				
Participation in advanced math courses during high school (excluded = no)				
Yes	2.12	6.43	1.19	1.80
Average math course grades	1.02	3.12	1.01	2.55
Grade during which student took last high school math course (excluded = grade 9 or 10)				
Grade 11	1.41	2.90	0.89	−0.64
Grade 12	1.89	5.46	1.21	1.04
Model χ^2 (df)	2,039.70 (47)		20,677.60 (47)	

Source: NELS Second Follow-up, 1992.

Note: Sample sizes are 12,784 for the logit model of the expectation of college attendance and 8,918 for the logit of the expectation of majoring in an S/E field among those individuals who expect to attend college. Models include missing data indicator variables for each of the covariates.

Table D3.c Change in the female-to-male odds ratio of expecting to major in S/E attributable to each explanatory factor

	Major in S/E	
Explanatory factor	"Low" (D_1)	"High" (D_2)
Race + high school program	−0.01	0.00
Math and science achievement	0.02	0.03
Math and science achievement high performance	0.00	0.02
Family of origin influences	0.00	0.01
Own family expectations and attitudes	0.00	0.00
Math attitudes	0.02	0.02
High school math course participation and grades	−0.01	−0.01
All factors	0.03	

Note: The entries represent the amount of change in the female-to-male odds ratio of expecting to major in S/E that is attributable to each explanatory factor or set of factors included in the model. The "Low" estimate (D_1) is the change in the exponentiated coefficient of sex after an explanatory factor or set of factors is removed from the full model (Model B7 in Table 3.2). The "High" estimate (D_2) is the increase in the exponentiated coefficient of sex after an explanatory factor or set of factors is added to the baseline model (Model B0 in Table 3.2). All calculations ignore sampling error.

Table D4.a Sex-specific distributions of explanatory variables for the sequential samples

	Total sample		Those who enroll in college		Those who attain a bachelor's degree	
	Female	Male	Female	Male	Female	Male
Sample size *(n)*	3,417	3,311	2,248	1,962	980	903
Background characteristics						
Educational expectations, spring 1982 (%)						
No college	56.95	58.78	38.28	33.30		
Non-S/E major	35.50	26.30	50.96	42.33		
S/E college major	7.55	14.91	10.76	24.37		
Educational status, fall 1982 (%)						
No college	41.65	47.47			n/a	n/a
Non-S/E major	51.83	35.69			84.73	64.99
S/E college major	6.53	16.84			15.27	35.01
High school program (%)						
Non–college preparatory	59.59	60.92	41.60	40.28	17.33	24.40
College preparatory	40.13	38.46	58.20	59.33	82.61	75.60
Missing	0.28	0.63	0.20	0.39	0.06	0.00
Math achievement score (mean)	0.05	0.27	0.38	0.75	0.92	1.19
Math achievement high performance (% yes)	4.41	9.20	7.28	15.97	14.50	27.36
Family of origin influences						
Father's educational attainment (%)						
Less than college	58.24	56.34	49.45	45.29	35.08	35.64
College or more	30.60	33.02	42.16	48.05	59.95	59.96
Missing	11.16	10.64	8.39	6.66	4.98	4.40
Mother's educational attainment (%)						
Less than college	67.27	65.08	58.23	56.38	46.39	49.77
College or more	26.82	26.04	37.79	37.94	51.54	45.97
Missing	5.91	8.87	3.98	5.67	2.07	4.27
Parental expectations for student's educational attainment (%)						
Less than college	37.25	32.46	23.85	17.61	5.91	5.58
College or more	47.65	46.61	65.34	69.06	88.78	86.13
Missing	15.10	20.93	10.81	13.33	5.30	8.28
Student's own family expectations and family vs. work attitudes, fall 1982						
Expected age at first marriage (mean)	24.71	26.05	25.25	26.43		
Expected number of children (%)						
None	6.50	7.41	6.56	5.97		
1 or 2	53.17	55.53	51.34	57.62		
3 or more	33.28	26.36	37.12	29.13		
Missing	7.04	10.70	4.99	7.28		

Table D4.a (continued)

	Total sample		Those who enroll in college		Those who attain a bachelor's degree	
	Female	Male	Female	Male	Female	Male
Family-work attitude scale (mean)	0.24	−0.22	0.15	−0.19		
Student's own family status and family vs. work attitudes, 1984						
Marital status (%)						
Married	14.50	5.12			1.34	0.17
Missing	0.22	0.21			0.13	0.00
Parental status (%)						
Have children	16.29	11.08			6.21	5.23
Missing	0.00	0.00			0.00	0.00
Family-work attitude scale (mean)	0.49	0.00			0.36	0.12
High school math grades and participation						
High school math course grades (mean)	79.41	77.07	81.37	79.30	85.01	83.98
Participation in advanced math courses during high school (%)						
Yes	17.16	18.97	26.73	31.19	43.76	43.83
Missing	10.13	10.53	6.80	8.11	5.68	6.26
Grade during which student took last high school math course (%)						
Grade 10	38.58	31.86	27.62	18.02	13.78	7.36
Grade 11	23.66	22.82	27.14	24.53	28.94	22.16
Grade 12	27.55	34.64	38.39	49.29	51.49	64.15
Missing	10.20	10.69	6.85	8.15	5.79	6.34
College GPA and course grades, 1984						
College course GPA (mean)	2.49	2.41			2.88	2.85
S/E vs. non-S/E college course grade scale (mean)	−0.21	0.20			−0.35	−0.36

Source: HSB Sophomore Cohort First Follow-up through Fourth Follow-up, 1982–1992.

Table D4.b Estimated coefficients from sequential logit models of enrollment and selection of S/E major among those who enrolled in college in the fall of 1982

	Enrollment		Selection of S/E major	
	exp(*b*)	*z*-ratio	exp(*b*)	*z*-ratio
Constant	0.11	−5.43	0.04	−4.62
Sex (female)	1.63	5.75	0.34	−8.89
Background characteristics				
Educational expectations (excluded = non-S/E major)				
No college	0.32	−10.18	1.54	2.21
S/E college major	0.79	−1.39	3.38	8.94
High school program (excluded = non–college preparatory)				
College preparatory	2.22	8.49	1.11	0.75
Math achievement score	1.57	8.12	1.44	3.60
Math achievement high performance	n/a	n/a	1.59	2.41
Family of origin influences				
Father's educational attainment (excluded = less than four years of college)				
College or more	1.37	3.07	0.80	−1.56
Mother's educational attainment (excluded = less than four years of college)				
College or more	2.00	6.41	0.90	−0.82
Parental expectations for student's educational attainment (excluded = less than four years of college)				
College or more	1.57	4.19	0.87	−0.65
Student's own family expectations and family vs. work attitudes				
Expected age at first marriage	1.04	2.52	0.97	−1.13
Expected number of children (excluded = none)				
1 or 2	2.50	5.15	0.74	−1.13
3 or more	3.16	6.01	0.79	−0.81
Family-work attitude scale	0.88	−3.37	0.86	−2.59
High school math grades and participation				
High school math course grades	1.01	2.88	1.02	3.26
Participation in advanced math courses during high school (excluded = no)				
Yes	1.58	3.29	1.38	2.36
Grade during which student took last high school math course (excluded = grade 10)				
Grade 11	1.41	3.29	0.82	−1.05
Grade 12	1.57	4.07	1.94	3.54
Model χ^2 (df)	1,053.27 (26)		423.9 (27)	

Source: HSB Sophomore Cohort First Follow-up through Fourth Follow-up, 1982–1992.

Note: Sample sizes are 6,728 for the logit of college enrollment and 4,210 for the logit of selection of S/E major among those who enrolled in college in the fall of 1982. Models include missing data indicator variables for each of the covariates.

Table D4.c Change in the female-to-male odds ratio of majoring in S/E attributable to each explanatory factor

Explanatory factor	Select an S/E major	
	"Low" (D_1)	"High" (D_2)
Educational expectations, spring 1982	0.04	0.04
High school program	0.00	0.00
Math achievement	0.02	0.05
Math achievement high performance	0.00	0.03
Family of origin influences	0.00	0.00
Own family expectations and attitudes	0.01	0.01
High school math course participation and grades	−0.03	−0.01
All factors	0.07	

Note: The entries represent the amount of change in the female-to-male odds ratio of majoring in S/E that is attributable to each explanatory factor or set of factors included in the model. The "Low" estimate (D_1) is the change in the coefficient of sex after an explanatory factor or set of factors is removed from the full model (Model B7 in Table 4.2). The "High" estimate (D_2) is the increase in the coefficient of sex after an explanatory factor or set of factors is added to the baseline model (Model B0 in Table 4.2). All calculations ignore sampling error.

Table D4.d Estimated coefficients from sequential logit models of degree attainment among all HSBSo respondents and S/E degree attainment among those who earned a bachelor's degree by 1988

	Degree		S/E degree	
	exp(b)	z-ratio	exp(b)	z-ratio
Constant	0.00	−12.24	0.00	−4.19
Sex (female)	1.03	0.30	0.49	−2.72
Background characteristics				
College major fall 1982 (excluded = non-S/E major)				
No college	0.29	−5.79	1.78	1.05
S/E college major	0.68	−3.03	81.15	16.96
High school program (excluded = non–college preparatory)				
College preparatory	2.55	8.38	1.53	1.20
Math achievement score	1.72	6.70	1.11	0.43
Math achievement high performance	n/a	n/a	1.39	0.98
High school math grades and participation				
High school math course grades	1.02	3.89	1.00	0.23
Participation in advanced math courses during high school (excluded = no)				
Yes	1.18	1.33	2.48	3.24
Grade during which student took last high school math course (excluded = grade 10)				
Grade 11	1.82	3.97	1.00	0.01
Grade 12	1.94	4.31	0.75	−0.49
Student's own family status and family vs. work attitudes, 1984				
Marital status	0.15	−5.11	0.50	−0.80
Parental status	0.69	−2.00	1.84	1.03
Family-work attitude scale	0.96	−1.04	0.95	−0.55
College GPA and course grades, 1984				
College course GPA	2.74	13.65	2.06	2.75
S/E vs. non-S/E college course grade scale	n/a	n/a	1.61	2.75
Model χ^2 (df)	720.58 (19)		354.60 (21)	

Source: HSB Sophomore Cohort First Follow-up through Fourth Follow-up, 1982–1992.

Note: Sample sizes are 6,728 for the logit model of degree attainment and 1,883 for the logit of S/E degree attainment among those individuals who attained a bachelor's degree by 1988. Models include missing data indicator variables for each of the covariates.

Table D4.e Change in the female-to-male odds ratio of degree receipt in S/E attributable to each explanatory factor

Explanatory factor	S/E degree	
	"Low" (D_1)	"High" (D_2)
College major, fall 1982	0.11	0.22
High school program	−0.02	−0.02
Math achievement	0.01	0.08
Math achievement high performance	0.01	0.06
High school math course participation and grades	−0.06	−0.03
Own family status and attitudes	−0.07	0.03
College GPA and course grade scale	−0.03	−0.02
All factors	0.14	

Note: The entries represent the amount of change in the female-to-male odds ratio of receiving an S/E degree that is attributable to each explanatory factor or set of factors included in the model. The "Low" estimate (D_1) is the change in the coefficient of sex after an explanatory factor or set of factors is removed from the full model (Model B7 in Table 4.3). The "High" estimate (D_2) is the increase in the coefficient of sex after an explanatory factor or set of factors is added to the baseline model (Model B0 in Table 4.3). All calculations ignore sampling error.

Table D5.a Estimated coefficients from three sequential logit models of postbaccalaureate choices among recent graduates (B&B)

	Graduate school or work vs. neither		Graduate school vs. work		Graduate school in S/E vs. non-S/E	
	exp(*b*)	*z*-ratio	exp(*b*)	*z*-ratio	exp(*b*)	*z*-ratio
Constant	25.83	12.20	0.39	−7.29	0.56	−2.50
Gender (Female)	1.03	0.08	1.02	0.10	0.77	−0.95
Bachelor's degree major (excluded = biological science)						
Engineering	1.50	1.03	0.77	−1.63	6.13	5.95
Mathematical science	2.87	2.33	0.57	−3.12	3.89	4.12
Physical science	1.74	1.05	2.22	3.82	6.80	5.75
Family status (excluded = unmarried)						
Married without children	0.74	−0.43	0.52	−2.85	1.75	1.40
Married with children	0.59	−0.71	0.78	−0.88		
Sex × (Family status)						
Married without children and female	5.59	1.36	0.66	−0.99	0.14	−2.46
Married with children and female	0.29	−1.38	0.35	−2.07		
Model χ^2 (df)	26.11 (8)		60.30 (8)		64.91 (6)	

Source: Baccalaureate and Beyond Longitudinal Study First Follow-up.

Note: Sample sizes are 2,086 for the logit model predicting the likelihood of either graduate school or work, 2,019 for the logit of the likelihood of enrollment in graduate school versus entering the labor force, and 506 for the logit of selection of an S/E major among those who enrolled in a graduate program.

Table D5.b Estimated coefficients from three sequential logit models of postbaccalaureate choices among recent graduates (NES)

	Graduate school or work vs. neither		Work vs. graduate school		Work in S/E vs. non-S/E	
	exp(*b*)	*z*-ratio	exp(*b*)	*z*-ratio	exp(*b*)	*z*-ratio
Constant	26.65	21.86	0.73	−5.60	0.84	−2.10
Sex (female)	0.90	−0.81	1.29	4.94	0.78	−3.13
Master's degree major (excluded = biological science)						
Engineering	2.25	6.43	2.38	18.12	6.58	23.93
Mathematical science	2.27	6.18	2.45	15.51	3.53	16.13
Physical science	1.15	1.22	0.87	−2.55	1.32	3.12
Year (excluded = 1978)						
1979	1.03	0.16	1.04	0.60	1.31	2.74
1980	0.92	−0.47	1.16	2.28	1.51	4.19
1982	0.52	−3.83	1.27	3.55	2.48	8.41
1984	0.62	−2.91	1.12	1.84	2.16	7.47
1986	0.81	−1.16	1.47	5.82	1.84	5.85
1988	0.77	−1.38	1.33	4.20	2.13	7.27
Family status (excluded = unmarried)						
Married without children	1.80	3.42	1.39	6.89	1.23	2.49
Married with children	1.46	1.60	2.32	10.77	1.37	2.70
Sex × (Family status)						
Married without children and female	0.31	−5.01	1.18	1.52	0.92	−0.58
Married with children and female	0.06	−9.48	1.10	0.43	0.50	−2.88
Model χ^2 (df)	415.10 (14)		1,033.03 (14)		1,081.01 (14)	

Source: 1978–1988 New Entrants Surveys.

Note: Sample sizes are 25,170 for the logit model predicting the likelihood of either graduate school or work, 24,305 for the logit model predicting the likelihood of working versus going to graduate school, and 15,861 for the logit of selection of an S/E occupation among those who work.

Table D6.a Estimated coefficients from three sequential logit models of post–master's degree choices among recent graduates

	Either graduate school or working		Work vs. graduate school		Work in S/E vs. non-S/E	
	exp(b)	z-ratio	exp(b)	z-ratio	exp(b)	z-ratio
Constant	30.10	13.96	0.96	−0.43	2.48	6.02
Sex (Female)	0.97	−0.12	1.44	3.82	0.68	−2.38
Master's degree major (excluded = biological science)						
Engineering	1.72	2.92	2.05	9.96	4.28	11.75
Mathematical science	1.24	1.01	2.69	10.84	2.13	5.76
Physical science	0.82	−1.10	1.06	0.73	1.77	4.20
Year (excluded = 1978)						
1979	0.89	−0.39	1.11	0.96	1.11	0.66
1980	1.05	0.16	1.12	1.16	1.61	2.98
1982	0.73	−1.21	0.89	−1.23	1.86	3.81
1984	0.87	−0.55	1.05	0.55	2.35	5.32
1986	0.96	−0.18	1.08	0.77	2.09	4.54
1988	0.91	−0.36	1.03	0.29	1.91	3.85
Family status (excluded = unmarried)						
Married without children	2.03	3.18	1.17	2.30	1.02	0.15
Married with children	3.07	4.59	2.20	10.81	0.65	−3.64
Sex × (Family status)						
Married without children and female	0.25	−3.78	1.27	1.47	0.90	−0.41
Married with children and female	0.06	−8.10	0.85	−0.76	0.86	−0.57
Model χ^2 (df)	233.77 (14)		372.77 (14)		239.44 (14)	

Source: 1978–1988 New Entrants Surveys.

Note: Sample sizes are 11,407 for the logit model predicting the likelihood of either graduate school or work, 11,040 for the logit model predicting the likelihood of working versus going to graduate school, and 7,459 for the logit of selection of an S/E occupation among those who work.

Table D7.a Estimated coefficients of a logit model predicting odds of employment and a linear model predicting log of earnings

	Employment		Earnings	
	exp(*b*)	*z*-ratio	*b*	*t*-ratio
Constant	225.11	6.87	6158.74	174.68
Sex (female)	2.09	3.84	0.93	−6.95
Age	0.96	−1.24	1.06	26.16
Age^2	1.00	0.18	1.00	−19.96
Race (excluded = white)				
Asian	0.73	−2.65	0.95	−7.93
Other	0.49	−5.38	0.94	−5.81
Education (excluded = less than Ph.D.)				
Ph.D.	1.25	1.83	1.13	18.66
Field (excluded = biological science)				
Engineering	0.81	−1.15	1.30	29.00
Mathematical science	0.73	−1.79	1.20	20.38
Physical science	0.87	−0.68	1.14	12.84
Employment sector (excluded = industry)				
Academic	1.11	0.58	0.80	−21.19
Government	2.17	3.55	0.90	−10.66
Other	0.94	−0.52	1.02	3.79
Weeks worked in 1989 (excluded = less than 45)				
45 to 49	n/a	n/a	1.15	7.59
50 and above	n/a	n/a	1.25	14.43
Hours typically worked in 1989 (excluded = less than 40)				
40–44	n/a	n/a	1.06	4.30
45 and above	n/a	n/a	1.16	11.44
Family status (excluded = unmarried)				
Married without children	2.53	7.73	1.07	9.83
Married with children	2.88	9.16	1.11	15.20
Sex × (Family status)				
Married without children and female	0.27	−4.95	0.93	−4.68
Married with children and female	0.19	−6.50	0.92	−5.19
Model fit	$\chi^2 = 212.12$ (16 df)		$R^2 = 23.33\%$	

Source: 5 percent 1990 PUMS.

Note: Sample size is 35,407 for the logit regression model predicting logged odds of employment. Sample size is 31,054 for the linear regression model predicting logged earnings.

Table D7.b Logit regression model predicting promotion: An event-history analysis of a cohort of scientists and engineers

	exp(b)	z-ratio
Constant	0.00	−2.94
Sex (female)	1.12	0.16
Year (excluded = 1984)		
1986	0.77	−1.15
1989	0.70	−1.63
Age	1.40	2.16
Age^2	1.00	−1.99
Race (excluded = white)		
Asian	0.61	−1.51
Other	1.13	0.33
Education^t (excluded = less than Ph.D.)		
Ph.D.	0.50	−2.89
Field of highest degree^t (excluded = biological science)		
Engineering	3.12	3.35
Mathematical science	4.33	3.93
Physical science	2.31	1.96
Other	1.26	0.28
Occupation field^t (excluded = biological)		
Engineering	0.28	−3.88
Mathematical	0.34	−3.01
Physical	0.84	−0.39
Employment sector^t (excluded = industry)		
Academic	0.21	−2.73
Government	0.82	−0.81
Other	2.59	2.96
Family status^t (excluded = unmarried)		
Married without children	0.55	−1.89
Married with children	1.04	0.14
Sex × (Family status)		
Married without children and female	0.88	−0.15
Married with children and female	0.22	−1.94
Model χ^2 (df)	75.83 (22)	

Source: 1982–1989 SSE.

Note: Regression was weighted. There are 6,183 person-periods for the logit model of the event-history analysis. Superscript t indicates variables that are time-variant.

Table D9.a Sex-specific means of explanatory variables (in percent) and estimated coefficients in the final negative binomial model of research productivity: Carnegie-1969

	Sample means		Parameter estimates	
	Women	Men	exp(b)	z-ratio
Constant			2.69	17.96
Sex (female)	100.00	0.00	1.00	−0.04
Field				
Biological science	52.57	34.43	(Excluded)	
Engineering	2.38	20.02	0.83	−6.85
Mathematical science	17.21	13.09	0.83	−4.74
Physical science	27.84	32.47	0.95	−1.92
Time between BS/BA and Ph.D.				
1–4 years	19.23	25.95	(Excluded)	
5–7 years	35.26	39.61	0.86	−6.63
8–10 years	14.80	19.05	0.80	−7.70
11 years and above	30.71	15.39	0.65	−11.10
Years of experience				
0–5	37.21	34.83	(Excluded)	
6–10	18.91	23.23	0.96	−1.17
11–20	25.69	27.93	0.80	−5.47
21–30	12.99	8.65	0.74	−5.74
31 and above	5.20	5.37	0.66	−5.99
Type of current institution				
High-quality university	10.88	18.37	(Excluded)	
Medium-quality university	19.28	30.45	0.85	−7.30
Low-quality university	16.47	22.51	0.72	−12.75
High four-year college	14.48	8.56	0.65	−11.16
Medium four-year college	12.33	8.75	0.52	−9.77
Low four-year college	25.79	10.58	0.47	−9.50
Junior college	0.78	0.79	0.57	−1.37
Rank				
Assistant professor	39.78	29.03	(Excluded)	
Associate professor	26.84	29.46	1.23	6.30
Full professor	25.76	38.98	1.52	10.10
Other	7.62	2.53	1.08	0.96
Teaching hours				
0–4 hours	22.18	35.88	(Excluded)	
5–6 hours	13.56	21.23	0.95	−2.04
7–8 hours	11.06	13.58	0.92	−2.78

Table D9.a (continued)

| | Sample means | | Parameter estimates | |
	Women	Men	exp(b)	z-ratio
9–10 hours	16.47	11.12	0.86	−3.68
11 hours and above	36.74	18.19	0.75	−7.06
Research funding				
Federal (dummy)	27.11	52.04	1.51	16.73
State/local (dummy)	2.15	10.35	1.04	1.39
Industrial (dummy)	1.94	10.23	1.27	8.63
Private foundation (dummy)	8.33	9.59	1.32	8.92
Own institution (dummy)	36.94	49.73	1.17	7.69
Research assistance				
Graduate assistant (dummy)	21.88	53.17	1.30	9.97
Family status				
Unmarried	56.88	9.00	(Excluded)	
Married without children	15.40	14.41	1.08	1.70
Married with children	27.72	76.59	1.12	2.89
Model χ^2 (df)			3,243.46 (32)	

Note: Sample size is 12,225. The negative binomial models include a parameter to correct for overdispersion in the dependent variable.

Table D9.b Sex-specific means of explanatory variables (in percent) and estimated coefficients in the final negative binomial model of research productivity: ACE-1973

	Sample means		Parameter estimates	
	Women	Men	exp(*b*)	*z*-ratio
Constant			2.67	13.79
Sex (female)	100.00	0.00	0.97	−0.37
Field				
Biological science	53.84	29.30	(Excluded)	
Engineering	0.67	19.94	0.84	−5.17
Mathematical science	19.14	17.13	0.89	−2.26
Physical science	26.35	33.64	1.04	1.10
Time between BS/BA and Ph.D.				
1–4 years	18.83	22.35	(Excluded)	
5–7 years	38.44	42.70	0.85	−5.91
8–10 years	17.90	18.78	0.77	−7.17
11 years and above	24.82	16.17	0.63	−9.06
Years of experience				
0–5	25.85	21.07	(Excluded)	
6–10	27.32	29.52	1.02	0.40
11–20	30.71	33.15	0.82	−3.94
21–30	9.88	11.85	0.68	−6.50
31 and above	6.23	4.41	0.73	−3.43
Type of current institution				
Research I	21.58	32.60	(Excluded)	
Research II	11.41	17.94	0.96	−1.52
Doctoral I	10.35	15.79	0.83	−5.16
Doctoral II	1.86	6.06	0.86	−3.61
Comprehensive I	18.27	15.79	0.50	−10.35
Comprehensive II	4.74	2.13	0.42	−5.17
Liberal arts I	15.23	4.79	0.40	−12.58
Liberal arts II	15.10	4.06	0.34	−6.69
Two-year college	1.48	0.83	0.57	−1.11
Rank				
Assistant professor	29.26	22.14	(Excluded)	
Associate professor	42.38	33.33	1.14	3.45
Full professor	26.08	43.96	1.43	7.35
Other	2.27	0.56	1.77	1.18

Table D9.b (continued)

Teaching hours				
0–4	14.50	22.59	(Excluded)	
5–8	24.71	36.97	1.02	0.82
9–12	33.84	25.40	0.94	−1.87
13–16	26.95	15.04	0.85	−3.05
Research funding				
Federal (dummy)	36.75	52.65	1.48	12.44
State/local (dummy)	3.34	10.95	1.00	−0.02
Industrial (dummy)	3.34	9.18	1.11	3.27
Private foundation (dummy)	5.82	10.32	1.27	7.73
Own institution (dummy)	30.02	31.82	1.11	4.08
Research assistance				
Graduate assistant (dummy)	29.68	49.79	1.42	11.45
Family status				
Unmarried	52.09	7.75	(Excluded)	
Married without children	21.97	14.24	1.05	0.87
Married with children	25.94	78.00	1.09	1.62
Model χ^2 (df)			1995.18 (33)	

Note: Sample size is 6,998. The negative binomial models include a parameter to correct for overdispersion in the dependent variable.

Table D9.c Sex-specific means of explanatory variables (in percent) and estimated coefficients in the final negative binomial model of research productivity: NSPF-88

	Sample means		Parameter estimates	
	Women	Men	exp(*b*)	*z*-ratio
Constant			3.55	5.88
Sex (female)	100.00	0.00	0.80	−1.42
Field				
Biological science	44.33	27.77	(Excluded)	
Engineering	7.07	20.09	1.11	0.92
Mathematical science	26.31	21.21	0.79	−2.16
Physical science	22.29	30.93	1.08	0.85
Time between BS/BA and Ph.D.				
1–4 years	11.86	14.99	(Excluded)	
5–7 years	31.02	47.03	0.77	−2.25
8–10 years	19.44	19.35	0.68	−2.64
11 years and above	37.69	18.63	0.77	−1.74
Years of experience				
0–5	16.88	13.04	(Excluded)	
6–10	25.38	16.41	1.01	0.04
11–20	43.83	36.16	0.89	−0.66
21–30	9.92	26.12	0.64	−2.30
31 and above	3.98	8.27	0.44	−3.35
Type of current institution				
Public research	34.35	32.16	(Excluded)	
Private research	12.57	12.32	1.08	0.70
Public doctoral granting	4.53	9.87	0.93	−0.68
Private doctoral granting	8.62	7.80	1.06	0.40
Public comprehensive	17.40	18.46	0.63	−3.35
Private comprehensive	9.60	7.95	0.72	−1.63
Liberal arts	5.33	7.79	0.41	−4.05
Public two-year	7.58	3.65	0.26	−3.09
Rank				
Assistant professor	29.25	19.28	(Excluded)	
Associate professor	37.81	26.96	1.09	0.62
Full professor	25.72	52.08	1.60	3.00
Other	7.22	1.68	1.27	0.46
Teaching hours				
0–4 hours	23.33	28.76	(Excluded)	
5–6 hours	24.33	19.44	1.01	0.14

Table D9.c (continued)

	Sample means		Parameter estimates	
	Women	Men	exp(b)	z-ratio
7–8 hours	9.49	10.54	0.90	−0.92
9–10 hours	13.41	12.47	0.71	−2.14
11 hours and above	29.44	28.80	0.59	−4.09
Research funding				
Federal (dummy)	39.50	36.62	1.68	6.33
State/local (dummy)	4.75	8.63	1.39	2.79
Industrial (dummy)	8.84	12.65	1.36	3.20
Private foundation (dummy)	14.06	9.53	1.23	1.79
Own institution (dummy)	13.97	13.07	1.25	2.45
Research assistance				
Graduate assistant (dummy)	71.45	76.51	1.27	2.18
Marital status				
Married (dummy)	60.80	86.37	1.15	1.46
Model χ^2 (df)			436.56 (32)	

Note: Sample size is 847. The negative binomial models include a parameter to correct for overdispersion in the dependent variable.

Table D9.d Sex-specific means of explanatory variables (in percent) and estimated coefficients in the final negative binomial model of research productivity: NSPF-93

	Sample means		Parameter estimates	
	Women	Men	exp(b)	z-ratio
Constant			4.15	7.92
Sex (female)	100.00	0.00	0.94	−0.73
Field				
Biological science	51.64	34.08	(Excluded)	
Engineering	9.10	19.94	0.90	−1.19
Mathematical science	19.25	20.70	0.80	−2.40
Physical science	20.01	25.28	0.89	−1.40
Time between BS/BA and Ph.D.				
1–4 years	7.44	16.80	(Excluded)	
5–7 years	43.71	45.68	0.72	−3.40
8–10 years	21.69	20.61	0.65	−3.88
11 years and above	27.16	16.91	0.60	−4.38
Years of experience				
0–5	27.92	14.94	(Excluded)	
6–10	21.27	13.38	0.87	−1.31
11–20	34.22	30.49	0.84	−1.33
21–30	13.66	32.03	0.65	−2.98
31 and above	2.93	9.16	0.55	−3.19
Type of current institution				
Public research	24.47	39.03	(Excluded)	
Private research	12.05	8.60	1.34	2.68
Public doctoral granting	9.29	10.79	0.89	−1.34
Private doctoral granting	5.56	6.15	0.93	−0.65
Public comprehensive	21.56	18.72	0.63	−4.66
Private comprehensive	8.32	5.53	0.49	−4.51
Liberal arts	12.09	6.56	0.54	−4.14
Public two-year	6.66	4.62	0.34	−4.01
Rank				
Assistant professor	35.86	19.41	(Excluded)	
Associate professor	30.83	26.74	1.06	0.58
Full professor	30.15	50.77	1.46	3.06
Other	3.16	3.08	1.08	0.26
Teaching hours				
0–4 hours	34.17	38.08	(Excluded)	
5–6 hours	17.39	18.23	0.93	−0.75

Table D9.d (continued)

	Sample means		Parameter estimates	
	Women	Men	exp(*b*)	*z*-ratio
7–8 hours	5.11	8.84	0.89	−0.98
9–10 hours	12.41	11.76	0.88	−1.25
11 hours and above	30.93	23.09	0.67	−4.44
Research funding				
Federal (dummy)	37.09	37.55	1.48	5.85
State/local (dummy)	9.78	9.56	1.34	3.25
Industrial (dummy)	6.96	16.07	1.38	4.37
Private foundation (dummy)	12.20	16.53	1.39	3.85
Own institution (dummy)	18.31	18.37	1.37	4.70
Research assistance				
Graduate assistant (dummy)	72.58	78.58	1.56	4.79
Marital status				
Married (dummy)	68.76	87.27	1.10	1.06
Model χ^2 (df)			795.26 (32)	

Note: Sample size is 1,845. The negative binomial models include a parameter to correct for overdispersion in the dependent variable.

Table D9.e Attribution of explanatory power to individual explanatory factors

Explanatory factor	Carnegie-1969		ACE-1973		NSPF-1988		NSPF-1993	
	"Low" (D_1)	"High" (D_2)	"Low" (D_1)	"High" (D_2)	"Low" (D_1)	"High" (D_2)	"Low" (D_1)	"High" (D_2)
Field	-0.028	-0.008	-0.013	-0.013	0.011	0.003	-0.030	-0.054
Time between BA/BS and Ph.D.	0.045	0.045	0.031	0.037	0.015	0.104	0.016	0.070
Years of experience	0.033	0.008	0.030	0.004	0.012	-0.001	-0.040	0.005
Type of current institution	0.039	0.138	0.112	0.217	0.014	0.031	0.020	0.090
Rank	0.054	0.031	0.036	0.023	0.060	0.092	-0.004	0.029
Teaching hours	0.015	0.117	0.003	0.075	-0.039	0.027	0.005	0.075
Research funding	0.040	0.181	0.007	0.086	-0.059	0.005	0.025	0.014
Research assistance	0.016	0.162	-0.008	0.083	0.003	0.017	0.018	0.055
Marital status	0.046	0.101	0.035	0.084	0.026	0.031	0.013	0.022
All factors $\exp(b^3) - \exp(b^0)$	0.417		0.339		0.106		0.127	

Note: The entries represent the amount of change in female-to-male ratio in productivity rate (r) that is attributable to each set of explanatory factors included in the model. The "Low" estimate (D_1) is the change in the exponentiated coefficient of sex after a set of factors is removed from the full model (Model 3 of Table 9.2). The "High" estimate (D_2) is the exponentiated increase in the coefficient of sex after an explanatory factor or set of factors is added to the model that includes only sex as an explanatory variable (Model 0 of Table 9.2). All calculations ignore sampling error.

Table D10.a Estimated coefficients of a logit model predicting odds of employment and a linear regression model predicting log of earnings

	Employment		Earnings	
	exp(b)	z-ratio	exp(b)	t-ratio
Constant	301.74	7.21	6,284.23	175.01
Sex (female)	1.08	0.56	0.89	−15.64
Age	0.95	−1.35	1.06	26.05
Age^2	1.00	0.37	1.00	−19.79
Race (excluded = white)				
Asian	1.33	2.02	0.98	−2.23
Other	0.65	−3.13	0.96	−4.22
Immigration status (excluded = U.S.-born)				
Foreign-born	0.53	−5.55	0.96	−5.38
Education (excluded = less than Ph.D.)				
Ph.D.	1.32	2.29	1.13	18.98
Field (excluded = biological science)				
Engineering	0.83	−1.04	1.30	29.14
Mathematical science	0.71	−1.94	1.20	20.32
Physical science	0.89	−0.59	1.14	12.88
Employment sector (excluded = industry)				
Academic	1.06	0.32	0.80	−21.29
Government	2.07	3.32	0.90	−10.86
Other	0.94	−0.51	1.02	3.80
Weeks worked in 1989 (excluded = less than 45)				
45 to 49	n/a	n/a	1.15	7.77
50 and above	n/a	n/a	1.25	14.46
Hours typically worked in 1989 (excluded = less than 40)				
40–44	n/a	n/a	1.06	4.23
45 and above	n/a	n/a	1.16	11.36
Family status (excluded = unmarried)				
Married without children	1.92	6.00	1.06	8.44
Married with children	2.15	7.31	1.09	14.31
English proficiency (excluded = speaks English proficiently)				
Does not speak English well	0.30	−4.39	0.81	−6.23
Sex × (Immigration status)				
Foreign-born and female	0.54	−2.95	0.98	−1.09
Model fit	$\chi^2 = 237.04$ (17 df)		$R^2 = 23.44\%$	

Source: 5 percent 1990 PUMS.

Note: Sample size is 35,407 for the logit regression model predicting logged odds of employment. Sample size is 31,054 for the linear regression model predicting logged earnings.

Table D10.b Logit model predicting promotion: An event-history analysis of a cohort of scientists and engineers

	exp(b)	z-ratio
Constant	0.00	−2.92
Year (excluded = 1984)		
1986	0.77	−1.15
1989	0.69	−1.63
Sex (female)	0.75	−0.64
Age	1.39	2.19
Age^2	1.00	−2.01
Race (excluded = white)		
Asian	0.47	−1.80
Other	1.00	0.01
Immigration status (excluded = U.S.-born)		
Foreign-born	1.59	1.36
Education^t (excluded = less than Ph.D.)		
Ph.D.	0.50	−2.92
Field of highest degree^t (excluded = biological science)		
Engineering	3.07	3.29
Mathematical science	4.24	3.91
Physical science	2.25	1.89
Other	1.16	0.18
Occupation field^t (excluded = biological science)		
Engineering	0.27	−3.91
Mathematical science	0.35	−2.89
Physical science	0.85	−0.37
Employment sector^t (excluded = industry)		
Academic	0.20	−2.87
Government	0.83	−0.77
Other	2.27	2.58
Family status^t (excluded = unmarried)		
Married without children	0.52	−2.07
Married with children	0.87	−0.53
Sex × (Immigration status)		
Foreign-born and female	0.43	−1.13
Model χ^2 (df)	79.83 (22)	

Source: 1982–1989 SSE.

Note: Regression was weighted. There are 6,183 person-periods for the logit model of the event-history analysis. Superscript t indicates variables that are time-variant.

Notes

1. Introduction

1. There are no concrete indications, however, that this concern is justified. Of course, part of the reason the United States is able to maintain its large scientific labor force is through immigration. The interaction between gender and immigration is discussed in Chapter 10.
2. See Keller (1985, 1992) and Harding (1986) for the feminist contention that women bring unique epistemological perspectives to science. See Koertge (1998) for a recent critique and Schiebinger (1999) for a recent review.
3. For convenience, we sometimes refer to science/engineering as science, and scientist/engineer as scientist, throughout the book.
4. This statement does not contradict the fact that some excellent samples have been created for the study of women in science. Prime examples are Cole (1979) and Long, Allison, and McGinnis (1993). Common to these studies is a research design that collects data from recipients of doctoral degrees in certain scientific fields.
5. The excellent study of Citro and Kalton (1989) led NSF to stop using this hybrid definition and to adopt two alternative definitions, one education-based and one occupation-based, as discussed in the next paragraph.
6. Our discussion ignores sampling variability and thus treats estimated statistics as population parameters.
7. Since the statistical models may be nonlinear, the indirect effect cannot always be computed as the simple product of the two direct effects C and B.

2. Math and Science Achievement

1. Findings of research based on broadly representative samples generally contradict those based on samples of select populations, such as Benbow's re-

search focusing on gender differences in mathematics abilities among gifted or precocious youth (Benbow and Stanley 1980, 1983a; Benbow 1988). Benbow (1988) reports significant gender differences in mathematics abilities favoring boys prior to age 12.

2. Traditional measures of sex differences in achievement rest on the assumption of normality of the within-sex distribution of test scores, as noted by Feingold (1992, p. 78). For simplicity, our discussion here also assumes normal distribution for math and science achievement scores.

3. Recent research has indicated that gender differences in science achievement vary by the subject matter of items on science achievement tests (Burkam, Lee, and Smerdon 1997; Dimitrov 1999; Lee and Burkam 1996). Gender differences in life science are found to be minimal, whereas in physical science gender differences are quite large and significant. For this analysis we do not distinguish life and physical science achievement. Since gender differences on physical science achievement tends to be much larger in magnitude, the gender differences we measure are likely to be dominated by the disparity in this subject-domain.

4. Note that males are more likely than females to drop out of high school. Since academically weak students are more likely to drop out, gender differences observed here may be negatively biased in favor of males because of selective attrition. To test if the increasing gender difference was due to differential attrition, we conducted this analysis restricting the samples to the cases that were nonmissing in each wave for each of the studies. Using these restricted samples, we found the same pattern of increasing male advantage in math achievement with age. Hence, we conclude that the age pattern of gender differences in achievement is not due to gender differences in attrition from high school.

5. This trend of narrowing gender differences over historical time was also found in the analysis using samples that were restricted to only those cases with nonmissing data at each observation of each study. See note 4.

6. We resist the temptation to interpret the findings for the LSAY2 cohort as a continuation of the decreasing trend in sex differences. The sample of the LSAY studies is significantly smaller and more selective than those of the other studies. The differences in the LSAY2 may also be due to differences in the instrument used for assessing achievement.

7. As will be shown in note 3 of Chapter 7, the female-to-male odds ratio is a close approximation of the sex ratio in proportions when a small fraction of a population has the characteristic of interest (in this case, being in the top 5 percent of the distribution) and when male and female populations are similar in size (see equation 7.1).

8. For an example of the level of contention in the interpretation of scientific research examining sex differences in spatial ability, see the responses to Caplan, MacPherson, and Tobin (1985) published in 1986 in *American Psychologist* (Burnett 1986; Caplan, MacPherson, and Tobin 1986; Eliot 1986; Halpern 1986; Hiscock 1986; Sanders, Cohen, and Soares 1986).

9. These variables were originally coded according to a six-category scale distinguishing "False," "Mostly false," "More false than true," "More true than false," "Mostly true," and "True." We collapse the categories of the original scale into a three-point scale where 1 = Agree, 2 = Ambivalent, and 3 = Disagree. These attitudinal measures were not collected as part of the NELS Second Follow-up.

10. The dummy variable for each specific course is coded 1 if participation in the course was indicated on the student's transcript. The availability of transcript data for each student is indicated by another dummy variable, coded 1 if the transcript data is missing.

11. High school course grades were translated from the 13-level coding scheme used in the transcript data file to a continuous variable ranging from 33 to 99 according to the grade scales reported by Jones et al. (1984, Appendix C). We used the middle grade scale based on 65 as a failing grade. We recoded the original variable by assigning each of the 13 grade categories the mean value of the range each letter grade represents. For example, A+ = 99, A = 96, A− = 93, and so on. Students who received a "Pass" were assigned the value equivalent to the letter grade B. The grade level "Fail" was assigned the value equivalent to an F. The categories "Incomplete," "Withdraw," and "Audit or Registered" were coded as missing. A separate dummy variable is included in the multivariate analysis, which is coded 1 for those students who did not enroll in any math/science courses or for whom the course grade information was missing from the transcript data.

12. This discussion suggests interaction effects between gender and variables measuring family attitudes. As discussed in footnote 16, we tested for such interactions but did not find them to be statistically significant.

13. Expected age at first marriage and expected age at first birth are categorical variables in the original data. We translated both variables into continuous measures by assigning to each category the midpoint of each age interval. The following coding scheme was used: "already married/had kids" or "before age 18" = 16, "18–21" = 19.5, "22–25" = 23.5, "26–29" = 27.5, "30 or older" or "don't expect to" = 35.

14. To create the family-work attitude scale, we use students' responses to four items that were included in the first and second follow-ups of the NELS. The wording of these items is as follows: "How important is each of the following to you in your life?" (a) "Being successful in my line of work;" (b) "Finding the right person to marry and having a happy family life;" (c) "Having lots of money;" and (d) "Having children." Students were asked to rate the degree of importance for each of these items on a three category scale: (1) "Not important," (2) "Somewhat important," and (3) "Very important." We created a scale of the importance of work-related aspects of life that ranges from one to six by simply adding students' responses on items (a) and (c). We created a parallel scale for students' attitudes about the importance of family-related aspects of life by combining responses to items (b) and (d). For each of these scales, a value of two indicates that a student responded that he/she consid-

ered each of the family- or work-related aspects of life "not important," and six indicates that he/she felt each was "very important." The final family-work attitude scale is created by taking the difference between the family and work attitude scales for each respondent. Survey respondents with missing values are coded as zero on the final family-work attitude scale and are distinguished in the multivariate analysis by the inclusion of a dummy variable that is coded 1 if family and work attitudes are missing.

15. We report linear regression coefficients adjusting for the pooled variance. After the adjustment, the coefficient of sex can be interpreted as the adjusted *d*-statistic: $d = b_{sex}/s_{M+F}$, where s_{M+F} represents the pooled within-sex standard deviation of achievement.

16. The results presented are from models that include only the additive effects of the set of covariates. We used the full additive model as a baseline for the assessment of significant gender-interaction effects, but we found no such effects.

17. We acknowledge that the "Asian or Pacific Islander" and "Native American Indian" racial/ethnic groups are quite different in math and science achievement. However, the very small number of cases in each of these categories made aggregation necessary.

18. The small discrepancy is due to variation in the sample definition. Whereas the full sample was used to compute the observed values of the indices in the earlier tables, the "unadjusted" values in Table 2.3 were based on a smaller sample that was used for the full regression model. Note that our analysis here focuses on whether the observed gender gap is explained by the explanatory variables. Aligning the sample for the baseline model to that for the full model allows us to pinpoint the explanatory power of the additional covariates.

3. Expectation of a Science/Engineering College Major

1. In the context of discussing students' educational expectations, we use the word *choice* to refer to a student's expression of the type of college major they *expect* to choose.

2. The possible responses to the question about postsecondary education enrollment were "Less than high school," "High school only," "Less than 2-year school," "More than 2-year school," "Trade school," "Less than 2-year college," "More than 2-year college," "Finish college," "Master's degree or equivalent," "Ph.D., M.D., or equivalent," and "I don't know." All students responding that they expected to "Finish college" or attain a postgraduate degree were coded as expecting to complete college. Students selecting one of the categories representing a lesser level of educational attainment or "I don't know" were coded as not expecting to complete college.

3. This item was coded in a closed-ended form with 23 categories. Six of the categories were considered S/E: agriculture, biological sciences, computer

science, engineering, mathematics, and physical sciences. The rest were considered non-S/E: architecture, art, business, communications, education, English, ethnic studies, foreign languages, health occupations, home economics, interdisciplinary studies, music, philosophy/religion, preprofessional, psychology, social sciences, and other.

4. The sample excludes original members of the NELS cohort who either dropped out of school or were "out of sequence," that is, who were enrolled in school but not in the twelfth grade at the time of the follow-up study.

5. The math and science achievement scores were standardized to the total sample of twelfth-graders (mean = 0, variance = 1), that is, before dropouts and out-of-sequence respondents were selected out of the sample.

6. All of the variables are based on responses provided by the students in 1992 except for family income, which was measured at the base year when the students were in the eighth grade.

7. Measures of participation and performance in high school science courses that parallel those measuring math course participation and performance were included in preliminary analyses of educational expectations. The measures of participation and performance in high school science courses were dropped from the final analyses for two reasons: (1) the high correlation between science and math on each of the measures of course participation and performance caused multicollinearity problems in the estimation of the models, and (2) the measures of math course participation and performance were found to have more explanatory power than those for science.

8. Since the same classification scheme was used for both the NELS and HSBSo, high school mathematics courses are categorized as advanced or not according to the classification of the HSBSo high school transcript study's secondary school course codes devised by West, Miller, and Diodato (1985, Appendix D). Courses identified as college preparatory courses for gifted-talented students and for math concentrators are classified as advanced.

9. In the calculation of the predicted probability of each educational expectation, the values of all the covariates are held constant at the sample means.

4. Attainment of a Science/Engineering Baccalaureate

1. The total sample size used for our analysis is 6,728 students: 3,311 men and 3,417 women.

2. We do not distinguish between degree attainment in the years 1986 and 1988: educational states during these observation years are collapsed. Although the majority of students (68 percent) in this cohort who attained a bachelor's degree by 1988 did so within four years of their high school graduation (i.e., by 1986), the remaining 32 percent of college graduates obtained their degrees in the following two years. Completing an undergraduate degree in four years is slightly more common in non-S/E fields than in S/E fields. By collapsing the observation of degree attainment across these years, we

avoid imposing a strict time schedule on the process of undergraduate education and allow for a larger variance in time to degree. Hence, we are able to observe a higher rate of degree attainment, especially among those who attain an S/E degree.

3. To clarify the language used in this discussion, "marginal probability" refers to the total probability of degree attainment. For most of the analysis in this chapter, the marginal probability of degree attainment is calculated separately for men and women. "Conditional probability of degree attainment" refers to the probability of degree attainment conditional on educational path.

4. Although we substitute males' distribution probabilities for females' in Table 4.1 one component at a time, the reader is cautioned that in reality the three distribution probabilities are constrained (summed to one) and thus cannot vary freely.

5. All of the indicators of family of origin influences were reported when the students were in high school.

6. The family-work attitude scale was measured in the spring of 1982, when students were still in high school, and is the same as the scale used for the analysis of the NELS data in Chapters 2 and 3.

7. Codebook B (posted at www.yuxie.com) lists the program codes and titles for high school mathematics courses and indicates which courses were classified as "advanced." This categorization was based on the classification of the HSBSo high school transcript study's secondary school course codes devised by West, Miller, and Diodato (1985, Appendix D). Those students who had participated in at least one advanced math course are coded 1 on this indicator.

8. College courses were coded as either S/E or non-S/E according to the Taxonomy of Postsecondary Courses published in *The New College Course Map and Transcript Files* (Adelman 1995). Codebook D (posted at www.yuxie.com) lists the College Course Map (CCM) program codes and titles for the college courses coded as S/E courses by each of the general S/E majors (biological science, physical science, engineering, computer science, and mathematics). College course grades are reported on a 4-point scale (0–4.0 range) for each course recorded on the students' transcript records. The college course grades scale is calculated as a student's average grade in S/E courses minus his/her average grade in non-S/E coursework. This scale measures students' course performance in S/E courses relative to their performance in non-S/E courses.

5. Career Paths after a Science/Engineering Baccalaureate

1. In addition, the structure of the data we use precludes an analysis based on the decision structure presented in Figure 5.2b. See the next section.

2. Note that the B&B survey was administered in 1994, whereas the NES surveys were conducted between 1978 and 1988. Indeed, as logit coefficients in Appendix Table D5.b show, the likelihood of entering graduate school versus the labor force among recent graduates with S/E bachelor's degrees significantly decreased over the years in which the NES data were collected.

3. In calculating the combined percentages, we acknowledge that the two datasets differ in the overall percentage in graduate education, with NES providing a higher estimate than B&B. However, this inconsistency should not severely compromise the interpretation, since our focus here is on cross-field differences.

4. This statement is also applicable for the logit regression models with O_1 as the dependent variable, except that in this case the comparison of results across the two datasets does not entail inversion.

5. We attribute this insignificance to the small sample size of the B&B data. The same odds ratios by family status are estimated from the NES data with higher reliability, and they are reported in Table 5.4.

6. From Appendix Table D5.a, it is easy to see that bachelor's degree graduates in biological science are less likely to be in S/E if they pursue graduate education. Women have a greater representation in biological science as a result of sex segregation by field, as revealed by the field-specific and gender-specific sample sizes in Tables 5.1 and 5.2.

7. More exactly, this statement should be interpreted to mean that women appear less likely to benefit from marriage than men. Examining the full coefficients of Model C3 in Appendix Table D5.a reveals that marriage has positive, albeit statistically insignificant, effects.

8. In additional analysis discussed later, we found significant interaction effects between gender and year. These interaction effects are such that the estimated gender gap in O_1 significantly declined over time, suggesting an increasing commitment to either graduate education or work among women who complete a bachelor's degree in S/E.

9. It is quite possible that this push factor may result from the economic pressure associated with marriage and parenthood, as further economic investment is required for graduate education. Indeed, if such economic pressure is the main reason, it would seem plausible that the pressure is lesser on married women than on married men. One problem with this interpretation, however, is that some individuals may decide to get married and have children if they anticipate working rather than entering graduate school. For the deterring effect of school enrollment on marriage, see Thornton, Axinn, and Teachman (1995).

10. In response to the declining supply of U.S.-trained undergraduates for S/E graduate programs, American universities have become heavily dependent on foreign students (NSF 1999, pp. 88–97). The intersection between immigration of scientists and women scientists will be discussed in Chapter 10.

6. Career Paths after a Science/Engineering Master's Degree

1. We note that the term *role-conflict* is not ideal. The term suggests that the conflict is at the individual level, but the problem may have structural causes at the societal level, such as socialization of stereotyped gender roles, gendered division of housework, lack of adequate childcare services, career timetables that conflict with the sequencing of women's family life course events, and discrimination against women with children.

2. If we were, for simplicity, to equate odds ratios to probability ratios, we could easily combine the estimates from Panels B and C to calculate the female-to-male ratio in the total probability of working in an S/E occupation (conditional on not being in State 5) as the product of the corresponding estimates in the two panels. For example, from Models B3 and C3, the female-to-male sex ratio in the total probability of being in an S/E occupation is approximately $1.52 \times 0.63 \approx 1$.

7. Demographic and Labor Force Profiles of Scientists and Engineers

This chapter was written by Yu Xie, Kimberlee Shauman, and Kimberly Goyette.

1. The 1960–1980 censuses collected information on years of schooling completed instead of degree attained. For the 1960 and 1970 data, we approximate degree attainment by years of schooling as follows: 16 or 17 = bachelor's degree, 18+ = master's or doctoral degree. The 1980 census added an additional category for the schooling variable, allowing us to approximate separate categories for master's degree holders (18 years of schooling) and doctoral degree holders (19+ years of schooling). By contrast, the 1990 census directly measured the highest degree attained.

2. We make this indirect inference because the census data do not contain information about field of degree and thus do not allow us to estimate the percentage of men and women with S/E degrees who work in S/E occupations.

3. The difference between a representation ratio and an odds ratio is that the representation ratio does not contain information pertaining to people outside the S/E labor force. One set of conditions under which we could approximate an odds ratio by a representation ratio is: (a) the population base is similar between men and women and (b) the overall proportion of representation for both sexes is low. Condition (a) is true if we consider all individuals (regardless of working status) as constituting the population base. Condition (b) is true because only 2–3 percent of the total labor force in the United States works in S/E occupations (calculated from NSF 1999, Appendix tables 1–2 and 1–5). Given the two conditions, we can show the equivalence between an odds ratio and its corresponding representation ratio. Let S stand for the total number of scientists/engineers, of which p proportion is women,

W for the total number of women, and M for the total number of men. The frequency cross-classification by S/E status and gender is then:

	Women	Men	Total
S/E	pS	$(1 - p)S$	S
Non-S/E	$W - pS$	$M - (1 - p)S$	$W + M - S$
Total	W	M	$W + M$

Condition (b) means that $M \approx W$. We further know that M and W are much greater than S. These two conditions lead to the following approximation for odds ratio (OR):

$$OR = \frac{pS/[(1-p)S]}{(W - pS)/[M - (1-p)S]} \approx \frac{p}{1-p}$$

[by conditions (a) and (b)], which is the female-to-male ratio in representation among incumbents of S/E occupations.

4. This is made possible by the very large sample size of the 5 percent PUMS. Statistics including scientists and engineers with at least a bachelor's degree are similar.
5. Note that the percentages referred to here pertain to proportions of scientists who *remain* divorced. Scientists who were divorced and then married are included in the category of being married.
6. The measure "with children" pertains to whether or not scientists' children are present in the same household, not whether or not scientists have had children.
7. Here, we use the terms *rate* and *odds* interchangeably. Because the magnitude of the promotion rate is very small, rates and odds are comparable.
8. Note that the scale for the rate is the probability of a promotion per interval, which could be two years (for 1982–1984 and 1984–1986) or three years (1986–1989). For simplicity, we aggregated the rates for three intervals into a single measure.
9. African-Americans are included in the "other" category, as are nonwhite Hispanic Americans. These racial groups were aggregated because their numbers were small.
10. This is true because the odds transformation of probabilities accentuates small differences at the tails near either 0 or 1. Also, the gender differences are estimated to be small because the PUMS sample is restricted to workers in the experienced labor force and thus excludes inactive scientists, who are more likely to be female.
11. However, it is possible that this small gap may reflect the selectivity of career-oriented women into high levels of education and S/E occupations.
12. Other scenarios could also explain the observed results. For example, career ambition may be positively correlated with marriage for men but uncorre-

lated for women, or career ambition may be negatively correlated with marriage for women but uncorrelated for men.

8. Geographic Mobility of Scientists/Engineers

1. Rosenfeld and Jones (1987, p. 495) further postulated that even single academic women may prefer to live in large cities "because it is there that a suitable pool of potential mates and social partners exist."

2. The occupation measure was taken in 1990, at the end rather than the beginning of the interval within which a migration may have taken place. This is an unfortunate limitation common to all migration research using census data. However, we exclude scientists who are currently enrolled in school. Since occupation is a relatively stable characteristic after the completion of formal education, we suspect that our results do not suffer much from this limitation.

3. Because linking was possible only for family members living in the same household, our variables concerning spouse and children refer to spouse and children living in the same household as the scientist.

4. When both husband and wife are doctoral scientists/engineers, their records are essentially duplicated, one with the husband as scientist/engineer and the other with the wife as scientist/engineer. The lack of independence between the individuals in these scientist-scientist couples results in underestimated standard errors. This nonindependence, however, should not produce biased parameter estimates in the multivariate analysis if the models are specified correctly.

5. We thank William Frey for advice and consultation on the creation of the coding scheme for geographic areas. When a PUMA consists of two or more metropolitan areas, or a combination of metropolitan and nonmetropolitan areas, we classify it as part of the largest metropolitan statistical area/primary metropolitan statistical area (MSA/PMSA). Completely rural PUMAs are retained according to the original PUMA codes.

6. We acknowledge the problem of collapsing never-married persons with those whose marriages have been terminated either through separation or divorce or through the spouse's death. Changes in marital status, such as the transition from married to separated or divorced, have been found to increase the mobility rates of individuals, especially women (Speare and Goldscheider 1987; Speare, Goldstein, and Frey 1975). We found, however, that the migration behavior of divorced and separated scientists was similar to that of never-married scientists.

7. The assignment of 0 to unmarried scientists is innocuous in our multivariate analyses because there is a dummy variable for marital status that uniquely identifies unmarried scientists as a group.

8. We focus our interpretation on the influence of children *before* the moves

made by the scientists in our sample. Some of the children age 0–6 may have been born after a move made during the 1985–1990 period; hence our estimation of the effect of children age 0–6 may reflect, in part, migration among childless scientists. We cannot account for this source of possible bias because we lack information about the sequence of childbearing and migration events during the five-year period.

9. Chi-square test statistic is 10.99 for 3 degrees of freedom.

10. Our sample is potentially biased in the conservative direction because it excludes women who were out of the labor force in 1990; that is, our statistics may overestimate the labor force attachment of all potential women scientists and thus understate sex differences.

9. Research Productivity

1. This conservative strategy is sensible given the lack of large and informative longitudinal datasets on doctoral scientists. A comprehensive study examining both career dynamics and publication histories would require data far richer (in terms of sample size and contained information) than that currently available.

2. This operationalization suffers from the problem of excluding permanent, doctoral-level, nonteaching researchers employed by universities. This exclusion is necessary for our study because the titles and statuses of such nonteaching researchers vary greatly across institutions. Insofar as our exclusion does not affect the relationship between sex and productivity (i.e., in the absence of three-way interaction), the exclusion does not bias our statistical results.

3. For two of the datasets used in our study (NSPF-1988 and NSPF-1993), information about publication in different formats was collected. However, for consistency with the other two datasets and other comparable studies, we use the simple publication count as our output measure.

4. Even with a short-term measure of publication rates, this research is not immune from the problem of reciprocal causality. We handle this problem in two ways: (1) through a series of hierarchical models moving from more exogenous controls to less exogenous controls and (2) by interpreting our models as descriptive rather than as causal.

5. The following coding scheme was used: none = 0, 1–2 = 1.5, 3–4 = 3.5, 5–10 = 7.5, more than 10 = 12.5.

6. Severe overdispersion is apparent, as the standard deviations rather than the variances of T and Y are close to the means of T and Y. This justifies our choice of the negative binomial model, which includes an additional random component to handle such overdispersion. See discussion in Xie and Shauman (1998); see also McCullagh and Nelder (1983, pp. 198–200) and Long (1997, pp. 230–38).

7. Testing for the statistical significance of the changes in sex differences is tantamount to testing for the interaction effects between sex and period in a regression analysis with pooled data. For the baseline negative binomial model without other covariates, the chi-square statistic for the interaction is 14.47 for 3 degrees of freedom and is significant at the $p < .01$ level.

8. See Xie and Shauman (1998) for a fuller discussion of the statistical approach.

9. Indeed, Cole's latest attempt (Cole and Singer 1991) focuses on the compounding process of small differences. Despite its elegance, Cole and Singer's theory of limited differences provides only a plausible hypothesis rather than an explanation for observed differences (for a similar critique, see Reskin 1992).

10. The institutional quality ratings in the Carnegie-1969 data, based on the Gourman Report of 1967 (Trow 1975), were contained in the data file made available for public use. In the ACE-1973 data file, institutions were rated according to the Carnegie Classification scheme. In NSPF-1988 and NSPF-1993, institutions were rated according to a modified Carnegie Classification.

11. Years of experience is defined as the difference between the Ph.D. and survey years.

12. The resource variables are dummy variables, coded as 1 if true and 0 otherwise.

13. Although Zuckerman (1991, pp. 35–36) maintains that women are no less likely to be located in prestigious research institutions than men, Long and Fox (1995, p. 51) clearly reject Zuckerman's claim. Also see Long (2001).

14. In the Carnegie-1969 dataset, for example, the change in the goodness-of-fit-statistic (G^2) is 1,143.8 for 10 degrees of freedom. Improvement in G^2 for Model 1 over Model 0 is smaller but highly significant for the other three datasets (629.1 for ACE-1973, 85.3 for NSPF-1988, and 200.0 for NSPF-1993, all with 10 degrees of freedom).

15. In Carnegie-1969, the change in G^2 between Models 2 and 1 is 3,939.0 for 19 degrees of freedom; the change is, respectively, 2,335.4, 355.5, and 708.7 in ACE-1973, NSPF-1988, and NSPF-1993, all with 20 degrees of freedom.

16. The change in G^2 between Models 3 and 2 for Carnegie-1969 is 16.38 for 2 degrees of freedom.

17. Of course, part of the reason for the nonsignificance is the relatively small sample size for NSPF-1988.

18. In our data, for example, the estimated productivity penalty for a heavy teaching load (11 or more hours per week as compared to 0–4 hours per week) has significantly increased during the period. See regression coefficients reported in Appendix Tables D9.a to D9.d.

19. The inclusion of the interaction resulted in a $\Delta G^2 = 0.78$, 1.98, 1.20, and 0.48, respectively, for the four datasets, all with 1 degree of freedom.

20. The statement was made by a reviewer of the original paper for the *American Sociological Review.*
21. In fact, this finding is not new. Blackburn, Behymer, and Hall (1978), Fox and Faver (1985), and Reskin (1978) all report smaller sex differences than the generalization of Cole and Zuckerman (1984) that women publish at 50 to 60 percent of the rate of men.

10. Immigrant Scientists/Engineers

This chapter was written by Kimberly Goyette, Yu Xie, and Kimberlee Shauman.

1. Natural logarithm is used. The exponential transformation of the entries yields the geometric means.
2. The sample size reported for the PUMS refers to those who worked full-time and reported positive earnings.
3. Here, we use the terms *rate* and *odds* interchangeably, because the rate of promotion is very small.

11. Conclusion

1. Of course, that women take major responsibility for childcare is an undeniable form of within-household gender stratification that benefits the husband and disadvantages the wife. However, we here suggest an important mechanism through which this stratification operates—children. When children are not present, our study suggests women scientists/engineers do not seem to suffer from marriage.
2. Note that these respondents were high school seniors in 1957. Women's economic role has dramatically expanded for more recent cohorts.
3. Rather, we tackled the issue of discrimination implicitly by using a conventional residual approach (e.g., Cole 1979), in which the residual gender difference after statistically adjusting for explanatory factors is taken as suggestive of the upper bound of the discrimination effect.

References

Adelman, Clifford. 1995. *The New College Course Map and Transcript Files: Changes in Course-Taking and Achievement, 1972–1993*. Washington, D.C.: U.S. Department of Education.

Ahern, Nancy C., and Elizabeth L. Scott. 1981. *Career Outcomes in a Matched Sample of Men and Women Ph.D.s: An Analytical Report*. Washington, D.C.: National Academy Press.

Allison, Paul D., and J. Scott Long. 1987. "Interuniversity Mobility of Academic Scientists." *American Sociological Review* 52:643–652.

——— 1990. "Departmental Effects on Scientific Productivity." *American Sociological Review* 55:469–478.

Allison, Paul D., J. Scott Long, and Tad K. Krauze. 1982. "Cumulative Advantage and Inequality in Science." *American Sociological Review* 47:615–625.

Alper, Joe. 1993. "The Pipeline Is Leaking Women All the Way Along." *Science* 260:409–411.

Alwin, Duane F., and Robert M. Hauser. 1975. "The Decomposition of Effects in Path Analysis." *American Sociological Review* 40:37–47.

American Association for the Advancement of Science (AAAS). 1992a. "Women in Science: First Annual Survey." *Science* 255:1365–1388.

——— 1992b. "Minorities in Science: Two Generations of Struggle." *Science* 258:1176–1235.

American Association of University Women Educational Foundation (AAUW). 1992. *How Schools Shortchange Girls*. Washington, D.C.: AAUW Educational Foundation and National Educational Association.

Armstrong, Jane M. 1981. "Achievement and Participation of Women in Mathematics." *Journal for Research in Mathematics Education* 12:356–372.

——— 1985. "A National Assessment of Participation and Achievement of

Women in Mathematics." Pp. 59–94 in *Women and Mathematics: Balancing the Equation,* edited by Susan F. Chipman, Lorelei R. Brush, and Donna M. Wilson. Hillsdale, N.J.: Lawrence Erlbaum Associates, Publishers.

Armstrong, Jane M., and Richard A. Price. 1982. "Correlates and Predictors of Women's Mathematics Participation." *Journal for Research in Mathematics Education* 13:99–109.

Astin, Helen S. 1969. *The Woman Doctorate in America: Origins, Career, and Family.* New York: Russell Sage Foundation.

Astone, Nan M., and Sara S. McLanahan. 1994. "Family Structure, Residential Mobility, and School Dropout: A Research Note." *Demography* 31:575–584.

Atkinson, Richard C. 1990. "Supply and Demand for Scientists and Engineers: A National Crisis in the Making." *Science* 248:425–432.

Bae, Yupin, Susan Choy, Claire Geddes, Jennifer Sable, and Thomas Snyder. 2000. *Trends in Educational Equity for Girls and Women.* NCES 2000–030. Washington, D.C.: U.S. Department of Education, National Center for Education Statistics.

Baker, David P., and Deborah P. Jones. 1993. "Creating Gender Equality: Cross-National Gender Stratification and Mathematical Performance." *Sociology of Education* 66:91–103.

Bayer, Alan E. 1973. "Teaching Faculty in Academe: 1972–73." *ACE Research Reports,* vol. 8. Washington, D.C.: American Council on Education, Office of Research.

Becker, Betsy J. 1989. "Gender and Science Achievement: A Reanalysis of Studies from Two Meta-Analysis." *Journal of Research in Science Teaching* 26:141–169.

Becker, Betsy J., and Larry V. Hedges. 1984. "Meta-Analyses of Cognitive Gender Differences: A Comment on an Analysis by Rosenthal and Rubin." *Journal of Educational Psychology* 76:583–587.

Becker, Gary S. 1981. *A Treatise on the Family.* Cambridge, Mass.: Harvard University Press.

Becker, Joanne R. 1981. "Differential Treatment of Females and Males in Mathematics Classes." *Journal for Research in Mathematics Education* 12:40–53.

Bellas, Marcia L. 1994. "Comparable Worth in Academia: The Effects on Faculty Salaries of the Sex Composition and Labor-Market Conditions of Academic Disciplines." *American Sociological Review* 59:807–821.

Benbow, Camilla P. 1983. "Adolescence of the Mathematically Precocious: A Five-Year Longitudinal Study." Pp. 9–29 in *Academic Precocity: Aspects of Its Development,* edited by Camilla P. Benbow and Julian C. Stanley. Baltimore, Md.: Johns Hopkins University Press.

——— 1988. "Sex Differences in Mathematical Reasoning Ability among the Intellectually Talented: Their Characterization, Consequences, and Possible Explanations." *Behavioral and Brain Sciences* 11:169–232.

——— 1992. "Academic Achievement in Mathematics and Science of Students between Ages 13 and 23: Are There Differences among Students in the Top One Percent of Mathematical Ability?" *Journal of Educational Psychology* 84:51–61.

Benbow, Camilla P., and Julian C. Stanley. 1980. "Sex Differences in Mathematical Ability: Fact or Artifact?" *Science* 210:1262–1264.

—— 1983a. "Sex Differences in Mathematical Reasoning Ability: More Facts." *Science* 222:1029–1031.

—— 1983b. "Differential Course-Taking Hypothesis Revisited." *American Educational Research Journal* 20:469–573.

Bentley, Richard J., and Robert T. Blackburn. 1992. "Two Decades of Gains for Female Faculty?" *Teachers College Record* 93:697–709.

Bernard, Jessie. 1964. *Academic Women.* University Park, Pa.: Pennsylvania State University Press.

Berryman, Sue E. 1983. *Who Will Do Science? Minority and Female Attainment of Science and Mathematics Degrees: Trends and Causes.* New York: Rockefeller Foundation.

Bianchi, Suzanne M., and Daphne Spain. 1986. *American Women in Transition.* New York: Russell Sage Foundation.

Bird, Gerald A., and Gloria W. Bird. 1985. "Determinants of Mobility in Two-earner Families: Does the Wife's Income Count?" *Journal of Marriage and the Family* 47:753–758.

Blackburn, Robert T., Charles E. Behymer, and David E. Hall. 1978. "Research Note: Correlates of Faculty Publications." *Sociology of Education* 51:132–141.

Blau, Francine D. 1998. "Trends in the Well-Being of American Women, 1970–1995." *Journal of Economic Literature* 36:112–165.

Bouvier, Leon F., and John L. Martin. 1995. *Foreign-Born Scientists, Engineers, and Mathematicians in the United States.* Washington, D.C.: Center for Immigration Studies.

Brush, Lorelei R. 1985. "Cognitive and Affective Determinants of Course Preference and Plans." Pp. 123–150 in *Women and Mathematics: Balancing the Equation,* edited by Susan F. Chipman, Lorelei R. Brush, and Donna M. Wilson. Hillsdale, N.J.: Lawrence Erlbaum Associates, Publishers.

Burkam, David T., Valerie E. Lee, and Becky A. Smerdon. 1997. "Gender and Science Learning Early in High School: Subject Matter and Laboratory Experiences." *American Educational Research Journal* 34:297–331.

Burnett, Sarah A. 1986. "Sex-Related Differences in Spatial Ability: Are They Trivial?" *American Psychologist* 41:1012–1013.

Caplan, Paula J., Gael M. MacPherson, and Patricia Tobin. 1985. "Do Sex-Related Differences in Spatial Ability Exist?" *American Psychologist* 40:786–799.

—— 1986. "The Magnified Molehill and the Misplaced Focus: Sex Differences in Spatial Ability Revisited." *American Psychologist* 41:1016–1018.

Carr, Deborah. 2000. "Interpretations of Career Successes and Failures among

Midlife Adults." Unpublished manuscript. Population Studies Center, University of Michigan, Ann Arbor, Mich.

Casserly, Patricia L. 1980. "Factors Affecting Participation in Advanced Placement Programs in Mathematics, Chemistry and Physics." Pp. 138–163 in *Women and the Mathematical Mystique*, edited by Lynn Fox, Linda Brody, and Dianne Tobin. Baltimore, Md.: Johns Hopkins University Press.

Casserly, Patricia L., and Donald Rock. 1985. "Factors Related to Young Women's Persistence and Achievement in Advanced Placement Mathematics." Pp. 225–247 in *Women and Mathematics: Balancing the Equation*, edited by Susan F. Chipman, Lorelei R. Brush, and Donna M. Wilson. Hillsdale, N.J.: Lawrence Erlbaum Associates, Publishers.

Catsambis, Sophia. 1994. "The Path to Math: Gender and Racial-Ethnic Differences in Mathematics Participation from Middle School to High School." *Sociology of Education* 67:199–215.

Chipman, Susan F., and Donna M. Wilson. 1985. "Understanding Mathematics Course Enrollment and Mathematics Achievement: A Synthesis of the Research." Pp. 275–328 in *Women and Mathematics: Balancing the Equation*, edited by Susan F. Chipman, Lorelei R. Brush, and Donna M. Wilson. Hillsdale, N.J.: Lawrence Erlbaum Associates, Publishers.

Citro, Constance F., and Graham Kalton (editors). 1989. *Surveying the Nation's Scientists and Engineers: A Data System for the 1990s.* Washington, D.C.: National Academy Press.

Clausen, John A. 1986. *The Life Course: A Sociological Perspective.* Englewood Cliffs, N.J.: Prentice-Hall.

Clemente, Frank. 1973. "Early Career Determinants of Research Productivity." *American Journal of Sociology* 83:409–419.

Cobb-Clark, Deborah. 1993. "Immigrant Selectivity and Wages: The Evidence for Women." *American Economic Review* 83:986–993.

Cohen, Jacob. 1977. *Statistical Power Analysis for the Behavioral Science,* 2d ed. New York: Academic Press.

Cole, Jonathan R. 1979. *Fair Science: Women in the Scientific Community.* New York: Columbia University Press.

Cole, Jonathan R., and Stephen Cole. 1973. *Social Stratification in Science.* Chicago: University of Chicago Press.

Cole, Jonathan R., and Burton Singer. 1991. "A Theory of Limited Differences: Explaining the Productivity Puzzle in Science." Pp. 277–310 in *The Outer Circle: Women in the Scientific Community,* edited by Harriet Zuckerman, Jonathan R. Cole, and John T. Bruer. New York: W. W. Norton and Company.

Cole, Jonathan R., and Harriet Zuckerman. 1984. "The Productivity Puzzle: Persistence and Change in Patterns of Publication of Men and Women Scientists." *Advances in Motivation and Achievement* 2:217–258.

——— 1987. "Marriage, Motherhood and Research Performance in Science." *Scientific American* 25:119–125.

———— 1991. "Marriage, Motherhood, and Research Performance in Science." Pp. 157–170 in *The Outer Circle: Women in the Scientific Community,* edited by Harriet Zuckerman, Jonathan R. Cole, and John T. Bruer. New York: W. W. Norton and Company.

Coleman, James S. 1988. "Social Capital in the Creation of Human Capital." *American Journal of Sociology* 94:S94–S120.

Committee on the Education and Employment of Women in Science and Engineering. 1979. *Climbing the Academic Ladder: Doctoral Women Scientists in Academe.* Washington, D.C.: National Academy of Science.

Committee on Women in Science and Engineering. 1991. *Women in Science and Engineering: Increasing Their Numbers in the 1990s.* Washington, D.C.: National Academy Press.

Crane, Diana. 1972. *Invisible Colleges: Diffusion of Knowledge in Scientific Communities.* Chicago: University of Chicago Press.

DaVanzo, Julie. 1977. *Why Families Move: A Model of the Geographic Mobility of Married Couples.* Washington, D.C.: U.S. Government Printing Office.

Davis, Cinda-Sue, Angela B. Ginorio, Carol S. Hollenshead, Barbara B. Lazarus, Paula M. Rayman, and Associates. 1996. *The Equity Equation: Fostering the Advancement of Women in the Sciences, Mathematics, and Engineering.* San Francisco, Calif.: Jossey-Bass.

Davis, James A. 1964. *Great Aspirations: The Graduate School Plans of America's College Seniors.* Chicago: Aldine Publishing Company.

———— 1965. *Undergraduate Career Decisions: Correlates of Occupational Choice.* Chicago: Aldine Publishing Company.

Denmark, Florence L., and Michele A. Paludi (editors). 1993. *Psychology of Women: A Handbook of Issues and Theories.* Westport, Conn.: Greenwood Press.

Dimitrov, Dimiter M. 1999. "Gender Differences in Science Achievement: Differential Effect of Ability, Response Format, and Strands of Learning Outcomes." *School Science and Mathematics* 99:445–450.

Duncan, R. Paul, and Carolyn C. Perrucci. 1976. "Dual Occupation Families and Migration." *American Sociological Review* 41:252–261.

Eccles, Jacquelynne S. 1984. "Sex Differences in Mathematics Participation." *Advances in Motivation and Achievement* 2:93–138.

———— 1989. "Bringing Young Women to Math and Science." Pp. 36–58 in *Gender and Thought: Psychological Perspectives,* edited by Mary Crawford and Margaret Gentry. New York: Springer-Verlag.

———— 1994. "Understanding Women's Educational and Occupational Choices: Applying the Eccles et al. Model of Achievement-Related Choices." *Psychology of Women Quarterly* 18:585–609.

Eccles, Jacquelynne S., Terry Adler, Robert Futterman, Susan B. Goff, Caroline M. Kaczala, Judith L. Meece, and Carol Midgley. 1985. "Self-Perceptions, Task Perceptions, Socializing Influences, and the Decision to Enroll in Mathematics." Pp. 95–121 in *Women and Mathematics: Balancing the Equation,* edited by Susan F. Chipman, Lorelei R. Brush, and Donna M. Wilson. Hillsdale, N.J.: Lawrence Erlbaum Associates, Publishers.

Eccles, Jacquelynne S., Terry Adler, and Judith L. Meece. 1984. "Sex Differences in Achievement: A Test of Alternate Theories." *Journal of Personality and Social Psychology* 46:26–43.

Eccles, Jacquelynne S., and Janis E. Jacobs. 1986. "Social Forces Shape Math Attitudes and Performance." *Signs: Journal of Women in Culture and Society* 11:367–380.

Eccles, Jacquelynne S., Janis E. Jacobs, and Rena D. Harold. 1990. "Gender Role Stereotypes, Expectancy Effects, and Parents' Socialization of Gender Differences." *Journal of Social Issues* 46:183–202.

Edmonston, Barry, and Jeffrey S. Passel (editors). 1994. *Immigration and Ethnicity: The Integration of America's Newest Arrivals.* Washington, D.C.: Urban Institute Press.

Elder, Glenn H., Jr. 1977. "Family History and the Life Course." *Journal of Family History* 2:279–304.

Eliot, John. 1986. "Comment on Caplan, MacPherson, and Tobin." *American Psychologist* 41:1011.

Entwisle, Doris R., Karl L. Alexander, and Linda S. Olson. 1994. "The Gender Gap in Math: Its Possible Origins in Neighborhood Effects." *American Sociological Review* 59:822–838.

Epstein, Cynthia F. 1974. "Reconciliation of Women's Roles." Pp. 473–489 in *The Family: Its Structures and Functions,* edited by Rose L. Coser. New York: St. Martin's Press.

Etzkowitz, Henry, Carol Kemelgor, Michael Neuschatz, and Brian Uzzi. 1994. "Barriers to Women's Participation in Academic Science and Engineering." Pp. 43–67 in *Who Will Do Science? Educating the Next Generation,* edited by Willie Pearson, Jr., and Alan Fechter. Baltimore, Md.: Johns Hopkins University Press.

Feingold, Alan. 1988. "Cognitive Gender Differences Are Disappearing." *American Psychologist* 43:95–103.

——— 1992. "Sex Differences in Variability in Intellectual Abilities: A New Look at an Old Controversy." *Review of Educational Research* 62:61–84.

——— 1994. "Gender Differences in Variability in Intellectual Abilities: A Cross-Cultural Perspective." *Sex Roles* 30:81–92.

Fennema, Elizabeth. 1980. "Sex-related Differences in Mathematics Achievement: Where and Why." Pp. 76–93 in *Women and the Mathematical Mystique,* edited by Lynn Fox, Linda Brody, and Dianne Tobin. Baltimore, Md.: Johns Hopkins University Press.

——— 1984. "Girls, Women, and Mathematics." Pp. 137–164 in *Women and Education: Equity or Equality?,* edited by Elizabeth Fennema and M. Jane Ayers. Berkeley, Calif.: McCutchan.

Fennema, Elizabeth, and Julia Sherman. 1977. "Sex-Related Differences in Mathematics Achievement, Spatial Visualization, and Affective Factors." *American Educational Research Journal* 14:51–72.

—— 1978. "Sex-Related Differences in Mathematics Achievement and Other Factors." *Journal for Research in Mathematics Education* 9:189–203.

Finn, Jeremy D. 1980. "Sex Differences in Educational Outcomes: A Cross-National Study." *Sex Roles* 6:9–26.

Fox, Mary F. 1981. "Patterns and Determinants of Research Productivity." Unpublished manuscript. Department of Sociology, University of Michigan, Ann Arbor, Mich.

—— 1995. "Women and Scientific Careers." Pp. 205–223 in *Handbook of Science and Technology Studies,* edited by Sheila Jasanoff, Gerald E. Markle, James C. Peterson, and Trevor Pinch. Thousand Oaks, Calif.: Sage Publications.

Fox, Mary F., and Catherine A. Faver. 1985. "Men, Women, and Publication Productivity: Patterns among Social Work Academics." *Sociological Quarterly* 26:537–549.

Frank, Robert H. 1978. "Family Location Constraints and the Geographic Distribution of Female Professionals." *Journal of Political Economy* 86:117–130.

Friedman, Lynn. 1989. "Mathematics and the Gender Gap: A Meta-Analysis of Recent Studies on Sex Differences in Mathematical Tasks." *Review of Educational Research* 59:185–213.

Gilbert, Melissa C. 1996. "Attributional Patterns and Perceptions of Math and Science among Fifth-Grade through Seventh-Grade Girls and Boys." *Sex Roles* 35:489–506.

Ginzberg, Eli, Sol W. Ginsburg, Sidney Axelrad, and John L. Herma. 1951. *Occupational Choice: An Approach to a General Theory.* New York: Columbia University Press.

Goldberg, Carey. 1999. "M.I.T. Admits It's Tough on Women." *New York Times,* March 28, sec. 4, WK2(L).

Goldin, Claudia D. 1990. *Understanding the Gender Gap.* New York: Oxford University Press.

—— 1997. "Career and Family: College Women Look to the Past." Pp. 20–58 in *Gender and Family Issues in the Workplace,* edited by Francine D. Blau and Ronald G. Ehrenberg. New York: Russell Sage Foundation.

Gornick, Vivian. 1990. *Women in Science: 100 Journeys into the Territory,* rev. ed. New York: Simon and Schuster.

Green, Patricia J., Sharon L. Myers, Pamela Giese, Joan Law, Howard M. Speizer, and Vicki S. Tardino. 1996. *Baccalaureate and Beyond Longitudinal Study: 1993/94 First Followup Methodology Report.* NCES 96–149. Washington, D.C.: National Center for Education Statistics.

Greene, Barbara A., Teresa K. DeBacker, Bhuvaneswari Ravindran, and A. Jean Krows. 1999. "Goals, Values, and Beliefs as Predictors of Achievement and Effort in High School Mathematics Classes." *Sex Roles* 40:421–458.

Gross, Jane. 1991. "Female Surgeon's Quitting Touches Nerve at Medical Schools." *New York Times,* July 14, sec. 1, 8(N), 10(L).

Gur, Ruben C., Lyn H. Mozley, P. David Mozley, Susan M. Resnick, Joel S. Karp,

Abass Alavi, Steven E. Arnold, and Raquel E. Gur. 1995. "Sex Differences in Regional Cerebral Glucose Metabolism during a Resting State." *Science* 267:528–531.

Haier, Richard J., and Camilla P. Benbow. 1995. "Sex Differences and Lateralization in Temporal Lobe Glucose Metabolism during Mathematical Reasoning." *Developmental Neuropsychology* 11:405–414.

Halpern, Diane F. 1986. "A Different Answer to the Question: 'Do Sex-Related Differences in Spatial Abilities Exist?'" *American Psychologist* 41:1014–1015.

Hanson, Sandra L. 1996. *Lost Talent: Women in the Sciences*. Philadelphia, Pa.: Temple University Press.

Harding, Sandra. 1986. *The Science Question in Feminism*. Ithaca: Cornell University Press.

Hargens, Lowell L., James C. McCann, and Barbara F. Reskin. 1978. "Productivity and Reproductivity: Fertility and Professional Achievement among Research Scientists." *Social Forces* 57:154–163.

Harnisch, Delwyn L. 1984. "Females and Mathematics: A Cross-National Perspective." *Advances in Motivation and Achievement* 2:73–91.

Hauser, Robert M., Shu-Ling Tsai, and William H. Sewell. 1983. "A Model of Stratification with Response Error in Social and Psychological Variables." *Sociology of Education* 56:20–46.

Haveman, Robert, Barbara Wolfe, and James Spaulding. 1991. "Childhood Events and Circumstances Influencing High School Completion." *Demography* 28:133–157.

Hedges, Larry V., and Amy Nowell. 1995. "Sex Differences in Mental Test Scores, Variability, and Numbers of High-Scoring Individuals." *Science* 269:41–45.

Hertz, Rosanna. 1986. *More Equal Than Others: Women and Men in Dual-Career Marriages*. Berkeley: University of California Press.

Hilton, Thomas L., and Valerie E. Lee. 1988. "Student Interest and Persistence in Science." *Journal of Higher Education* 59(5):510–526.

Hiscock, Merrill. 1986. "On Sex Differences in Spatial Abilities." *American Psychologist* 41:1011–1012.

Hochschild, Arlie R. 1989. *The Second Shift: Working Parents and the Revolution at Home*. New York: Viking.

——— 1994. "Inside the Clockwork of Male Careers." Pp. 125–140 in *Gender and the Academic Experience,* edited by Kathryn P. M. Orlans and Ruth A. Wallace. Lincoln: University of Nebraska Press.

Hodge, Robert W., Paul M. Siegel, and Peter H. Rossi. 1964. "Occupational Prestige in the United States, 1925–63." *American Journal of Sociology* 70:286–302.

Hughey, A. M. 1990. "The Incomes of Recent Female Immigrants to the United States." *Social Science Quarterly* 71(2):383–390.

Hyde, Janet S. 1981. "How Large Are Cognitive Gender Differences? A Meta-Analysis Using w and d." *American Psychologist* 36:892–901.

Hyde, Janet S., Elizabeth Fennema, and Susan J. Lamon. 1990. "Gender Difference in Mathematical Performance: A Meta-Analysis." *Psychological Bulletin* 107:139–155.

Hyde, Janet S., Elizabeth Fennema, Marilyn Ryan, Laurie A. Frost, and Carolyn Hopp. 1990. "Gender Comparisons of Mathematics Attitudes and Affect; A Meta-Analysis." *Psychology of Women Quarterly* 14:299–324.

Ingels, Steven J., Sameer Y. Abraham, Rosemary Karr, Bruce D. Spence, and Martin R. Frankel. 1990. *National Education Longitudinal Study of 1988. Base Year: Student Component Data File User's Manual.* NCES 90–464. Washington, D.C.: U.S. Department of Education, Office of Educational Research and Improvement.

Ingels, Steven J., Leslie A. Scott, Judith T. Lindmark, Martin R. Frankel, and Sharon L. Myers. 1992. *National Education Longitudinal Study of 1988. First Follow-up: Student Component Data File User's Manual, Volume I.* NCES 92–030. Washington, D.C.: U.S. Department of Education, Office of Educational Research and Improvement.

Ingels, Steven J., Kathryn L. Dowd, John D. Baldridge, James L. Stipe, Virginia H. Bartot, and Martin R. Frankel. 1994. *National Education Longitudinal Study of 1988. Second Follow-up: Student Component Data File User's Manual.* NCES 94–374. Washington, D.C.: U.S. Department of Education, Office of Educational Research and Improvement.

International Association for the Evaluation of Educational Achievement. 1985. *Second Study of Mathematics: Summary Report for the United States.* Champaign, Ill.: Stipes Publishing Company.

Jacklin, Carol N. 1989. "Female and Male: Issues of Gender." *American Psychologist* 44:127–133.

Jacobs, Janis E., and Jacquelynne S. Eccles. 1992. "The Impact of Mothers' Gender-Role Stereotypical Beliefs on Mothers' and Children's Ability Perceptions." *Journal of Personality and Social Psychology* 63:932–945.

Jacobs, Jerry A. 1989. *Revolving Doors: Sex Segregation and Women's Careers.* Palo Alto, Calif.: Stanford University Press.

—— 1995. "Gender and Academic Specialties: Trends among Recipients of College Degrees in the 1980s." *Sociology of Education* 68:81–89.

Jones, Calvin, Shirley Knight, Marjorie Butz, Ioanna Crawford, and Bruce Stephenson. 1984. *High School and Beyond Transcript Survey (1982) Data File User's Manual.* NCES 84–205. Washington, D.C.: National Center for Education Statistics.

Kahle, Jane B. (editor). 1985. *Women in Science: A Report from the Field.* Philadelphia: The Falmer Press.

Kahle, Jane B., and Marsha L. Matyas. 1987. "Equitable Science and Mathematics Education: A Discrepancy Model." Pp. 5–41 in *Women: Their Underrepresentation and Career Differentials in Science and Engineering,* edited by Linda S. Dix. Washington, D.C.: National Academy Press.

Kanter, Rosabeth M. 1977. *Men and Women of the Corporation.* New York: Basic Books.

Kavrell, Suzanne M., and Anne C. Petersen. 1984. "Patterns of Achievement in Early Adolescence." *Advances in Motivation and Achievement* 2:1–35.

Keller, Evelyn F. 1985. *Reflections on Gender and Science.* New Haven: Yale University Press.

——— 1992. *Secrets of Life, Secrets of Death: Essays on Language, Gender, and Science.* New York: Routledge.

Kerckhoff, Alan C. 1993. *Diverging Pathways: Social Structure and Career Deflections.* Cambridge: Cambridge University Press.

——— 1996. "Building Conceptual and Empirical Bridges between Studies of Educational and Labor Force Careers." Pp. 37–56 in *Generating Social Stratification: Toward a New Research Agenda,* edited by Alan C. Kerckhoff. Boulder, Colo.: Westview Press.

Kloosterman, Peter. 1990. "Attributions, Performance Following Failure, and Motivation in Mathematics." Pp. 96–127 in *Mathematics and Gender,* edited by Elizabeth Fennema and Gilah C. Leder. New York: Teachers College Press.

Koch, James V. 1987. "The Incomes of Recent Immigrants: A Look at Ethnic Differences." *Social Science Quarterly* 68:294–310.

Koertge, Noretta. 1998. "Feminism: A Mixed Blessing to Women in Science." Pp. 189–202 in *Women in Science: Meeting Career Challenges,* edited by Angela M. Pattatucci. Thousand Oaks, Calif.: Sage.

Landinsky, Jack. 1967. "Occupational Determinants of Geographic Mobility among Professional Workers." *American Sociological Review* 32:253–264.

Laws, Judith L. 1976. "Work Aspiration of Women: False Leads and New Starts." Pp. 33–49 in *Women and the Workplace: The Implications of Occupational Segregation,* edited by Martha Blaxall and Barbara Reagan. Chicago: University of Chicago Press.

Leahey, Erin, and Guang Guo. 2001. "Gender Differences in Mathematical Trajectories." *Social Forces* 80:713–732.

Lee, Valerie E., and David T. Burkam. 1996. "Gender Differences in Middle-Grade Science Achievement: Subject Domain, Ability Level, and Course Emphasis." *Science Education* 80:613–650.

Lee, Valerie E., David T. Burkam, and Becky A. Smerdon. 1997. "Debunking the Myths: Exploring Common Explanations for Gender Differences in High-School Science Achievement." Paper presented at the 1997 annual meeting of the American Educational Research Association, Chicago.

Lee, Valerie E., Xianglei Chen, and Becky A. Smerdon. 1995. "The Influence of School Climate on Gender Differences in the Achievement and Engagement of Young Adolescents." Unpublished manuscript. University of Michigan, Ann Arbor, Mich.

Lee, Valerie E., Helen M. Marks, and Tina Byrd. 1994. "Sexism in Single-Sex and Coeducational Independent Secondary School Classrooms." *Sociology of Education* 67:92–120.

Levin, Sharon G., and Paula E. Stephan. 1991. "Research Productivity Over the Life Cycle: Evidence for Academic Scientists." *American Economic Review* 81:114–132.

Libman, Joan. 1991. "Sudden End to a Trailblazing Career." *Los Angeles Times,* June 7, E1.

Lichter, Daniel T. 1980. "Household Migration and the Labor Market Position of Married Women." *Social Science Research* 9:83–97.

——— 1982. "The Migration of Dual-Worker Families: Does the Wife's Job Matter?" *Social Science Quarterly* 63:48–57.

——— 1983. "Socioeconomic Returns to Migration among Married Women." *Social Forces* 62(2):487–503.

Lieberson, Stanley. 1985. *Making It Count: The Improvement of Social Research and Theory.* Berkeley, Calif.: University of California Press.

Linn, Marcia C., and Janet S. Hyde. 1989. "Gender, Mathematics, and Science." *Educational Researcher* 18:17–27.

Linn, Marcia C., and Anne C. Peterson. 1985. "Emergence and Characterization of Sex Differences in Spatial Ability: A Meta-Analysis." *Child Development* 56:1479–1498.

Littleton, Karen. 1996. "Girls and Information Technology." Pp. 81–96 in *Equity in the Classroom: Towards Effective Pedagogy for Girls and Boys,* edited by Patricia F. Murphy and Caroline V. Gipps. Washington, D.C.: Falmer Press.

Long, J. Scott. 1978. "Productivity and Academic Position in the Scientific Career." *American Sociological Review* 43:889–908.

——— 1990. "The Origins of Sex Differences in Science." *Social Forces* 68(4):1297–1316.

——— 1992. "Measures of Sex Differences in Scientific Productivity." *Social Forces* 71:159–178.

——— 1997. *Regression Models for Categorical and Limited Dependent Variables.* Thousand Oaks, Calif.: Sage Publications.

——— (editor). 2001. *From Scarcity to Visibility: Gender Differences in the Careers of Doctoral Scientists and Engineers.* Washington, D.C.: National Academy Press.

Long, J. Scott, Paul D. Allison, and Robert McGinnis. 1979. "Entrance into the Academic Career." *American Sociological Review* 44:816–830.

——— 1993. "Rank Advancement in Academic Careers: Sex Differences and the Effects of Productivity." *American Sociological Review* 58:703–722.

Long, J. Scott, and Mary F. Fox. 1995. "Scientific Careers: Universalism and Particularism." *Annual Review of Sociology* 21:45–71.

Long, Larry H. 1972. "The Influence of Number and Ages of Children on Residential Mobility." *Demography* 9:371–382.

——— 1974. "Women's Labor Force Participation and the Residential Mobility of Families." *Social Forces* 52:343–348.

Maccoby, Eleanor E. 1995. "The Two Sexes and Their Social Systems." Pp. 347–365 in *Examining Lives in Context,* edited by Phyllis Moen, Glen H. Elder,

Jr., and Kurt Luscher. Washington, D.C.: American Psychological Association.

Maccoby, Eleanor E., and Carol N. Jacklin. 1974. *The Psychology of Sex Differences*. Palo Alto, Calif.: Stanford University Press.

MacLeod, Jay. 1987. *Ain't No Makin' It: Aspirations and Attainment in a Low-Income Neighborhood*. Boulder, Colo.: Westview Press.

Maret, Elizabeth, and Barbara Finlay. 1984. "The Distribution of Household Labor among Women in Dual-Earner Families." *Journal of Marriage and the Family* 46:357–364.

Marini, Margaret M., and Mary C. Brinton. 1984. "Sex Typing in Occupational Socialization." Pp. 192–232 in *Sex Segregation in the Workplace: Trends, Explanations, Remedies*, edited by Barbara F. Reskin. Washington, D.C.: National Academy Press.

Markham, William T., and Joseph H. Pleck. 1986. "Sex and Willingness to Move for Occupational Advancement: Some National Sample Results." *Sociological Quarterly* 27:121–143.

Marwell, Gerald, Rachel Rosenfeld, and Seymour Spilerman. 1979. "Geographic Constraints on Women's Careers in Academia." *Science* 205:1225–1231.

Matyas, Marsha L. 1985. "Factors Affecting Female Achievement and Interest in Science and in Scientific Careers." Pp. 27–48 in *Women in Science: A Report from the Field*, edited by Jane B. Kahle. Philadelphia: Falmer Press.

Matyas, Marsha L., and Linda Skidmore Dix (editors). 1992. *Science and Engineering Programs: On Target for Women?* Washington, D.C.: National Academy Press.

Maxwell, Nan L. 1988. "Economic Returns to Migration: Marital Status and Gender Differences." *Social Science Quarterly* 69:108–121.

McCullagh, P., and J. A. Nelder. 1983. *Generalized Linear Models*, 2d ed. New York: Chapman and Hall.

McIlwee, Judith S., and J. Gregg Robinson. 1992. *Women in Engineering: Gender, Power, and Workplace Culture*. Albany, N.Y.: State University of New York Press.

McLanahan, Sara S., and Gary D. Sandefur. 1994. *Growing Up with a Single Parent: What Hurts, What Helps*. Cambridge: Harvard University Press.

McLure, Gail T., and Ellen Piel. 1978. "College-Bound Girls and Science Careers: Perceptions of Barriers and Facilitating Factors." *Journal of Vocational Behavior* 12:172–183.

Meece, Judith L., Jacqueline E. Parsons, Caroline M. Kaczala, Susan R. Goff, and Robert Futterman. 1982. "Sex Differences in Mathematics Achievement: Toward a Model of Academic Choice." *Psychological Bulletin* 91:324–348.

Merton, Robert K. 1973. *The Sociology of Science: Theoretical and Empirical Investigations*, edited by Norman W. Storer. Chicago: University of Chicago Press.

Meyer, Margaret R. 1989. "Gender Differences in Mathematics." Pp. 149–159 in

Results from the Fourth Mathematics Assessment of the National Assessment of Educational Progress, edited by Mary M. Lindquist. Reston, Va.: National Council of Teachers of Mathematics, Inc.

Meyer, Margaret R., and Mary S. Koehler. 1990. "Internal Influences on Gender Differences in Mathematics." Pp. 60–95 in *Mathematics and Gender,* edited by Elizabeth Fennema and Gilah C. Leder. New York: Teachers College Press.

Miller, Jon D., Thomas B. Hoffer, Robert W. Suchner, Karen G. Brown, and Cynthia Nelson. 1992. *LSAY Codebook: Student, Parent, and Teacher Data for Cohort One for Longitudinal Years One through Four (1987–1991).* Dekalb, Ill.: Northern Illinois University.

Mincer, Jacob. 1978. "Family Migration Decisions." *Journal of Political Economy* 86:749–773.

Morgan, Laurie A. 1998. "Glass-Ceiling Effect or Cohort Effect? A Longitudinal Study of the Gender Earnings Gap for Engineers." *American Sociological Review* 63:479–493.

Mullis, Ina V. S., and Lynn B. Jenkins. 1988. *The Science Report Card: Elements of Risk and Recovery.* Princeton, N.J.: Educational Testing Service.

National Opinion Research Center (NORC). 1993. *1992–93 National Study of Postsecondary Faculty (NSOPF-93), Restricted Access Data File, Project Documentation Excerpts.* Chicago, Ill.: National Opinion Research Center.

National Science Foundation (NSF). 1986. *Women and Minorities in Science and Engineering.* NSF 86–301. Washington, D.C.: National Science Foundation.

———— 1992. *Women and Minorities in Science and Engineering: An Update.* NSF 92–303. Washington, D.C.: National Science Foundation.

———— 1994. *Women, Minorities, and Persons with Disabilities in Science and Engineering: 1994.* NSF 94–333. Washington, D.C.: National Science Foundation.

———— 1996. *Women, Minorities, and Persons with Disabilities in Science and Engineering: 1996.* NSF 96–311. Washington, D.C.: National Science Foundation.

———— 1999. *Women and Minorities, and Persons with Disabilities in Science and Engineering: 1998.* NSF 99–338. Washington, D.C.: National Science Foundation.

———— 2000. *Women and Minorities in Science and Engineering.* NSF 00–327. Washington, D.C.: National Science Foundation.

North, David S. 1995. *Soothing the Establishment: The Impact of Foreign-Born Scientists and Engineers on America.* New York: University Press of America.

Nowell, Amy, and Larry V. Hedges. 1998. "Trends in Gender Differences in Academic Achievement from 1960 to 1994: An Analysis of Differences in Mean, Variance, and Extreme Scores." *Sex Roles* 39:21–43.

Oakes, Jeannie. 1990. "Opportunities, Achievement, and Choice: Women and

Minority Students in Science and Mathematics." *Review of Research in Education* 16:153–222.

Office of Technology Assessment (OTA). 1989. *Educating Scientists and Engineers: Grade School to Grad School.* Washington, D.C.: Office of Technology Assessment.

O'Rand, Angela M. 1996. "Structuration and Individualization: The Life Course as a Continuous Multilevel Process." Pp. 3–16 in *Generating Social Stratification: Toward a New Research Agenda,* edited by Alan C. Kerckhoff. Boulder, Colo.: Westview Press.

O'Rand, Angela M., and Margaret L. Krecker. 1990. "Concepts of the Life Cycle: Their History, Meanings, and Uses in the Social Sciences." *Annual Review of Sociology* 16:241–262.

Pallas, Aaron M., and Karl L. Alexander. 1983. "Sex Differences in Quantitative SAT Performance: New Evidence on the Differential Coursework Hypothesis." *American Educational Research Journal* 20:165–182.

Pattatucci, Angela M. (editor). 1998. *Women in Science: Meeting Career Challenges.* Thousand Oaks, Calif.: Sage.

Pedraza, Silvia. 1991. "Women and Migration: The Social Consequences of Gender." *Annual Review of Sociology* 17:303–325.

Peek, Charles W. 1995. "Sources of Gender and Racial/Ethnic Stratification in Non-Academic Science and Engineering." Unpublished dissertation. University of Michigan, Ann Arbor, Mich.

Peterson, Penelope L., and Elizabeth Fennema. 1985. "Effective Teaching, Student Engagement in Classroom Activities, and Sex-related Differences in Learning Mathematics." *American Educational Research Journal* 22:309–335.

Peterson, Trond. 1992. "Alternative Ways of Modeling Mobility." *Contemporary Sociology* 21:636–639.

Portes, Alejandro, and Ruben G. Rumbaut. 1990. *Immigrant America: A Portrait.* Berkeley, Calif.: University of California Press.

Powers, Daniel A., and Yu Xie. 2000. *Statistical Methods for Categorical Data Analysis.* New York: Academic Press.

Reid, Pamela T., and Michele A. Paludi. 1993. "Developmental Psychology of Women: Conception to Adolescence." Pp. 193–212 in *Psychology of Women: A Handbook of Issues and Theories,* edited by Florence L. Denmark and Michele A. Paludi. Westport, Conn.: Greenwood Press.

Reskin, Barbara F. (editor). 1984. *Sex Segregation in the Workplace: Trends, Explanations, Remedies.* Washington, D.C.: National Academy Press.

——— 1978. "Scientific Productivity, Sex, and Location in the Institution of Science." *American Journal of Sociology* 83:1235–1243.

——— 1992. "Women in Science: Conflicting Views on Where and Why." *Contemporary Sociology* 21:571–573.

Reskin, Barbara F., and Heidi I. Hartmann (editors). 1986. *Women's Work, Men's Work.* Washington, D.C.: National Academy Press.

Reskin, Barbara F., and Patricia A. Roos. 1990. *Job Queues, Gender Queues: Explaining Women's Inroads into Male Occupations.* Philadelphia: Temple University Press.

Reyes, Laurie H. 1984. "Affective Variables and Mathematics Education." *Elementary School Journal* 84:558–581.

Riccobono, John, L. B. Henderson, G. J. Burkheimer, C. Place, and J. R. Levinsohn. 1981. *National Longitudinal Study: Base Year (1972) through Fourth Follow-Up (1979) Data File Users Manual Volume I.* Washington, D.C.: National Center for Education Statistics.

Rogers, Lesley. 1983. "Hormonal Theories for Sex Differences—Politics Disguised as Science: A Reply to Debold and Luria." *Sex Roles* 9:1109–1113.

——— 2001. *Sexing the Brain.* New York: Columbia University Press.

Rogers, Lesley, and Joan Walsh. 1982. "Shortcomings of the Psychomedical Research of John Money and Co-Workers into Sex Differences in Behavior: Social and Political Implications." *Sex Roles* 8:269–281.

Rosenfeld, Rachel A. 1991. "'Outcomes Analysis' of Academic Careers." Review prepared for the Office of Scientific and Engineering Personnel, National Research Council. Department of Sociology, University of North Carolina.

Rosenfeld, Rachel A., and Jo Ann Jones. 1987. "Patterns and Effects of Geographic Mobility for Academic Women and Men." *Journal of Higher Education* 58:493–515.

Rossi, Alice S. 1965. "Women in Science: Why So Few?" *Science* 148:1196–1202.

——— 1972. "Women in Science: Why So Few?" Pp. 141–153 in *Towards a Sociology of Women,* edited by Constantina Safilios-Rothschild. Lexington, Mass.: Xerox College Publishing.

Ryder, Norman B. 1965. "The Cohort as a Concept in the Study of Social Change." *American Sociological Review* 30:843–861.

Sadker, Myra, and David Sadker. 1995. *Failing at Fairness: How Our Schools Cheat Girls.* New York: Simon and Schuster.

Sandberg, David E., Anke A. Ehrhardt, Claude A. Mellins, Susan E. Ince, and Heino F. L. Meyer-Bahlburg. 1987. "The Influence of Individual and Family Characteristics upon Career Aspirations of Girls during Childhood and Adolescence." *Sex Roles* 16:649–668.

Sandefur, Gary D. 1985. "Variations in Interstate Migration of Men across the Early Stages of the Life Cycle." *Demography* 22:353–366.

Sanders, Barbara, Marsha R. Cohen, and Mary P. Soares. 1986. "The Sex Differences in Spatial Ability: A Rejoinder." *American Psychologist* 41:1015–1016.

Schiebinger, Londa. 1999. *Has Feminism Changed Science?* Cambridge, Mass.: Harvard University Press.

Schunk, Dale H. 1981. "Modeling and Attribution Effects on Children's Achievement: A Self-Efficacy Analysis." *Journal of Educational Psychology* 73:848–856.

——— 1982. "Effects of Effort Attribution Feedback on Children's Perceived Self-Efficacy and Achievement." *Journal of Educational Psychology* 74:548–556.

Selby, Cecily C. (editor). 1999. *Women in Science and Engineering: Choices for Success.* New York: New York Academy of Sciences.

Sells, Lucy W. 1980. "The Mathematics Filter and the Education of Women and Minorities." Pp. 66–75 in *Women and the Mathematical Mystique,* edited by Lynn Fox, Linda Brody, and Dianne Tobin. Baltimore, Md.: Johns Hopkins University Press.

Sewell, William H., Archibald O. Haller, and Alejandro Portes. 1969. "The Educational and Early Occupational Attainment Process." *American Sociological Review* 34:82–92.

Sewell, William H., and Robert M. Hauser. 1975. *Education, Occupation, and Earnings.* New York: Academic Press.

Seymour, Elaine, and Nancy M. Hewitt. 1997. *Talking about Leaving: Why Undergraduates Leave the Sciences.* Boulder, Colo.: Westview Press.

Sharps, Matthew J., Jana L. Price, and John K. Williams. 1994. "Spatial Cognition and Gender: Instructional and Stimulus Influences on Mental Image Rotation Performance." *Psychology of Women Quarterly* 18:413–426.

Shauman, Kimberlee A., and Yu Xie. 1996. "Geographic Mobility of Scientists: Sex Differences and Family Constraints." *Demography* 33(4):455–468.

——— 1998. "Explaining Sex Differences in Publication Productivity among Postsecondary Faculty." Paper presented at the Conference for Women in Research Universities, Cambridge, Mass. November.

Shaywitz, Bennett A., Sally E. Shaywitz, Kenneth R. Pugh, R. Todd Constable, Pawel Skudlarski, Robert K. Fulbright, Richard A. Bronen, Jack M. Fletcher, Donald P. Shankweiler, Leonard Katz, and John C. Gore. 1995. "Sex Differences in the Functional Organization of the Brain for Language." *Nature* 373:607–609.

Sherman, Julia, and E. Fennema. 1977. "The Study of Mathematics by High School Girls and Boys: Related Variables." *American Educational Research Journal* 14:159–168.

Shihadeh, Edward S. 1991. "The Prevalence of Husband-Centered Migration: Employment Consequences for Married Mothers." *Journal of Marriage and the Family* 53:432–444.

Sonnert, Gerhard. 1995a. *Gender Differences in Science Careers: The Project Access Study,* with assistance of Gerald Holton. New Brunswick, N.J.: Rutgers University Press.

——— 1995b. *Who Succeeds in Science? The Gender Dimension,* with assistance of Gerald Holton. New Brunswick, N.J.: Rutgers University Press.

——— 1999. "Women in Science and Engineering: Advances, Challenges, and Solutions." Pp. 34–57 in *Women in Science and Engineering: Choices for Success,* edited by Cecily Cannan Selby. New York: New York Academy of Sciences.

Sorensen, Annemette. 1983. "Children and Their Mother's Career." *Social Science Research* 12:26–43.

Spain, Daphne, and Suzanne M. Bianchi. 1996. *Balancing Act: Motherhood, Marriage, and Employment among American Women.* New York: Russell Sage Foundation.

Speare, Alden, Jr. 1970. "Home Ownership, Life Cycle Stage, and Residential Mobility." *Demography* 7:449–458.

Speare, Alden, Jr., and Frances K. Goldscheider. 1987. "Effects of Marital Status Change on Residential Mobility." *Journal of Marriage and the Family* 49:455–464.

Speare, Alden, Jr., Sidney Goldstein, and William H. Frey. 1975. *Residential Mobility, Migration, and Metropolitan Change.* Cambridge, Mass.: Ballinger Publishing Company.

Spenner, Kenneth I., and Rachel A. Rosenfeld. 1990. "Women, Work, and Identities." *Social Science Research* 19:266–299.

Stake, Jayne E., and Charles R. Granger. 1978. "Same-Sex and Opposite-Sex Teacher Model Influences on Science Career Commitment among High School Students." *Journal of Educational Psychology* 70(2):180–186.

Steinkamp, Marjorie W., and Martin L. Maehr. 1983. "Affect, Ability and Science Achievement: A Quantitative Synthesis of Correlational Research." *Review of Educational Research* 53:369–396.

——— 1984. "Gender Differences in Motivational Orientations toward Achievement in School Science: A Quantitative Synthesis." *American Educational Research Journal* 21:39–59.

Stephan, Paula E., and Sharon G. Levin. 1992. *Striking the Mother Lode in Science: The Importance of Age, Place, and Time.* New York: Oxford University Press.

Stier, Haya. 1991. "Immigrant Women Go to Work: Analysis of Immigrant Wives' Labor Supply for Six Asian Groups." *Social Science Quarterly* 72(1):67–82.

Straker, Anita. 1986. "Should Mary Have a Little Computer?" Pp. 149–152 in *Girls into Maths Can Go,* edited by Leone Burton. London: Holt, Rinehart, and Winston.

Stuart, Alan, and J. Keith Ord. 1991. *Kendall's Advanced Theory of Statistics, Volume 2: Classical Inference and Relationship,* 5th ed. New York: Oxford University Press.

Takaki, Ronald. 1989. *Strangers from a Different Shore: A History of Asian Americans.* Boston: Little, Brown.

Tang, Joyce. 1993. "The Career Attainment of Caucasian and Asian Engineers." *Sociological Quarterly* 34(3):467–496.

——— 2000. *Doing Engineering: The Career Attainment and Mobility of Caucasian, Black, and Asian-American Engineers.* Lanham, Md.: Rowman and Littlefield Publishers.

Terwilliger, James S., and Janet C. Titus. 1995. "Gender Differences in Attitudes and Attitude Changes among Mathematically Talented Youth." *Gifted Child Quarterly* 39:29–35.

Thornton, Arland, William G. Axinn, and Jay D. Teachman. 1995. "The Influence of School Enrollment and Accumulation on Cohabitation and Marriage in Early Adulthood." *American Sociological Review* 60:762–774.

Tobin, Kenneth, and Pamela Garnett. 1987. "Gender Related Differences in Science Activities." *Science Education* 71:91–103.

Treiman, Donald J., and Heidi I. Hartmann. 1981. *Women, Work, and Wages: Equal Pay for Jobs of Equal Value.* Washington, D.C.: National Academy Press.

Trow, Martin (editor). 1975. *Teachers and Students: Aspects of American Higher Education.* New York: McGraw-Hill.

Tuma, Nancy B., and Michael T. Hannan. 1984. *Social Dynamics: Models and Methods.* San Francisco: Academic Press.

Turner, Ralph H. 1964. "Some Aspects of Women's Ambition." *American Journal of Sociology* 70:271–285.

Useem, Elizabeth L. 1992. "Middle Schools and Math Groups: Parents' Involvement in Childrens' Placement." *Sociology of Education* 65:263–279.

Valian, Virginia. 1999. *Why So Slow? The Advancement of Women.* Cambridge, Mass.: The MIT Press.

Vasegh-Daneshvary, Nasser, Alan M. Schlottmann, and Henry W. Herzog, Jr. 1987. "Immigration of Engineers, Scientists, and Physicians in the U.S. High Technology Renaissance." *Social Science Quarterly* 68:311–325.

Waldfogel, Jane. 1997. "Working Mothers Then and Now: A Cross-Cohort Analysis of the Effects of Maternity Leave on Women's Pay." Pp. 92–126 in *Gender and Family Issues in the Workplace,* edited by Francine D. Blau and Ronald G. Ehrenberg. New York: Russell Sage Foundation.

Ward, Kathryn B., and Linda Grant. 1995. "Gender and Academic Publishing." Pp. 172–212 in *Higher Education: Handbook of Theory and Research,* vol. 11, edited by John C. Smart. New York: Agathon.

Ware, Norma C., and Valerie E. Lee. 1988. "Sex Differences in Choice of College Science Majors." *American Education Research Journal* 25:593–614.

Ware, Norma C., Nicole A. Steckler, and Jane Leserman. 1985. "Undergraduate Women: Who Chooses a Science Major?" *Journal of Higher Education* 56(1):73–84.

Wasserman, Elga. 2000. *The Door in the Dream: Conversations with Eminent Women in Science.* Washington, D.C.: Joseph Henry Press.

Welch, Wayne W., Ronald E. Anderson, and Linda J. Harris. 1982. "The Effects of Schooling on Mathematics Achievement." *American Educational Research Journal* 19:145–153.

West, Jerry, Wendy Miller, and Louis Diodato. 1985. *An Analysis of Course-Taking Patterns in Secondary Schools as Related to Student Characteristics.* NCES 85–206. Washington, D.C.: National Center for Educational Statistics.

Westat. 1979. *United States Personnel and Funding Resources for Science, Engineering, and Technology: Survey of Recent Science and Engineering Graduates, 1978. A User's Guide to the Machine Readable Data File.* Rockville, Md.

Wigfield, Allan, and Jacqueline S. Eccles. 1992. "The Development of Achievement Task Values: A Theoretical Analysis." *Developmental Review* 12:265–310.

Williams, Joan. 2000. *Unbending Gender: Why Family and Work Conflict and What to Do about It.* London: Oxford University Press.

Wilson, Robin. 1999. "An MIT Professor's Suspicion of Bias Leads to a New Movement for Academic Women." *Chronicle of Higher Education* 46(Dec 3, 1999):A16–A18.

Wolfe, Lynda K., and Nancy E. Betz. 1981. "Traditionality of Choice and Sex Role Identification as Moderators of the Congruence of Occupational Choice in College Women." *Journal of Vocational Behavior* 18:43–55.

Yee, Doris, and Jacquelynne S. Eccles. 1988. "Parent Perceptions and Attributions for Children's Math Achievement." *Sex Roles* 19:317–334.

Xie, Yu. 1989. "The Process of Becoming a Scientist." Unpublished dissertation. University of Wisconsin, Madison, Wis.

—— 1996. "A Demographic Approach to Studying the Process of Becoming a Scientist/Engineer." Pp. 43–57 in *Careers in Science and Technology: An International Perspective,* edited by the National Research Council. Washington, D.C.: National Academy Press.

Xie, Yu, and Kimberlee Akin. 1994. "Sex Differences in Research Productivity: Solving the Puzzle?" Population Studies Center Research Report 94–322. Ann Arbor: University of Michigan.

Xie, Yu, and Kimberlee A. Shauman. 1997. "Modeling the Sex-Typing of Occupational Choice: Influences of Occupational Structure." *Sociological Methods and Research* 26:233–261.

—— 1998. "Sex Differences in Research Productivity: New Evidence about an Old Puzzle." *American Sociological Review* 63:847–870.

Zahs, Daniel, Steven Pedlow, Marjorie Morrissey, Patricia Marnell, and Bronwyn Nichols. 1995. *High School and Beyond Fourth Follow-Up Methodology Report.* Washington, D.C.: National Center for Education Statistics.

Zuckerman, Harriet. 1991. "The Careers of Men and Women Scientists: A Review of Current Research." Pp. 27–56 in *The Outer Circle: Women in the Scientific Community,* edited by Harriet Zuckerman, Jonathan R. Cole, and John T. Bruer. New York: W. W. Norton and Company.

Zuckerman, Harriet, Jonathan R. Cole, and John T. Bruer (editors). 1991. *The Outer Circle: Women in the Scientific Community.* New York: W. W. Norton and Company.

Index